The Female Circumcision Controversy

An Anthropological Perspective

Ellen Gruenbaum

PENN

University of Pennsylvania Press

Philadelphia

10 9 8 7 6 5 4

Published by
University of Pennsylvania Press
Philadelphia, Pennsylvania 19104-4011

Library of Congress Cataloging-in-Publication Data
Gruenbaum, Ellen.
    The female circumcision controversy : an anthropological perspective
/ Ellen Gruenbaum.
        p.   cm.
    Includes bibliographical references and index.
    ISBN 0-8122-3573-8 (cloth : alk. paper) — ISBN 0-8122-1746-2 (pbk. : alk. paper)
    1. Female circumcision.   I. Title.
GN484 .G78 2000
392.1 — dc21   00-041803

For my parents,

Ruth and Luther Gruenbaum

Contents

Introduction
Grappling with the "Female Circumcision" Controversy

To outsiders, the practice euphemistically known as "female circumcision" is shocking. That people surgically alter the genitals of young girls and women, usually in painful and unhygienic procedures that can cause grave harm to their health, seems truly horrible. Why do loving parents allow such things to happen? How can they bring themselves to celebrate these events? How can they justify the practice when occasionally a girl dies from the injuries?

The horror female circumcision evokes is grist for outrage, electrifying a cry for urgent change. At the new millennium, there are still millions of girls and women in dozens of countries who bear the scars of cutting done to their genitalia early in life. Worldwide, it is estimated that an additional two million girls too young to give their consent undergo some form of female genital cutting each year. How can this be?

This book offers an exploration of the female circumcision practices themselves, the reasons they are done, examples of the social contexts, the health, social, and sexual consequences, and the controversies surrounding the process of change. It addresses many of the most frequent questions and challenges I have encountered in teaching and lecturing about these topics, with the intention to improve understanding, reduce simplistic denunciation, and provide a solid grounding for those who decide to support reform efforts. For people outside the cultural contexts where female circumcision is still practiced, developing understanding requires much more than merely knowing the facts or arriving at a philosophic position for or against. To allow readers more opportunity to consider the social contexts and the human experience, I include narratives and examples from my ethnographic research in Sudan.

The Practices Known as "Female Circumcision"

"Female circumcision" is one term used for the cutting and removal of tissues of genitalia of young girls to conform to social expectations. There is tremendous variation in the practices and their meaning. In some cultural contexts, these operations are done on very young children, including infants and toddlers (Shandall 1967, Toubia 1993, Abdal Rahman 1997). Anne Jennings has reported southern Egyptian girls undergoing the procedure at age one or two (1995:48). Most commonly, it is done to young girls between the ages of four and eight. But there are other cultural contexts (e.g., the Maasai of eastern Africa) where it is young teens, around the time of marriage (fourteen to fifteen or even older), who are circumcised.

While I consider it important to resist generalizing about the types of genital alterations around which the controversy unfolds, the variant forms can be differentiated and grouped. The least severe forms of the operations (excluding those that merely wash or prick the clitoris or prepuce without removal of any tissues) are those where a small part of the clitoral prepuce ("hood") is cut away, analogous to the foreskin removal of male circumcision. Toubia asserts that in her years of medical practice in Sudan, Egypt, and the United Kingdom, she never saw any circumcisions that precisely fit this description (1996). Nevertheless, it is referred to elsewhere, at least as a theoretical possibility, and is discussed later in this volume. This form is grouped with those that include the cutting, pricking, or partial removal (or "reduction") of the clitoris under the rubric of "*sunna* circumcision." This term "sunna circumcision" is in fact applied to a wide variety of surgeries, and the term itself offers serious problems of interpretation of the meaning, propriety, and religious associations of the surgeries. The basic translation of the word "sunna" is "tradition," and it usually connotes the traditions of Islam's Prophet Mohammed, meaning those things that he did or advocated during his lifetime.[1] In Sudan, some use the term "sunna" for even more severe forms of female circumcision than the reductions just described.

Full clitoridectomies are termed "excision" or "intermediate" by most writers. These are more severe forms of surgery that include removal of the prepuce, the clitoris, and usually most or part of the labia minora, or inner lips. In Sudan this form is usually called *sunna* even though it is more serious than what some writers mean by *sunna*. The reason for this is that the folk classifications, in many areas at least, consist of only two

---

[1] Muslims believe the Holy Qur'an to be God's direct revelation and the first source of guidance concerning righteous living; the example set by the Prophet Mohammed in his lifetime and handed down in the writings known as the Hadith is a secondary source. Thus Muslims are expected to respect and follow these sunna of the Prophet as much as possible.

forms, sunna and pharaonic circumcision, even though the operations vary a great deal from one circumciser to another and the sunna terminology seems to be applied to any circumcisions that are not "pharaonic." Midwives and others also use an imprecise term, *nuss* ("half"), for some of the in-between forms.

Pharaonic circumcision entails the removal of all the external genitalia — prepuce, clitoris, labia minora, and all or part of the labia majora — and infibulation, or stitching together, of the vulva. Once healed, this most extreme form leaves a perfectly smooth vulva of skin and scar tissue with only a single tiny opening, preserved during healing by the insertion of a small object such as a piece of straw, for urination and menstrual flow. The extremely small size of the opening makes first sexual intercourse very difficult or impossible, necessitating rupture or cutting of the scar tissue around the opening. In a variation of infibulation that is slightly less severe, the trimmed labia minora are sewn shut but the labia majora are left alone. Reinfibulation is done after childbirth.

In short, the variety of operations defy easy categorization, and the descriptive terminologies that are comparative — generated from outside the frame of meaning of those who do them, to aid medical descriptions for example — cannot be expected to reflect categorizations that are meaningful from any specific cultural perspective. Whether a writer's typology has three categories or some other number depends on the purposes of the study, whether it is for health education, ethnographic description, or medical analysis. I often use the two common Sudanese terminologies, sunna and pharaonic, because these are significant to the debates about cultural and religious authenticity discussed later, but I also discuss variations and innovations in these surgeries. These two categories parallel Sudanese physician Nahid Toubia's dichotomous classification of "reduction" operations and "covering" operations (Toubia 1994).

What Should Be the General Term for These Practices?

The term "female genital mutilation" has become more widely accepted since the 1990s. "Mutilation" is technically accurate because most variants of the practices entail damage to or removal of healthy tissues or organs. But for most people, the term "mutilation" implies intentional harm and is tantamount to an accusation of evil intent. Some of my Sudanese friends have been deeply offended by the term, and it is their reaction as much as the connotations of that term that have influenced my preference for the term that is very commonly used when speaking or writing in English: female circumcision. "Female circumcision," however, echoes the term for the removal of the foreskin in the male, which is generally considered nonmutilating (Toubia 1993:9). The term "female circumcision" is therefore rejected by many people because "circumcision" seems to trivialize the damaging act and the huge scale of its practice.

Neither term — mutilation or circumcision — is a translation of the Arabic word most commonly used for female circumcision in Sudan. *Tahur* (or its variations such as *tahara*) is usually translated as "purification" and connotes the achievement of cleanliness through a ritual activity. But in fact there is little about the rather matter-of-fact performance of the surgical act that one would associate with ritual in a religious or mystical sense. Thus using a term that connotes ritual seems both inaccurate and inadequate to the broad range of meanings and contexts of the practices. And some are offended by it, as it could give the impression that practitioners are unreflective or not rational.

"Clitoridectomy" and "infibulation" are somewhat more precise descriptive terms, but a term that encompasses both types of surgeries and other variations is also needed. "Female genital operations" or "genital surgeries" are accurate terms and can be used in some contexts, but they do not adequately differentiate these practices from therapeutic medical surgeries, whereas to call them "*traditional* female genital operations" evokes the simplified interpretation I challenge in this book. Shortening "female genital mutilation" to the more clinical-sounding FGM is an alternative now used widely by many, including Toubia, writing in the United States for an international audience. She adds, however, the eminently sensible thought that using the terms of reference of the communities where the practice occurs is a "starting point from which to initiate the process of change" (1993:9); she herself varies her terminology in her writing. The term "female genital cutting" (FGC) has been used by some writers and seems to be gaining greater acceptance.

The term "female circumcision" is often used here, despite its clearly euphemistic character, to avoid the connotations of evil intentions or wanton mayhem associated with the term "mutilation." I am fully cognizant of its inadequacies.

Health Risks

All the forms of female circumcision share certain risks. First, the unhygienic circumstances in which circumcision operations are often carried out, together with the minimal training of many circumcisers, pose serious risks. Infection of the wound is common when unsterilized instruments are used or if cleanliness is not meticulously attended to. Hemorrhage (uncontrolled bleeding) is sometimes difficult to stop if the circumciser has cut too deep. Shock can occur, and septicemia (blood poisoning) can also result. In the days after the surgery, some girls experience retention of urine because of pain, swelling, fear of pain, or obstruction of the urethral opening. Problems such as adhesions of labial tissue (where not entirely removed), vaginal stones, and vaginal stenosis (narrowing) are also reported.

The forms that include infibulation offer additional serious health consequences. Obstruction of menstrual flow can occur in cases in which the scar tissue obstructs the vagina, and an adolescent girl may find menses prevented, with the unsuccessful discharge backing up and distending her uterus. El Dareer described a case in Sudan in which pregnancy was suspected, much to the shame and fear of the girl's mother, until the true nature of the problem was discovered: the fifteen-year-old girl, who had never menstruated, had such a small opening she had difficulty passing urine and her menstrual discharge had been completely obstructed, perhaps because of vulvo-vaginal atresia (absence of an opening). An incision released the large quantity of fetid blood (1982:37). El Dareer also heard reports of a similar case in which the girl was said to have been killed for the sake of family honor. Even those whose menstrual flow is not obstructed often report painful menstruation, probably not only because of the usual cramps but also because of the tightness of the infibulation and frequent infections.

Later, first intercourse is complicated by infibulation because either painful tearing or unhygienic cutting (by the husband or a midwife called in to assist) commonly occurs. Obstructed intercourse resulting from a tight introitus or painful intercourse (dyspareunia) and chronic pelvic inflammation that might affect penetration or frequency can also result in infertility (Shandall 1967; Verzin 1975; for case descriptions, see El Dareer 1982).

During pregnancy and childbirth, the infibulated opening creates other difficulties. Infections of the vagina or urinary tract may contribute to miscarriage. Chronic pelvic infections are considered a major factor in infertility cases, and infertility is a socially disastrous condition throughout the regions where circumcision is practiced (see Inhorn 1994, 1996). The most severe, life-threatening, long-term complication of infibulation is obstructed labor. Fibrous, inelastic tissues of the vulva may require excessive bearing down during the second stage of labor, exhausting the mother and stressing the infant (El Dareer 1982:38). During childbirth, a midwife must be present to cut the inelastic scar tissue across the vaginal opening when the baby is in position for delivery (crowning) and sew the tissue together again after delivery. This cut is basically an episiotomy that is cut upward (anterior), rather than downward (posterior). Lateral or bilateral episiotomy to widen the vagina is also sometimes necessary (Abdalla 1982:26). Keloid scarring and cysts are not uncommon at the site of the infibulations, which can make the episiotomies themselves, as well as the restitching and healing, difficult. The risks of excessive bleeding and infections from all the cutting needed and the unavailability of medical facilities for emergencies in most rural areas of Africa pose survival risks for mothers. To reduce the risks of childbirth, some women greatly reduce their nutritional intake during pregnancy, a practice that may have the opposite effect.

Delays in the cutting during labor (e.g., if the midwife does not arrive in time or the traditional birth attendant lacks the experience to judge the timing), in addition to posing a risk to the survival of mother and infant, can also cause severe perineal lacerations or damage to vaginal tissue, often resulting in vasicovaginal fistulae, a serious medical problem wherein a passage is created between the vagina and the urinary bladder or other parts of the body cavity, including the rectum (see Shandall 1967, Mudawi 1977, Verzin 1975). For some women the result is a most embarrassing condition rendering her unable to retain urine and producing constant leakage. In rural areas where pads or absorbent cotton are not available in the market or are beyond the means of a family, the woman may be unable to preserve basic hygiene and may suffer the consequence of social avoidance, ostracism, or divorce (El Dareer 1982:38).

Infibulation is also related to an apparently high prevalence of urinary tract and other chronic pelvic infections. If urine cannot be passed easily and there is only a single pinhole-sized opening for both bladder and vagina, some women experience the backing up of urine into the vagina, which is particularly dangerous during pregnancy. One can easily imagine how a woman with such a condition — or any woman who finds it difficult, slow, or painful to pass urine — might be tempted to cut down on her fluids, drinking too little for good health in a hot climate. In many rural areas, latrines are nonexistent and hidden places, as well as opportunities, for uninterrupted urination may be few. When traveling by bus or truck, the lack of facilities at stops may force women to hide under their long veils and urinate in the open; many prefer the discomfort of holding their urine for many hours.

Such conditions and inadequate fluid intake could be contributing factors to the high rates of urinary tract infections reported: Shandall has reported a prevalence rate of 28 percent of northern Sudanese women affected by urinary tract infections (1967, see also Boddy 1998a:53).

The limited epidemiological information available on maternal mortality, stillbirths, and neonatal mortality in the countries affected by female circumcision practices gives cause for concern, though clear demonstrations of the relationship of these results to incidence of female circumcision await better data. Nevertheless, there is every reason to believe that reduction of the incidence and severity of female circumcision could contribute to improvement of the health and survival of women and children. (For more on medical consequences, see Abdalla 1982; Boddy 1982, 1989, 1998; Cook 1976; Dorkenoo and Elworthy 1992; Dorkenoo 1994; El Dareer 1982; Verzin 1975; Rushwan et al. 1983; Shandall 1967; Toubia 1993, 1994; Van der Kwaak 1992).

Psychological risks have also been discussed by some writers and depicted in fiction (e.g., Walker 1992, El Saadawi 1980a, Abdalla 1982). Abdalla states that psychological reactions range from "temporary trauma and permanent frigidity to psychoses," and she hypothesizes an effect on the personality development of the young girls, a "totally neglected" topic (1982:27). There have been a few studies of mental health sequelae and the issue is being addressed in the literature (e.g., Baashar et al. 1979; Grotberg 1990, Toubia 1993). Baashir notes that the physical complications often produce psychological effects, for example, the "toxic confusional states" resulting from shock or tetanus, and there are also longer-term psychiatric sequelae to the physical complications, which can lead to "chronic irritability, anxiety reactions, depressive episodes and even frank psychosis" (quoted in Abdalla 1982:27). More research would be useful on female circumcision trauma in relation to later depression, fear of intimacy, and sexual dysfunction. Psychological consequences clearly can be expected to vary considerably, depending on cultural meanings that are taught and whether girls are prepared for the operations.

Reviewing the horrendous health risks, one can understand the intense outpouring of condemnation that ensued when the practices became more widely known by people outside the societies involved. That they have been nevertheless strongly defended and variously interpreted is the source of the intense controversy.

The Extent of Female Circumcision Practices

Various writers estimate that there are more than 100 million women and girls whose bodies have been altered by some form of female circumcision. Toubia estimates 114.3 million (1993:25). About 2 million are considered at risk for undergoing the procedure each year. Some form of female genital cutting is practiced in about twenty-eight countries in Africa.

But the procedure is not limited to Africa. Many more countries need to be concerned, as medical practitioners and social services providers find themselves dealing with circumcised women of immigrant populations now living in North America, Europe, South America, and Australia. Although new cases among immigrants are believed to be few, public health education of immigrants is needed and caregivers need preparation. Circumcision may also spread as people come to believe, however erroneously, that it is required by their religion, as in the case of Muslim populations in South Asia and Indonesia that have adopted circumcision. Several countries of Europe, south and southeast Asia, and North America, together with Brazil and Australia are said to have practicing populations that are "less than 1 percent" (Toubia 1993:34).

In Africa, statistics on prevalence of circumcision, its types, and the rates of new cases have been difficult to determine, as data are uneven (see Toubia 1993, 1995; Amnesty International 1997; Hosken 1978, 1982, 1998). According to data drawn from national surveys, small studies, country reports in *WIN News,* and anecdotal information, the affected countries have prevalence rates (i.e., the percentage of cases in the appropriate female age groups) that range from as high as 98 percent to as low as 5 percent. Some countries have none. The moderate rates of some countries may reflect an average of high prevalence in one area (perhaps certain ethnic groups) with low prevalence in another.

The countries with the highest total estimated prevalence are Somalia (98 percent), Djibouti (95–98 percent), Egypt (97 percent), Mali (90–94 percent), Sierra Leone (90 percent), Ethiopia (90 percent), Eritrea (90 percent), Sudan (89 percent for the northern two-thirds of the country), Guinea (70–90 percent), Burkina Faso (70 percent), Chad (60 percent), Côte d'Ivoire (60 percent), Gambia (60 percent), and Liberia (60 percent). Also very high, with estimates of 50 percent each, are Benin, Central African Republic, Guinea Bissau, Kenya, and Nigeria. Countries where fewer than one-third of women and girls are affected include Mauritania (25 percent), Ghana (15–30 percent), Niger (20 percent), Senegal (20 percent), Togo (12 percent), Tanzania (10 percent), Uganda (5 percent), and Zaire (5 percent). The remaining countries of northern Africa and southern Africa are considered "nonpracticing countries." (See Map 1.)

Nearly a third of the cases in Africa are in Nigeria, not because of high prevalence but because of its large population; the country accounts for 30.6 million of the 114.3 million cases for Africa as a whole, according to Toubia (1993:25). Just seven countries of northeast Africa (Egypt, Sudan, Eritrea, Ethiopia, Djibouti, Somalia, and Kenya) contain half of the circumcised women and girls in Africa.

Infibulation, the most severe form of female circumcision, is most common in that same region of northeast Africa, including Somalia, Djibouti, eastern Chad, central and northern Sudan, southern Egypt, and parts of Ethiopia and Eritrea (see also Hicks 1993). The people of Djibouti have practiced infibulation almost exclusively. For Somalia, circumcision is virtually universal, and at least 80 percent are infibulated. For the northern two-thirds of Sudan, where El Dareer's research team conducted interviews, 98 percent had circumcisions, but only 2.5 percent were sunna, while 12 percent were intermediate and 83 percent were infibulated. At the time of the interviews in 1979 and 1980, only 1.2 percent reported no circumcisions (El Dareer 1982:1). In Egypt the prevalence of infibulation is high mostly in the south near Sudan. Similarly, the areas of Eritrea and Ethiopia where infibulation is found are those near Sudan, Somalia, and Djibouti, where infibulation is predominant.

Although the amount of information is growing, mapping the areas where the various forms are practiced today and indicating prevalence is challenging, given the unevenness of data. Unfortunately, some of the maps that are being used in publications draw upon earlier efforts that incorporated anecdotal accounts that, at least for the areas of Sudan with which I am familiar, are not fully supported by ethnographic information. Because comprehensive epidemiological research has not been carried out everywhere and health data in general is often inaccurate in areas underserved by health care systems, all existing maps (including Map 1) must be understood as crude approximations of the pattern of prevalence; they do not reflect the increases or decreases in incidence (rate of new circumcisions in age groups at risk) that may or may not be occurring because of public health efforts and cultural change.

Clitoridectomy in the West

Damaging female genital surgeries are not limited to just a few countries of the world, nor have they always been linked to cultural traditions. A few years ago one of my European-American students told me that her grandmother had been circumcised as a child, growing up in the American South. She was not alone.

In a surgery performed in Berlin in 1822 (reported in *The Lancet* in 1825), a fourteen-year-old "idiotic" patient was said to have been cured of her "excessive masturbation and nymphomania" after being "declitorized" (Huelsman 1976:127). Not only did she discontinue "self-pollution," but the "intellectual faculties of the patient began to develop themselves, and her education could now be commenced," allowing her to begin to "talk, read, reckon, execute several kinds of needle-work, and a few easy pieces on the piano forte" (quoted in Huelsman 1976:127–28). According to Huelsman, the first four decades that *The Lancet* was in publication (i.e., after 1825), there were numerous case histories of patients "declitorized for a variety of medical reasons," including hypertrophy, tumors, and "infantile, adolescent or adult masturbation regarded as excessive" (1976:128).

Elizabeth A. Sheehan offers a fascinating account of one of the European medical advocates of selective female genital cutting in the mid-nineteenth century, Isaac Baker Brown (Sheehan 1997), who was active

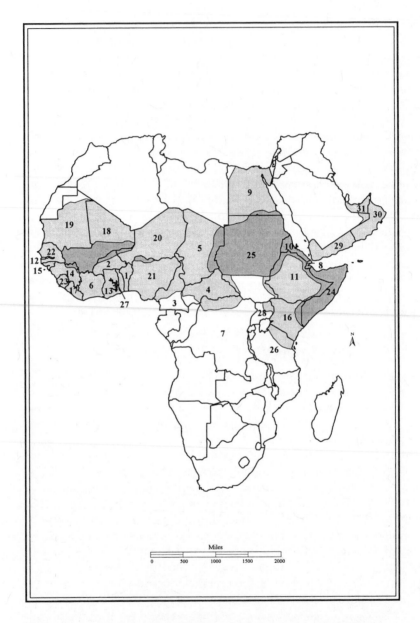

Map 1. Types of Female Genital Cutting in Africa and Arabian Peninsula. Shaded areas indicate prevalence of some form of "female circumcision." Darker shading indicates prevalence of infibulation.
See Map Key on facing page.

during the period of greatest popularity of biomedical declitorization in England during the 1860s (Huelsman 1976:29). Although removal of clitorises in cases of disease was known in European medicine for centuries, Brown's ideas emerged in an era of debate over whether the clitoris had any role at all in the female enjoyment of sex; some came to consider its removal as a "harmless operative procedure" (a phrase that was used in 1866, see Sheehan 1997: 328). An expert in various operations on the female sexual organs, Brown had founded the London Surgical Home for Women. From the observation that many of the female epileptics in his institution masturbated, Isaac Baker Brown developed a theory of causality that masturbation led to a progression of stages from "hysteria" to epilepsy and eventually "idiocy or death." Particularly frightening in the long history of European understanding of women's psychology is Brown's assertion that danger signs of such possible degeneration might include becoming "restless and excited, or melancholy and retiring, listless, and indifferent to the social influences of domestic life." "Often a great disposition for novelties is exhibited, the patient desiring to escape from home, fond of becoming a nurse in hospitals . . . To these symptoms in the single female will be added, in the married, distaste for marital intercourse" (Brown 1866, quoted in Sheehan 1997: 327).

Brown's cure for such "feminine weaknesses" was removal of the clitoris. Recommending chloroform and scissors rather than a knife for the removal, Brown described cases of immediate improvement of his

---

Key for Map 1

COUNTRY

		16	Kenya
1	Benin	17	Liberia
2	Burkina Faso	18	Mali
3	Cameroon	19	Mauritania
4	Central African Republic	20	Niger
5	Chad	21	Nigeria
6	Côte d'Ivoire	22	Senegal
7	Democratic Republic of Congo	23	Sierra Leone
8	Djibouti	24	Somalia
9	Egypt	25	Sudan
10	Eritrea	26	Tanzania
11	Ethiopia	27	Togo
12	Gambia	28	Uganda
13	Ghana	29	Yemen
14	Guinea	30	Oman
15	Guinea-Bissau	31	United Arab Emirates

patients. There was widespread acceptance of his theories and some acceptance of his surgeries, both in Britain and North America. In modern times, even as late as the 1940s, biomedical physicians in England and the United States have done clitoridectomies for the treatment and prevention of masturbation and other "deviant" behaviors and psychological conditions such as "hysteria," particularly for mental patients (Ehrenreich and English, 1973:34).

Ethnographic Research

Although this book is intended to offer breadth on the practices in their variant forms, I also offer data from my ethnographic research on rural women in communities in Sudan. This northeast African country is a valuable case because the most severe form of the surgeries — infibulation — is widely practiced there.

Over a period of more than two decades, I was able to spend about five and a half years in Sudan, which afforded me the opportunity to reflect on, and conduct ethnographic research on, female circumcision (see Map 2 for specific locations). My first trip to Sudan began in 1974, when my husband and I took teaching jobs at the University of Khartoum. The language of instruction at the university was English, but to delve into the society we studied Arabic and gradually became more proficient at speaking Sudanese Arabic. During the next several years, we lived in two urban contexts that afforded ample opportunities for participant observation: Khartoum, the capital city, and Wad Medani, the capital of Gezira Province, where my husband, Jay O'Brien, worked for a year at the University of Gezira. Some of my observations are drawn from these urban experiences, but I was fortunate to have opportunities for rural research in several parts of the country. (See Map 2, page 145.)

In 1975–76, I worked with the Economic and Social Research Council of the National Council for Research on the Jonglei Research Team that focused on the region in southern Sudan where the ill-fated Jonglei Canal was planned. Our multidisciplinary team collected data to enable us to analyze political, economic, and cultural patterns, local interest in development projects, and existing environmental adaptations and migration patterns of local herding, agricultural, hunting, and fishing practices. There I interviewed (with an interpreter) eighty women of the noncircumcising Nuer ethnic group on their work roles and reproductive histories (Gruenbaum 1990). We interviewed in a sample of Nuer communities clustered south of the confluence of the Sobat River with the White Nile in Jonglei Province, and I did participant observation in the village of Ayod, a Nuer community in Jonglei Province.

For the Sudanese Ministry of Social Affairs, I led a survey team to study the utilization of health and social services in Sudan's premier area for irrigated agricultural development and cotton production, Gezira Province (located south of Khartoum in the peninsula formed by the Blue Nile and White Nile), and I conducted community case studies in Wad Sagurta and Abdal Galil villages. That 1977 research, together with archival research before and after it and additional research visits to Abdal Galil village, contributed to my dissertation on the impact of the Gezira Irrigated Scheme on health and health services in Sudan (Gruenbaum 1982).

In 1976–77, I also participated in research in two villages on the Rahad River, east of the Blue Nile, where my husband, Jay, and a colleague were studying economic organization and labor migration. The villages of Um Fila and Hallali afforded a rich opportunity to compare ethnic differences in female circumcision practices, as well as patterns of family life (Gruenbaum 1979).

I went to Sudan for a short period of follow-up field research in 1989 that included work in the cities of Khartoum and Wad Medani and the villages of Abdal Galil in Gezira Province and a new village, Garia Wahid, where the families from Um Fila and Hallali had been resettled for a development project, the Rahad Irrigation Project. Although I was only able to spend a few hours at the old Um Fila site with the families who had declined to relocate, the weeks of research in Garia Wahid afforded valuable insights into the process of change and the interethnic influences that were taking place.

In 1992, I returned to Abdal Galil in Gezira and Garia Wahid in the Rahad and also spent brief periods in the cities of Khartoum and Wad Medani. Although the time was short, just a little over a month, I was able to note the changes and to focus on interviews with people already well known to me.

Whenever possible, I have taken opportunities to continue discussing female circumcision and change efforts with Sudanese and other African women in international contexts. Most memorable was the Beijing Conference in 1995, when I had the opportunity to spend many hours over several days in the company of both northern and southern Sudanese women representing the whole political spectrum, including progovernment factions, internal dissidents, and exiles.

Taboo Subject?

It was not my intention to study the topic of female circumcision originally. In fact, I did not know about these surgeries prior to my decision to go to Sudan for the first time in 1974. It was not until the last few weeks before my husband and I were to depart that I learned of pharaonic

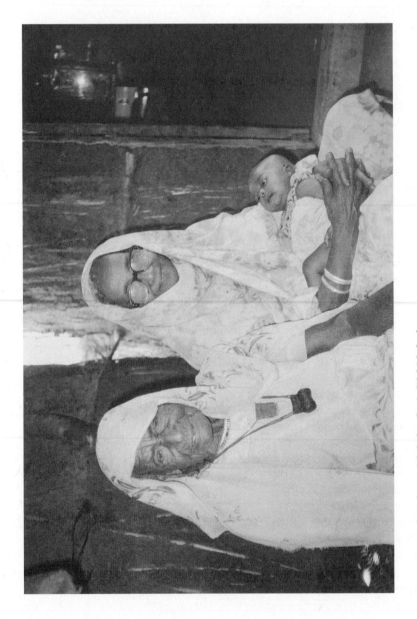

Kenana grandmothers with baby, Garia Wahid, Sudan.

circumcision. The wife of one of my graduate school professors, who had spent three years in Sudan in the 1960s, shocked me with the news. At our going-away party, she told me that most Sudanese women had undergone genital surgeries during childhood, that midwives removed the girls' clitorises and all or part of their labia and then left them sewn shut, except for a very small opening for urination and menstruation preserved by insertion of a piece of straw during the healing process.

A stark image. I recall feeling vaguely nauseous. Could she be mistaken? What a horrendous secret! Why hadn't I come across this before? I had no reason to doubt her information, but I found myself unable to believe it completely, wondering if — and hoping — that it might by then be a thing of the past.

It is perhaps a similar experience of shock upon learning about female circumcision that has led outsiders to label this a taboo subject that cannot be discussed (e.g., Hosken 1982). After all, we wonder, why isn't a fact of this importance generally known? One might conclude it has been kept secret, making the term "taboo" — associated with forbidden or secret activities — seem particularly apt.

But female circumcision is not a secret at all. In Sudan everyone knows about it. In 1994, I discussed this concept of circumcision as a secret or taboo with Sudanese legal scholar and change supporter, Asma M. Abdal Halim, who agreed: "It's *not* a secret; we celebrate it!" (personal notes, Sisterhood Is Global Conference, Bethesda, Maryland, September 1994).

Why might a visitor conclude the topic is "taboo"? Probably because the subject is not likely to be brought up in conversations with outsiders. People have been reluctant to speak of it. First, it relates to sexual anatomy and sexuality, neither of which is a common conversation opener with people from outside one's culture or social milieu. Indeed, sexuality is not a frequent topic of conversation among women in my Sudan experience and in the accounts of others. It is rarely mentioned in mixed company, though it is not suppressed among friends and in environments where people feel safe. Second, among people where circumcision practices and the reality of being scarred is part of everyday existence, it is unremarkable, taken for granted, and therefore unlikely to be spoken of among casual acquaintances visiting from foreign countries. In the United States, where until recently the circumcision of infant males was so general that doctors often performed it on newborns without even bothering to ask the parents, the fact that men are circumcised scarcely merits comment. Upon meeting a visitor from another country, an unlikely conversational gambit for an American to offer would be, "Oh, by the way, in our country we cut the foreskins off male babies. What about in your country?" Probably not. Does that mean it is "taboo"? I don't think so. It is more or less the same for people from Sudan, Somalia, and other countries in which female circumcision is common.

There is another reason the subject has seemed hush-hush: the fear of outsiders' condemnations. People dealing with foreigners were well advised to keep their female circumcision practices quiet or, when discussed, downplay their extent. Certainly during the colonial period (roughly the nineteenth and first half of the twentieth centuries), the attitudes of missionaries, colonial administrators, and medical workers were highly negative. European and North American attitudes that viewed many even less harmful indigenous customs in Africa as "barbaric" or "uncivilized" were not based on universally accepted values but are now understood to have been ethnocentric and often calculated attempts to justify actions and attitudes that were racist, ethnocentric, and exploitative. Were European activities in conquering and militarily "pacifying" African peoples, installing European-owned plantations and mines on their lands, destroying their cultures, and importing a new religion always beneficial to Africans? It would be naive to think so, though at the time these "white man's burden" and "civilizing mission" ideologies were used successfully to gain support in Europe for conquest and exploitation.

From a contemporary, postcolonial perspective, such attempts at justification are transparent and can be confidently criticized. It should not be too surprising that external condemnations of female circumcision, like the old colonial ideologies, might be similarly criticized as being unjustified and offensive. In short, African societies have experienced European/North American ethnocentrism in its most cynical and destructive forms, and it should be no wonder that practices that diverge so markedly from European/North American values have not been advertised to Europeans and North Americans.

Where female circumcision is practiced, it has not been some hidden ritual of which people are guiltily ashamed, as some writers seem to suggest. Dr. Nahid Toubia has pointed out that critics have tended to mystify the whole subject and assume that female circumcision is "something inherited from an untraceable past that has no rational meaning and lies within the realm of the untouchable sensitivity of traditional people" (1985:150). In her interview by Terry Gross on the radio program *Fresh Air* (recorded in 1996), Toubia noted that the subject of female circumcision "is not taboo," rather, "it is *painful*." When women feel they are in a safe environment, they are "desperate to talk about it," she has found.

The view that female circumcision is simply an irrational tradition suggests that the practitioners are somehow less rational than people in "modern" societies and justifies a heavy-handed approach that strives to teach (or preach to) people who are seen as "ignorant." In my view, an elitist and ethnocentric attitude does not offer much hope for productive dialogue and mutual understanding. Female circumcision is neither a taboo subject—the fact that "we" didn't know much about it does not mean it was secret—nor is it done without thought.

That said, I must also note that some people with insider status who are ardent activists against the practices do accuse those who allow complacency of succumbing to a taboo. For example, Somali activist Raqiya Haji Dualeh Abdalla comments, with reference to "the ancient custom of genital mutilation of women":

Almost no one, so far, has had the courage to speak openly about it because of the taboo attached to sexual matters.

This taboo and secrecy surrounding the continuation of this brutal practice, the unwillingness of those involved in it to face reality, and the excuse that cultural practices are sacrosanct, are no longer convincing to many Somali women today. (Abdalla 1982:2)

Abdalla writes to motivate action, and the use of this word *taboo* seems intended to jolt her Somali sisters into action, lest they be branded as backward thinking. Others refer to female circumcision as a "silent issue."

The Khartoum Context

After I moved to Khartoum in 1974, it took me many months to develop a perspective on my own horrified reaction to female circumcision. During those first months in Sudan's capital city, the subject rarely came up with my Sudanese colleagues or students. The elegant Sudanese women at the university wore Western dresses covered by sheer, white, wraparound veils called *tobes* that modestly covered their heads and bodies nearly to the floor but did not conceal their hair, forearms, or faces. Women students in Khartoum generally spoke softly, carried themselves gracefully, walking in twos and threes, seldom alone, their high-heeled shoes or sandals clicking on the tiled corridors. Many wore bouffant hairstyles that lifted their tobes into impressive crowns framing their faces, and most wore some jewelry.

Their modest elegance was in stark contrast to women's styles at the U.S. universities I had attended (Stanford and the University of Connecticut); I was used to jeans and sweatshirts or dressing up in pants suits or miniskirts. My friends and I seldom wore earrings, and my jewels in those days consisted of "love beads" left over from California in the 1960s. Our feminism emphasized health, outdoorsy looks, and a strong, witty intellectual style, with relatively little interest in, and even distaste for, what we saw as traditional feminine delicacy. By contrast, in this middle-class milieu of 1970s Khartoum, femininity was clearly marked, stylized, and valued. The women (about 10 percent of the students in those days) always sat in the front of the classrooms, a location that allowed them to concentrate on the lecture and afforded them the chance to discreetly rearrange and adjust their tobes after class without having to make eye contact with the male students while doing so.

It was difficult to imagine that it was these women who were the ones who practiced female circumcision. And could these affable, joking, confident men at the university be the fathers, husbands, and brothers who expected women to be circumcised?

I remember sitting with our friend and colleague Mohammed on one of those very hot, slow afternoons after lunch at the University of Khartoum Staff Club. Most offices closed about 1:30, and Jay and I usually drove our battered Volkswagen home by 2:30 or so, but we had decided to wait that day until the weather cooled off a little. We sat inside, away from the blinding tropical brightness outdoors and as close as we could get to the evaporative cooler that was built into the wall. Jay always complained that the ceiling fans—meant to circulate the cooled air—were so slow that the flies rode around on them. That day I believed him.

"Ya, Salim!" Mohammed called. He knew all the waiters' names. The middle-aged man in a worn *jalabiya*, loose turban, and scuffed leather loafers took our order for another round of Pepsis and then returned with the heavy tray. "Sorry, no more ice," he said as he set the thick, refillable bottles in front of us. They were barely cool to the touch.

Mohammed insisted on paying for all of them, treating us like guests again, even though we had been there for several months. More than once we had been accused of not respecting their cultural values if we tried to resist someone's hospitality. Even after I learned the Arabic for "No, by God, it's my turn," and Jay could say "By the divorce!" (which meant "I'll divorce my wife if you don't let me pay," which always got a laugh), we still did not often succeed in paying. To get a turn, one of us usually had to find the waiter in the corridor and pay him halfway through the meal before the others knew about it.

We learned much about Sudan from Mohammed. He often spoke passionately about politics, criticizing the latest policy of the minister of social affairs or passing on one of the many President Nimeiri jokes with which Sudanese expressed their dissatisfactions with the government. At first I was surprised that he would speak so frankly to foreigners. But he had spent several years as a graduate student in Britain and had traveled widely to international conferences, so he had numerous foreign friends and a cosmopolitan outlook. He was quite at home, however, in the small villages of Sudan. He was a man who combined a strong sense of cultural pride with a genuinely global view of humanity: we humans were all in this together, he seemed to be saying, so why bother hiding anything?

That day our conversation turned to the situation of women. His wife was a homemaker, though she had finished high school, had been abroad with him for part of the time, and spoke English fairly well. When we visited them, their home seemed very traditional to us. Several female relatives who lived nearby came and went through the women's entrance and stayed on the private side of the house, while Jay had to stay with Mohammed on the formal side of the house, which consisted of the living room and courtyard by the main entrance. Although Mohammed's wife, dressed in a colorful tobe, had ventured in to greet Jay, she seemed to prefer the company of the children and other women who were helping her prepare the meal while Mohammed relaxed with us. Did he prefer this division of labor and space, I wondered?

In fact, Mohammed was critical of the situation of women in his own culture. Many aspects of women's roles didn't matter much to him — separate entrances at the mosques and whether one wore a tobe or not — those were just traditional. "When people are ready to leave those things, they will. But for now they are comfortable with them." He thought the division of labor in the family might also change.

But there were two things that Mohammed thought were real injustices: the limited educational opportunities for girls and female circumcision. As the father of several daughters, he wanted them to have excellent educations and good career opportunities. Since most schools — except for a few of the elementary schools — were sex segregated, there were far fewer schools for girls than boys. Whenever a village or town set out to build its first school, it was almost always for boys. Only many years later would the girls get a school. Mohammed's urban residence and influential occupation meant that his daughters would get elementary school places, but the competition was very tough for the much smaller number of places available at each higher level.

Mohammed told us that he was also worried about female circumcision for his daughters. He had told the women of his family that he did not want them to be circumcised. I naively assumed that in a culture where the males are clearly dominant, his decision would be enough to protect them.

Not so. He was afraid that if he left the country to go to the conference he was planning to attend, the grandmothers would simply arrange everything and have the older two daughters circumcised in his absence. He was sure his wife would not oppose her own mother.

"Wouldn't they be afraid you would be angry?"

"Of course. But they just go along with me when I'm here. Among themselves they say it's not men's business."

"But isn't it illegal?"

"Oh, yes. Since the British law of 1946. But what difference does that make?" He laughed and shrugged. "I couldn't have my own mother arrested, or my mother-in-law. If they do it, I'd just have to accept it."

He took another sip of his Pepsi. "Anyway," he continued, "I think I've figured out a way to take the family along for a vacation while I'm at the conference."

Entering the Debates

I presented my first paper on the topic of female circumcision in 1980 and rapidly began to appreciate the intensity of this controversy. The fact that I had known little about female circumcision before my departure for Sudan in 1974 was not because it had never been written about. Indeed, in the British colonial period in Sudan, it was a topic of interest to policy-makers, government reformers, and activist groups. Nevertheless, it does not appear to have caught tremendous notice in scholarship, probably because most of the previous writing on the subject was to be found in medical journals that offered little social contextualization and this writing had not filtered into the consciousness of the women's movement. With women's studies only recently coming on the scene in the late 1960s and early 1970s, no one had yet undertaken the project to sort out for the public the information that was there to be gleaned from the medical articles and from existing ethnographic sources.

I would also note that during the early decades of the twentieth century, and to some degree even to the present, ethnographic writings usually were not written to be accessible to public policymakers. Instead, the image of anthropologists was that they cared only about obscure, "primitive," "tribal" people and that such people were not of great interest to, or were seen as inferiors by, the dominant cultures of the developed countries, particularly in the period before the civil rights movement and the wholesale termination of overt colonial control of African countries. Anthropologists' policy contributions often were directed to governing such people in colonial settings, offering insights into our evolution as a species, or at times assisting in cultural profiling to aid in war and counterinsurgency. Of course that is only one part of our history as a discipline. But although we and our forebears have been passionate about documenting cultural differences and have treasured the peoples whose stories we have come to know, we have not been immune from the use and misuse of our knowledge for less than lofty purposes.

Given that context, it is understandable that it was not until the momentum of the women's movement that more information began to be available. In 1975 the *American Ethnologist* carried an important article by Rose Oldfield Hayes based on research in Sudan that linked the practice of "female genital mutilation" with fertility control, women's roles, and patrilineal social structure. Here at last was an accessible argument that offered information and linked it to social context.

It was in this period, after I returned from my first research trip to Sudan, that I had been invited to present my paper. Like Hayes, my position was a feminist one that sought to explain the context and provide understanding of this as a women's issue that was constrained by patriarchal relations and global inequality of opportunity. My paper evoked intense interest that led me to publish it (Gruenbaum 1982b). But I also encountered other reactions.

First, I found that several of the women scholars of Middle Eastern origin were intensely critical of this topic entering the Western discourse on the Middle East at that time. They considered it an inappropriate topic for outsiders because it tended to sensationalize and stigmatize their cultures. I agreed with them that the general public and scholars in the United States knew too little about Islam, the Arab-Israeli conflict, Arab cultural heritage, and the daily life of the many peoples of the Middle East/North Africa. They had a valid point: talking about this shocking practice could contribute to stereotyping, rather than promoting understanding.

The positions that Rose Oldfield Hayes (1975), Marie Bassiii Assaad (1980), Janice Boddy (1982), and I (1982) had offered in our analyses recognized the value of the practices in their cultural contexts — not very pleasant or healthy, perhaps, but a significant element of the culture. Although Cloudsley (1983) gave the original version of her book the pointed subtitle *Victims of Circumcision,* she too documented its cultural significance.

None of these analyses was an apologist stance; anthropologists who wrote at that time recognized that change was happening and was likely to continue, perhaps at a gradual pace. We wrote as analysts rather than activists, but with an eye toward conditions that might lead to change (e.g., Gruenbaum 1982b). I strongly argued, as I continue to do, that there is a lengthy agenda of life struggles facing the poor people of the societies in question and we must not neglect to address their other dire problems like war, displacement, famines, high rates of disease and infant and child mortality, lack of educational opportunities, and economic exploitation (see also Morsy 1991). Harmful traditional practices are on the list, but from the perspective of rural women, they may not be at the top of the social change agenda.

Some of the Western feminist scholars who studied the affected countries made the decision to suppress this topic in their own writing and teaching. That was not only because Middle Eastern and African women asserted that it was not our place to bring it up, but also because many of us who had worked so hard in our teaching and writing to promote interest in and understanding of the cultures of Africa and the Middle East discovered that once this topic was mentioned, we could not discuss much else. The effect was, as Hale (1994) and Fleuhr-Lobban (1995) have discussed, a tendency to silence oneself on this topic, even among those who knew a great deal about it, leaving this issue to a footnote or not mentioning it at all.

Meanwhile, most social scientists from Egypt and Sudan rarely mentioned female circumcision in their work during the 1970s and early 1980s. Only a few Middle Eastern feminists wrote about it in English or translated works, with Egyptian novelist, doctor, and political activist Nawal El Sadaawi being a noteworthy example. The chapter entitled "The Circumcision of Girls" in her book *The Hidden Face of Eve* (1980) was particularly influential, as was the section describing her memories of her own circumcision, which was excerpted for *Ms.* magazine in the early 1980s. Its publication brought greater attention to the subject among North American feminists. But the most extensive and explicit analyses by Middle Eastern social scientists came later, for example, Morsy's work on Egypt (1993) and her rejoinder to Gordon (1991).

Fran Hosken is credited with presenting the bombshell that generated much of the popular awareness of the seriousness and wide prevalence of these practices (discussed further in Chapter 8). In particular, her 1980 publication of *The Hosken Report: Genital and Sexual Mutilation of Females* (see also the third edition 1982) offered new information, a multicountry perspective, and an impassioned plea that aid missions, church groups, and international organizations should take a firm stand, including the withholding of aid, to require governments of the affected countries "to prevent the operations." Hers was a take-no-prisoners approach that justified even forceful external interference.

While I differed with her analysis and tactics, Hosken did succeed in opening up to a broad audience a debate that was inevitable: how best to promote change. Her radical "eradication now!" position contrasted sharply with the gradualist program of medicalization that Sudanese reformers were pursuing in the 1970s — providing better hygiene and safety by performing these procedures in doctors' offices, providing midwives with medical supplies to do them better, and trying to persuade people to do less severe forms. (Today public health programs refer to such approaches as "harm reduction," pursued when eradication seems an impossible or distant goal.) Several other writers in the 1980s were also strongly oriented toward change (Sanderson 1981, Koso-Thomas 1987, Accad 1989, originally published in 1982 in French).

For impassioned change agents, however, reform programs are considered an obstacle and contextual analysts are viewed as apologists (a position I examine in the final chapter). From this perspective, we should stop using cultural "excuses" for human rights abuses of women and children. Gordon advocated that we anthropologists "draw the line" at female circumcision (1991), and increasingly anthropologists are willing to consider doing so (e.g., Fleuhr-Lobban 1995).

Novelists, journalists, other writers, and filmmakers joined the discourse in the 1990s. Hanny Lightfoot-Klein's "Prisoners of Ritual" (1989) was just the first of many provocative titles that aroused tremendous public interest. Words like "crimes," "pain," "brutal ritual," and "torture" figured prominently in titles; examples include "The Ritual: Disfiguring, Hurtful, Wildly Festive" (French 1997) and "Battling the Butchers" (Brownworth 1994). Alice Walker's novel *Possessing the Secret of Joy* (1992) and Walker and Pratibha Parmar's book and film *Warrior Marks* (1993) persuaded large numbers of people that a highly damaging, oppressive "ritual" was being inflicted without reflection, based on male domination and ignorance. With all of this awareness of the issue, anthropologists owe it to the public to offer their best ideas and analysis.

Recent analytical work and public education writing by anthropologists (and our kindred social scientists) has developed in a very gratifying direction, generally offering the contextualized analyses while accepting and contributing to ideas for change. Writers such as Scheper-Hughes (1991) and Gruenbaum (especially 1996) stress that circumcision practices are already changing and that the peoples affected are "arguing this one out" for themselves. Obermeyer (1999), Abusharaf (1998), Hale (1994), Hicks (1993), Lane and Rubinstein (1996), Boddy (1998b), Walley (1996), and the contributors to the new edited volume by Shell-Duncan and Hernlund (2000) all offer examples of contextualized analysis that neither condemns those who practice female circumcision nor endorses the continuation. This new body of literature could perhaps be characterized as being calm and optimistic about the prospects for change, while urging critics and reformers to make serious attempts to understand the contexts.

Feminist anthropologists who are committed to ameliorating the social injustices of the world and especially those based on women's subordination must grapple with ethical dilemmas. Our respect for and analysis of the ways that humans have adapted culturally to many environments and social situations throughout our human past should not eclipse the fact that as human social actors, we are also engaged in the process of forming the human future. As feminist anthropologists, we should be involved in trying to find our way forward to a harmonious and sustainable future that allows autonomy for individuals and social groups but moves toward resolving conflicts in these differing world views and social practices.

No one has all the answers, but many fruitful avenues are being pursued. One area of possible dialogue is the expansion of the agenda of the human rights movement. In 1997, I became involved with the American Anthropological Association's Committee for Human Rights. It was my hope that the human rights discourse might contribute to alleviating human suffering, but of course it is never easy to map such terrain. Human rights discourse requires anthropologists to consider conflicts between group rights and individual rights, between one group's valued traditions and religious beliefs and the traditions and beliefs of others. The human rights movement internationally has at times allowed one set of cultures to be hegemonic, leaving it open to accusations of ethnocentrism, clearly counter to our anthropological tradition of cultural relativism (Messer 1993, Nagengast 1997, Walter 1995). Cultural hegemony cannot be the foundation if there is to be acceptance of universalist stances. But it will be even more difficult to resolve these issues as the human rights agenda expands into areas well beyond condemning oppressive actions of states, venturing into cultural practices and human rights to health and well-being (see Chapter 8).

The process of exploring the female circumcision debates is valuable in developing one's own position and becoming able to contribute in some way to promoting understanding and working for better lives for women. To explore these issues in our writing is not the same as trying to "speak for" others or become their unauthorized "allies." Nor is it intended to tell "them" what to do or pretend that some imaginary superior "we" has the answer to the questions of when and how to pursue change. Instead, grappling with difficult questions is a human moral imperative, or try to understand our world and to promote discussion and understanding across the boundaries that divide people.

Humanitarian Values and Cultural Relativism

Upon learning of these female circumcision practices, people from outside the cultures commonly conclude that the continuation of such harmful practices violates humanitarian values. Certainly, for those committed to improving women's rights globally and for those working on international health, the agenda seems clear: we respond with an urgent desire to stop the practices.

Yet if these practices are based on deeply held cultural values and traditions, can outsiders effectively challenge them without challenging the cultural integrity of the people who practice them? Cognizant as we have become, at the dawn of the millennium, of the injustice of exercising cultural hegemony and of the greater insight achievable when multiple viewpoints are consulted and disparate voices heard, can we adopt a position that declines to challenge any cultural practices? Under what circumstances and through what means is it permissible to attempt to alter fundamentally the beliefs and practices of others? And even if the ethical justifications are found, how effective will condemnations of a cultural practice be, particularly if they appear to condemn an entire people and their cultural values?

Simplistic condemnations are not only ineffectual but can also stimulate strong defensive reactions. On many occasions, the pious pronouncements of outsiders against cultural practices deemed "backward" or "barbaric" have provoked a backlash, with people staunchly defending their traditions against criticism. Jomo Kenyatta, who was trained in anthropology and later became president of Kenya, wrote a book entitled *Facing Mount Kenya* (1959, originally published in 1938), in which he argued strongly in favor of female circumcision, viewing British colonial criticism of it as essentially cultural imperialism. More recently, at the 1975 international conference in Denmark sponsored by the United Nations for the International Decade for Women, female circumcision became a major focus of controversy at the conference when some of the African women present took umbrage at the denunciations of anticircumcision political activists such as Fran Hosken; non-African women such as Hosken were accused of inappropriate cultural interference. As this discussion has continued to flourish in international gatherings into the present, even African women who are activists against the practice do not usually welcome outsiders preaching pompously against their societies' traditions.

Critical opposition is potentially experienced as hostile ethnocentrism. Ethnocentric assessments that view the practices of others through the perspective of one's own culture are often innocuous misunderstandings. To see cultural differences naively from one's own cultural perspective is neither preventable nor necessarily harmful. But frequently ethnocentric views lead not only to misconceptions but also to strongly negative judgments of differences. That sort of ethnocentrism has a different tone entirely, one of scolding, distaste, condescension, and condemnation. Insofar as it is unreflective, such ethnocentrism contributes to prejudices, particularly when the cultural differences concern strongly held values.

In the argument against female circumcision, people have too often latched onto some single cause that can be condemned. This may enhance one's conviction of the need for change, but if it does not include an understanding of how the practitioners view the issue, it will not bring us any closer to seeing how change can occur. A sound analysis requires looking at female circumcision from many angles, listening to what women who do it have said about it, and trying to understand the reasons for resistance to change. Doing that does not make us advocates for the practices. It simply recognizes that without a more sympathetic "listen," we miss the fundamental causes and the concrete obstacles to change.

The Prime Directive

Like the Hippocratic Oath to do no harm and *Star Trek*'s "prime directive" not to interfere with indigenous cultures of other worlds, cultural anthropologists have valued the rights of peoples to pursue their traditional practices and values.[2] This is not to say that in the past cultural anthropologists were not affected by ethnocentrism. Indeed there are many examples of disparagement and condemnation of customs to be found in earlier writings of cultural anthropologists. But anthropologists have struggled to clarify their perspective, recognizing the impossibility of totally "value-free" social science and yet pursuing a stance capable of greater objectivity than ethnocentrism affords. Any missionary zeal to change "the other" into a copy of the model of "civilized" culture offered by one's own culture is understood to truncate one's ability to understand.

Thus the anthropological antidote to ethnocentrism became cultural relativism — judging each culture within its own context rather than by the values of others. I regard cultural relativism not as an ultimate ethical stance but as a mental technique to assist people to avoid negative judgments of, say, food preferences, manners of greeting, or marital customs. Such a perspective is clearly necessary for carrying out ethnographic field research. While a cultural relativistic approach embodies certain ethical dilemmas, it is a beneficial starting point for promoting intercultural understanding. Although a useful mental exercise to free one from unreflective ethnocentrism, cultural relativism usually requires a degree of suspension of one's ethical values. How far can or should one go with this?

Female circumcision offers a major test of whether it is possible to reconcile cultural relativist respect for cultural diversity with the desire to improve the lives of girls and women across cultural boundaries. It raises the question of whether the outsider's desire to influence cultural prac-

---

[2] The challenge that the female circumcision controversy poses to these values is deeply significant. For a short discussion of the topic in relation to *Star Trek*, see Anderson (1997).

tices constitutes ethnocentric interference or humanitarian solidarity. It demands consideration of how respect for cultural variation, which seems to imply noninterference, can be made to allow a constructive role for outsiders in social change.

The Limits to Cultural Relativism

One way to explore the issue of limits is to turn to some of the most extreme examples that can be imagined and see how individuals' ethical values respond to these cases. Let us consider for a moment slavery. In slavery systems, one person owns and controls the fate of another, his or her freedom, work, sexuality, and well-being. In doing so, the owner may be following a socially permitted institution of another time and place, and he or she may consider slavery to be right and just. Applying cultural relativism would allow for better understanding and explanation of how that owner might manage to feel morally upright. An even more extreme example would be genocide. While it is jarring to think about it, those who have engaged in genocide or ethnic cleansing may have reasons for doing these things that they consider proper, such as perhaps a belief that it is God's will or that racial/ethnic purity and homogeneity are the proper state of existence and the ancestral rights of inhabitants of a region.

But is it necessary to accept slavery or genocide as legitimate human institutions simply because certain cultures at particular historical junctures have justified them? Surely not. But to dismiss such views as purely crazy or "backward" is also to fail to appreciate the incredible complexity of the human mind, which can find justifications for behavior that in the light of a more general sense of human morality is clearly disgusting and outrageous. It is also clear that trying to understand the causes of such practices may prove valuable in preventing them in the future.

In my view, human beings should reflect upon and criticize historical events, whether they are directly involved in them or not. The exercise of understanding how those who practice slavery or genocide think about and justify the practices could be extremely valuable both to the under- standing of humanity, a fundamental goal of anthropology, and to practi- cal efforts to prevent these practices. For issues less likely to be altered by legislation or war, understanding why it may be in the interests of certain groups to continue practices judged harmful by others is a basic prereq- uisite for any efforts to convince others to change.

My point is that in order to benefit from the insights of the suspended judgment used in cultural relativism, individuals need not disavow all ethical considerations. And if an individual's ethics are derived from a

particular religious or cultural tradition, that does not automatically dis-
qualify them as ethnocentric. Indeed, when there is dialogue, many of
our culturally based human values can be seen to transcend cultures.

Genocide and slavery provide stark examples of cross-cultural ethical
judgments; the response to other practices is not as clear to many of us.
Consider infanticide. Although one might believe it is wrong to kill or
abandon a healthy, unwanted infant after it is born, it is possible to arrive
at understanding and sympathy for the moral position of a mother who
has committed infanticide without oneself approving of infanticide as a
customarily tolerated practice. In a situation of rural isolation, poverty,
maternal malnutrition, cultural permission, and no apparent alternatives, a mother may be faced with a situation in which a new baby presents
an unacceptable risk to the survival of her fourteen-month-old child who
is also dependent on her milk. Early weaning of a toddler in a situation
where other sources of milk or nutritious weaning foods are not available
could easily lead to that child's death through malnutrition and conse-
quent infectious diseases. In fact, "kwashiorkor," the name for a severe
nutritional deficiency disease, means "second-child disease," indicating
that the disease is related to early weaning after the arrival of a new infant
(Wood 1979:73). Faced with the risk of losing an older child to whom she
and her family are already attached and in whom she has invested a great
deal of effort, a mother might understandably consider protecting that
child from the competition of a new, unwanted infant. If in addition the
new infant has some disadvantage — a physical handicap, say, or being
female in a social situation where sons are vital — the mother might make
the difficult choice of infanticide, for which she would not be considered
immoral in that society. (For one such example, see Chagnon 1983. See
also Scheper-Hughes's study of motherhood in the impoverished conditions of urban Brazil, *Death Without Weeping*, 1992.)

In the case of infanticide, pronouncing a moral judgment is really
beside the point. What is to be gained by calling such a mother a mur-
derer? Will an external condemnation serve as a deterrent to future such
incidents? Or would changing the economic, educational, nutritional,
and other social opportunities be a more effective route to change?

Where change is desirable and urgent, pronouncing moral judgments
may have a place. But while it may be psychologically satisfying to pass
judgment on the practices of others, it is not particularly useful unless the
person is already in agreement with you. With issues like female circumcision, utilizing relativism is often more fruitful because it requires contextualization and inhibits crude ethnocentric prejudices that interfere
with effective dialogue. Exploring the context produces clues about what
changes would be necessary to allow for changes in the unfortunate
practice and what factors might create obstacles to change. Infanticide

can disappear when change occurs in the conditions that fostered it, as when economic conditions improve, allowing for more adequate nutrition. One can also expect that changes in cultural conditions, such as the strong preference for sons (which is itself frequently based on old-age security considerations of parents) found in many cultures where female infanticide has been accepted, could also help to reduce infanticide. If rural communities offered better opportunities for children and if a government introduced policies to allow girls the same educational and employment opportunities as boys, this could facilitate a cultural transition away from male-child preference. But under what conditions would a government introduce such policies? And is it acceptable for state power to interfere with cultural preferences? Can a state be assumed to represent the legitimate interests of the peoples it governs, even if some groups oppose the cultural standards imposed?

Strong cultural relativists question whether it is justified to strive to change the culture of others or whether a basic right of cultural self-determination prohibits external interference. In this view, to offer or impose changes rooted in the values and cultural traditions of powerful external forces constitutes cultural imperialism. Wasn't this exactly the sort of justification used by European powers to conquer and subjugate other regions of the world?

The arguments that it was the "white man's burden" to carry out a "civilizing mission" in Africa and other lands are now well understood as the ideological cover used to justify economic and social exploitation of subjugated peoples. The idea that "native" peoples should be Christianized and civilized served to garner public opinion in Europe for invasion and establishment of colonial domination around the world. With this justification, willful destruction of indigenous lifeways was carried forth for centuries as powerful countries imposed their economic systems and social values on peoples whose traditional cultures did not deserve the opprobrium they received. And Christianity, capitalism, and related governmental forms have been dogged by numerous economic, moral, and social problems of their own.

Thus it is appropriate to be cautious about the assumption that what seems self-evident and obviously "right" and "wrong" to a Western "us" is universally so. Shifting viewpoints can produce different understandings of the apparent purposes of social actions. Anthropologists, with their deep training in cultural sensitivity, may be more diligent in looking for ulterior motives and unforeseen effects of culture change initiatives undertaken by reformers, public health educators, and others working for change and development. Yet ultimately anthropologists, too, are affected by their own cultural backgrounds and beliefs.

Mahnaz Afkhami, a feminist activist with the Sisterhood Is Global Institute, has noticed that even those Western feminists who attempt to exercise cultural sensitivity at times display what she calls "arrogance": "I have seen a lot more sensitivity from Western feminists in the last few years, but . . . sometimes their attempts at cultural awareness and sensitivity can go too far, as we see among those Western women who say that female circumcision . . . is just another cultural practice. But this cultural relativism is just another example of . . . arrogance. . . . It is as if Western feminists are saying 'okay, a whole set of norms apply to us and our culture, and a whole other set of norms applies to these other cultures' " (Afkhami 1996:17).

Thus the analysis of the causality and roots of female circumcision practices is intricately linked to the need to assess and evaluate change efforts in terms of their intent and effect. Is an effort to change based partly on ethnocentric values? Or is it a response to human needs? Is it responsive to the priorities for change of the population affected by a policy? Can the policy be effective if it is perceived as ethnocentric?

There is no clear rule for how to decide when one is applying a universal moral standard and when one is seeing the world through the moral values of one's own culture. Although there are philosophers who confidently assert universal moral principles, it is nevertheless quite difficult to persuade people with strongly held beliefs to accept any one set of "universal" values. Assertion, appeals to reason, or complex logical arguments cannot easily dislodge beliefs rooted in culture, faith, emotion, a different philosophical perspective, or lack of knowledge.

This dilemma is at the core of the female circumcision controversy. Although many people have achieved strong, clear views, others do not accept their reasoning or have strong views of their own. A fruitful dialogue requires a clearer understanding on all sides, not strongly stated moral judgments.

As immigrants have brought female circumcision practices with them to the countries of Europe and North America, and as the interconnectedness of the world's peoples increases, the issue of the harm to the health of women and girls becomes a global concern. The insider/ outsider differences in standpoint blur, intensifying the need to achieve some consensus on universal human rights to guide policy. It is incumbent upon North Americans and Europeans to become informed about female circumcision — to overcome misconceptions, to understand possible routes toward change, and to identify a constructive role in change efforts. But it is equally important to keep in mind the differing perspectives that people might hold from their own backgrounds because this is the substrate upon which the arguments, policies, and change efforts must grow.

Exploring the female circumcision controversy requires an investigation of ethnic, moral, religious, and gender role issues to promote greater understanding of the people who continue these practices and to consider how change is taking place.

Cultural Debates

Mohammed (in my earlier example) was not unique in his desire to foster improvements in the situation of women in Sudan. Indeed, a strong women's organization, the Sudanese Women's Union, has been politically active since the 1940s and includes many feminist, as well as nationalist, goals in its agenda (Hale 1996).

Yet in the 1990s, accusations that women's rights advocates have adopted "Western values" are not uncommon. Nationalism in Africa often has included rejection of some elements of European culture and social structure, but this has intensified in certain contexts under the Islamist movement. Often referred to as "Islamic fundamentalism," a term disliked by most Muslims, this Islamist movement is characterized by a desire to adopt what is thought to be a more authentic adherence to Islamic practice, including using Islamic law as the law of the state, and in some situations imposing Islamist understanding of proper dress and social rules on all members of society, or all Muslims at least. "Western" can then become an ideological stigma, symbolic for the Islamists of a rejection of the Islamic faith. In countries like Sudan, where an Islamist-oriented government came to power in 1989 and imposed many such policies and promulgated teaching and media efforts to gain popular acceptance, those who prefer to wear less restrictive clothing or otherwise challenge the legal initiatives of those in power have found themselves labeled "Westernized." This label implies their views or practices are illegitimate for a Muslim or for any Sudanese and sets them up for discrimination and worse. In some countries where the Islamist movement has taken hold more as a social movement, there may be more tolerance for diversity of personal practice and opinions, as seems to be the case in Egypt. Many of the extreme elements of the movement do not accept this diversity as a final state of society, however, and are working toward the goal of an Islamist state.

Although European and North American feminists have strongly advocated equality for women, including social changes to allow them greater dignity and autonomy and the elimination of sharp social constraints on roles and behaviors, the labeling of these desires as "Western" is misplaced. Throughout the world, women's equality has been a goal for reformers for decades, often predating the European and American movements. Indeed, Muslims frequently claim that the revelation of the Qur'an to Mohammed in the seventh century was a major boost to the status of women. In the past century, many Arab women (Muslim and otherwise) have written works that are clearly feminist in intent (Badran and Cooke 1990), and one of the first feminist "role reversal" novels was written in 1905 by Rogaia Sakhawat Hossain, a Muslim woman in what is now Bangladesh: *Sultana's Dream* (Hossain 1988). And although there were contentious debates at the Fourth World Conference on Women held in Beijing in 1995 about whether equality for women should be a goal in the Platform for Action document, most Muslims who opposed the term "equality" could accept the compromise term "equity." They argued that equity—with its implications of appropriateness to the context, allowing for a special role for each sex and different rules for men and women—rather than formal equivalency was preferable. According to their position, men should not have superiority, but men and women could have differing roles without preventing fair and equitable treatment of women. "Equality" to them implied that they would need to violate religious values such as male responsibility for support of family, the latter constituting the justification for such practices as giving women a smaller share of inheritance. The compromise on wording enabled people from all the participating countries to agree to promote women's welfare without agreeing on the particular legal, religious, or cultural approach.

The drive for change in women's roles and improvement in women's status is not simply the result of external "Western" influences but is a consequence of the dynamic of the inherent cultural contradictions in each culture. Culture is always contested (Sanday and Goodenough 1990), rife with debates, and crosscut by the viewpoints of different classes, age groups, genders, and other social divisions. Individuals' lack of behavioral conformity to cultural ideals offers evidence of this, as do the disagreements over ideas and the debates about how to interpret myths, traditions, rules, and religious teachings.

In posing a model of contested culture on these questions, I offer an alternative to the oversimplified "traditional/modern" or worse, "Western/non-Western," dichotomies that have plagued the analysis of cultural differences. The ways in which dialogues take place across our imaginary "cultural boundaries" are structured by the contested nature of culture—which ideas are listened to, discussed, adopted, or rejected is influenced by the problems faced by individuals and groups and whether the ideas offer satisfying resolutions to existing social conflicts. The women and men of the societies in which circumcision is now practiced are arguing this issue out for themselves (see Gruenbaum 1996), and their ideas are as diverse and varied as the political discourse on women's issues is anywhere. They are not dependent on the "West" for feminist ideas, nor can "traditional" and "modern" ideas be posed as monolithic

alternatives. This book offers my understanding of the relationship between female circumcision and the status of women, from both a global
perspective and more specifically as I have come to understand it in
Sudan.

Why Do People Do It?

There is no simple answer to this question. People have different and
multiple reasons. Female circumcision is practiced by people of many
ethnicities and various religious backgrounds, including Muslims, Christians,[3] and Jews,[4] as well as followers of traditional African religions. For
some it is a rite of passage. For others it is not. Some consider it aesthetically pleasing. For others, it is mostly related to morality or sexuality.

Understanding the diversity of reasons is the central issue if there is to
be any hope for cross-cultural understanding, fruitful dialogue, or effective change efforts. Thus the central chapters focus on these questions.

Chapter 2 examines the cultural meanings associated with the practices, including beliefs about them and ritual aspects. Comparison with
other forms of body alteration, especially male circumcision and subincision practices, is included. The main examples are drawn from my field
research in one rural Sudanese community. Religion is often used as a
justification for continuing or discontinuing a cultural practice, and circumcision is no exception. Because female circumcision is practiced by
people of several religions, the issue requires an exploration of the rele-
vant religious teachings and controversial interpretations.

In Chapter 3, I address morality and marriage expectations, including
the significance of virginity expectations, the contribution of female circumcision to the preservation of virginity, and its role in the promotion
of marital fidelity. The key question is whether circumcision status affects
marriageability in the cultures where it is practiced.

If culture is so important in the perpetuation of female circumcision
from one generation to the next, the cultural differences among ethnic
groups might be expected to coincide with differences in practices,
meanings, and ability to change. But insofar as ethnic identity might then
be partially defined by the practices, we can also expect that tenacity

---

[3] According to Leila Ahmed, "in Egypt it [clitoridectomy] is as common among Christians as among Muslims" (1992:176). Nahid Toubia, as a Sudanese Christian, discussed the
extent of the practice among Christians in the Arabic-speaking northern part of the country in her radio interview for *Fresh Air* in 1996, in which she commented on her own
mother's determination, as she matured, to prevent it for her younger daughters. See also
Toubia 1993:31–32 on Islam, Christianity, and Judaism. Additional discussion of Islam and
female circumcision is found in Chapter 2, below.

[4] Mainly the Ethiopian Jews known as the Falashas, many of whom now live in Israel.

to female circumcision practices based on ethnic identity might rival gender identity as an important obstacle to change efforts. Also, as people shift their ethnic identities through social class realignments, intermarriage, and migration, what happens to their circumcision practices? These are the issues pursued in Chapter 4.

One of the most salient issues about female circumcision in the writings of Western feminist authors is sexuality, which is the subject of Chapter 5. What are the effects of different forms of the surgeries on male and female sexual responses? Is the preoccupation with sexuality an indication of Western ethnocentrism?

Chapters 7 and 8 offer a perspective on the efforts to make fundamental changes in the practices. The first addresses grassroots change, while the second, the final chapter, looks at international covenants and social movements, current approaches to public health education, and practical suggestions for those committed to fostering change.

Dilemmas of Research and Reporting on Female Circumcision

Although one goal of this book is to consider the diversity of practices, contexts, and meanings, it cannot offer a comprehensive review of the full range of circumcision practices and their ethnographic contexts. I have drawn heavily on my own ethnographic research, however. I am fortunate that my examples from Sudan encompass a variety of ethnic, regional, and social class groups and span a period of years of significant social changes. From the diversity within one country and from selected comparisons with other areas, it will be evident that there is no single meaning or reason for female circumcision and there may be multiple routes to change.

In my field notebooks, I had jotted some thoughts on my frustration with fieldwork. How can anyone, I had written, ever achieve the level of confidence in their generalizations embodied in the style of the classic anthropological ethnographies, such as those of Evans-Pritchard? The old ethnographies give the impression that the researcher was omniscient, observing every detail of behavior, understanding every motive, able to generalize confidently about meanings and trends.

Contemporary anthropologists have been critical of that style, arguing that the knowledge is not authoritative, general, and timeless, but based on observations at one point in time. The strong postmodern critique of the study of the "other" recognizes that writing about culture is inherently interpretative and therefore influenced by the observer's predispositions and opportunities.

But to write about female circumcision, which is considered inherently harmful and a violation of women's and girls' human rights, poses an additional dilemma for feminist anthropologists. The feminist commitment to giving voice to — but not presuming to speak for — the experiences of women, as well as the commitment not only to do no harm but also to contribute to empowerment, seems straightforward enough when dealing with many women's issues. Domestic violence, children's welfare, and equal opportunities and pay are all examples where giving voice to women's dissatisfactions is usually supportive of a desire for change and improvement of the situation. But what about a harmful practice advocated by women?

The usual response in the 1960s and 1970s in the United States women's movement was that women who accepted subordination might be said to have a "false consciousness" and that should not be considered morally blameworthy. Consciousness-raising groups were very popular as a means for providing a support group in which one could express one's suffering, anger, difficulties, and doubts. The groups offered an opportunity to reflect on one's analysis of the realities and one's interpretation of fairness. What I always found significant about this process was that it relied heavily on open discussion, exploration of personal experience, and emotional support. It did not rely on preaching by an "enlightened" leader, passing judgment on other women, or demands for immediate changes in behavior. If a woman could not face the conflict over housework with her spouse, for example, she was not chastised, but offered sympathy, support, and suggestions by others who knew how difficult it might be. Personal growth, developing the courage to confront difficult changes, or just the release of knowing one is not alone were the results. Consciousness was raised by allowing one's own insights and by listening to others to develop new perspectives.

For the most part, Western feminists have found themselves in a dilemma in dealing with female circumcision. To label women of a different culture as having a "false consciousness" for advocating circumcision sounds like a delegitimization of the culture or beliefs of others. And even if that criticism is restrained, there are major barriers to entering into a "consciousness-raising" process with advocates of circumcision, not the least of which are language, location, culture, and religion. Thus too often the result has been a pedagogy of missionizing, telling others what they ought to do differently for reasons justified only by the "enlightened" outsiders' beliefs.

As I argue in this book, there is a role for anyone interested in contributing to the process of change. But the starting point is to work on understanding concrete situations in which female circumcision is practiced, as well as exploring and understanding one's own reactions. I offer my experiences as one place to start.

Chapter 1
Patriarchy

My first female circumcision party occurred shortly after my husband Jay and I moved into a house in the Khartoum neighborhood known as As-Sajjana, just south of Qurashi Park. We were younger then — it was the mid-1970s — and still in the glow of the excitement of our second year living in this dusty, hot city. Here our milk was delivered by a man wearing a flowing white jalabiya and turban, riding on a donkey. The neighbors' goats ate the garbage dumped in the central square beyond our walls, somehow turning it into milk for the evening tea. We joined the rhythm of the neighborhood, more or less, awakened each morning around 4:30 by the call to prayer, enhanced by the loudspeaker from the minaret of the nearby mosque, and retiring in the evening to the sounds of the neighbors' radios or visitors on the other side of the wall that divided our courtyards.

From our lawn chairs on the second-floor balcony, we could see a lot of neighborhood life. We had covered the balcony rail with straw mats to afford ourselves a little more privacy than the builder of the rather fancy, modern, red-brick house had provided and had decorated with four large clay pots of bougainvilleas from a nursery near the Nile. From the balcony we could see barefoot children playing soccer on the smooth, dusty field and school kids in uniforms wandering home. Itinerant glass-bottle buyers and broom sellers called their trades in nasal chants as their donkeys trotted their routes through the neighborhood. Creaky old cars (like our ancient orange VW bug) had to drive slowly down the bumpy dirt road to avoid scattered broken bricks and drainage ditches. In the mornings we saw women in colorful tobes returning to their homes with baskets of purchases from the market. At noon and at sunset men, and a few women, hurried to the mosque to pray at the appointed times, especially on the holy day, Friday.

In the glaring sun, these public moments burned images into our minds. But one of the reasons we had decided to move to this house from our first apartment, in a high-rise building near the airport, was to be more involved in a neighborhood. Watching was not enough, so we walked a lot, practiced our Arabic by chatting with shopkeepers, bought fresh fried *tamiya* (felafel) in the evenings from a man preparing it at a nearby corner, and introduced ourselves to the neighbors in the small mud-brick houses on either side of us. But it was not easy to become a part of this neighborhood, as different as we were and living in a house so clearly above (both in height and in social class) the neighborhood norm.

So Jay and I were very pleased the day a neighbor came by and invited us to a party that evening. We eagerly accepted his invitation and promised to be there. He indicated a house across the open space a little way down the street, where a couple of men were at work setting up a string of electric lights at the entrance and across their courtyard inside the wall.

The evening party was to be the formal occasion to celebrate his daughter's circumcision; the actual operation itself and the initial celebration among the women had already taken place in the morning. We had heard women's joyful ululation earlier, coming from that direction. Ululation is a sound like no other—a high-pitched, very loud vocalization, almost trill-like in its rhythmic variations in intensity and pitch. When performed simultaneously by several women, it announces to anyone within earshot (a long way in our open neighborhood of houses with open windows) that something significant and joyful is occurring—childbirth, circumcision, a bride's dance, a reunion. The sound can also drown out many other sounds such as cries of intensity of effort or pain. It is distinctly joyful and contrasts sharply with the other form of neighborhood announcement of a significant event, women's keening wail of grief upon receiving news of a death. So this time the ululation was a girl's circumcision.

During the afternoon a truck delivered stacks of blue metal chairs that were taken into the courtyard of the house. The houses on that side of the open space were almost identical: modest government housing originally built for the guards employed at the prison—hence the name of the neighborhood, As-Sajjana (those who work in the *sijin*, prison). Each home had an entrance through the outside wall into an inner courtyard and at least two rooms. The basic living conditions were good. There was running water, electricity, and some drainage, though the sewage system was something of a mystery. Our own toilets flushed, but our next-door neighbor, like most others, still had a bucket latrine inside the front wall that had to be emptied from time to time by workers who accessed it from the street by opening a small, pale-green wooden cover. The interior walls of most of the houses were smooth and painted. Some families had added rooms, verandas, and animal pens over the years, leaving some courtyards rather crowded. Most families still had dirt floors, though some had upgraded a visiting area — a veranda or one of the rooms — to cement tile. Most houses had water-resistant mud-and-dung roofs.

Jay and I waited until we saw from our balcony that evening prayers were finished at the mosque and that many of the guests had begun to arrive at the party. We had been to other sorts of parties with our students and faculty colleagues from the university, so we knew people would be well dressed, perfumed, and festive. We went over in our usual modified Western dress — I usually wore a long colorful jalabiya. The Sudanese considered this garment modest enough for a foreigner, but it was easier to manage than the Sudanese women's wrap-around tobe.

By that time, the hired musicians had set up and were singing the lilting Sudanese songs that were so popular, accompanied by violin and 'oud (a round-bodied string instrument related to the lute). We found chairs and tables set out in the courtyard for the men (and me). Something light and delicious to eat and cold drinks were brought to each table.

Eventually, I headed for the back courtyard, as I usually did on social occasions, to look for the women. I found my next-door neighbor Fatma there — she and several other neighbors had been helping prepare the food and were now relaxing with glasses of aromatic tea. She greeted me warmly and seemed pleased to see me there. She took me to a small, freshly painted bedroom to congratulate the girl who had been circumcised that morning.

The girl seemed to be trying to lie still and quiet as her visitors greeted her, but she intermittently moaned and writhed in discomfort. She looked older than I had expected. I was embarrassed to discover that people were putting small gifts of money under her pillow. My pockets were empty. But I offered my greetings and did my best to reproduce the blessing I had heard another woman say.

"They waited too long," Fatma told me quietly as we left the room. "She's nearly eleven. Older ones suffer more."

All of them must suffer, I thought, but I said nothing. Fatma had of course experienced this herself, so she certainly could empathize with the child. But I detected no hint of rebellion or resentment. It seemed too soon in our acquaintance to question her further, but the impression I had was that Fatma seemed quite accepting of this practice. In fact, it became my hypothesis in the many future conversations I had on this topic that for Sudanese women, *tahur* (purification, the colloquial term for both male and female circumcision) was seen as just another part of life — not a troublesome custom, but an assumed, normal reality. The impression was reinforced over and over in future conversations: any difficulties or pain that might be associated with female circumcision were, like the pain of childbirth, just one of the burdens and joys that go with being female.

I returned to the courtyard where the musicians were playing. In my absence, Jay had been served some whisky,[1] apparently in honor of his being foreign because no one else had any. This must have been an expensive party for a family of modest means. When we got up to say good-bye, our host was beaming with pride, probably from the success of his party as much as from his daughter's rite of passage.

What could explain the tenor of the event? Why the conspicuous consumption in celebration of the circumcision of a daughter?[2] The pride, pain, sympathy, and acceptance all seemed intertwined. As an outsider, I found it difficult to comprehend. So it was to this puzzle that I returned again and again in the years that followed.

Cultural Expressions of Male Domination

Why do societies permit and promote actions that interfere with the wholeness of the body? The mutilating female genital "circumcisions" — in whatever form — clearly violate the bodily integrity of girls and women. Male circumcision violates the bodily integrity of boys and men. A sentence such as the latter, however, is usually followed by "but . . ." Male circumcision seems far less harmful than female circumcision, and there is therefore a tendency to dismiss it as a totally different sort of phenomenon, despite the strong similarities in reasons given for performing male and female genital operations. For example, a pediatrician and certified Mohel(et) (circumciser of males in the Jewish tradition), Dorothy Greenbaum, wrote to the *Anthropology Newsletter* to say she had "read with interest and disapproval . . . comments . . . aligning the custom of entering a Jewish male child into the covenant of Abraham and the painful, crippling genital mutilation practiced by societies in which women are sexually and socially oppressed" (1997:2). Her comments elevate the one practice to a sacred rite and denounce the other as nothing but a mutilation intended to cripple and oppress, "a morally reprehensible behavior."

Greenbaum's stand, rooted in her own cultural and religious values, is strongly moral and explicitly condemnatory, allowing no space for suspending judgment to exercise cultural relativism: "I will not be a voyeur to preventable tragedy," she stated. Many outsiders, of course, share this

[1] This was prior to the enforcement of the Shari'a law and the prohibition of alcohol under the government of Jaafar Nimeiri in 1983.

[2] Sudanese anthropologist El Wathig Kameir noted a marked increase in "conspicuous consumption" at such urban parties in the 1970s.

view. But they also too often share her spare and simple explanation that female circumcision is an intentional (or subconscious) patriarchal action whose goal or consequence is the oppression of women. Too many observers who reach this conclusion offer little in the way of argument or evidence. And it can easily be imagined that female circumcision was conceived by men in some long-ago generation as a way of keeping women from having the full measure of their power and freedom and was passed down through the generations by male dominance and the ideologies of patriarchy.

This is an appealing argument that seems accurately to reflect both the latent functions (effects) and the correlates of the practice: indeed, in societies where it is practiced women are subordinated and males wield greater social power. Male sexual pleasure and family honor seem to be more universally acknowledged as important, and women's sexuality, autonomy, reproductive abilities, and economic rights are usually subordinated to the control of fathers, brothers, husbands, and other men in their societies.

Patriarchy does not hold up well as a sufficient causal explanation, particularly because pervasive patriarchal social institutions exist widely, far beyond circumcising societies, but women's and children's social and economic subordination appears to be a necessary condition for the perpetuation of female circumcision practices.

So, is it patriarchy? "Patriarchy" is a term with a number of interpretations, but its basic meaning is "rule by the father(s)." It is frequently equated with male dominance. There is of course no society in which all males have authority or power over all females. Think of the male two year old and his competent older sister, adult mother, and grandmother. Each of these females no doubt has significant say over the small boy. And yet that same male child when older may well move into a position of considerable control over these women. Many cultures have even institutionalized that transition from childhood dependence and lack of power and authority to new roles with authority over women as the boys become men. Joan Bamberger's examination of this issue offers the classic insight into why the transition into adulthood is so much more elaborate for boys than for girls in so many cultures in which the gender division of labor assigns the primary responsibility for child care to women (1974). Bamberger notes that whereas boys' initiation rituals often involve grueling physical ordeals, lengthy group educational sessions with adult men (lasting weeks or months) to learn lore, rituals, behaviors, and attitudes appropriate to men, in contrast girls' transitions to womanhood are rather brief, sometimes individualized, and in some societies no more than a fifteen-minute ritual on the occasion of a girl's first menstruation. Bamberger's conclusion is that males in a patriarchal culture must go through a far more wrenching experience than girls—they must learn how to assert control and domination over the females who have until then had a large degree of power over them. It is a role reversal that is at the core of the dominating male role, and it requires a severing or redefining of what is probably the closest relationship most humans experience, the relationship with his mother (and other female nurturers). One classic example of this transition in the mother-son relationship is found in the film *Maasai Women* (Llewellyn-Davies 1983), in which young men having completed the manhood rituals gather with their mothers in a location far from the settlements and engage in all sorts of entirely inappropriate joking and wild behavior to break down the former relationship of female authority and help both mothers and sons get used to their future reversed roles.

In Bamberger's South American examples, girls more often merely carry on, continuing the roles they have been learning in apprenticeship to their mothers—doing women's tasks, acting as caregivers to children, and being subordinate to men, but adding a new role in sexuality as they mature.

When we reflect on patriarchy in this way, it is also evident that age is part of the core power relations. Indeed, patriarchy is not simply a system of rule by males over females, but a more complex set of relationships that result in domination by older men over both younger men and females. But there is other domination and authority here as well: females over children, older women over younger women, older children over younger children, boys as they grow up increasingly asserting themselves over girls, even older sisters who used to have authority, and so on. Even in the most strongly male-dominated culture, where women might be said to be very subordinated, young men often do not feel that they have power.[3]

Patriarchy is not a single, uniform pattern. The degree of male domination, female autonomy, hierarchy among males, and other factors is quite variant and includes manifestations that defy any conclusion that patriarchy is a universal impulse of the species. For some time, anthropol-

---

[3] This can also help to account for the anger some young men in my university classes in the United States have expressed when confronted by accounts of women's disadvantages. They often do not feel any more advantaged than young women and conclude that feminism is unfair, blaming men for something they are not doing. In fact, young men experience their own sort of social disadvantage, based on their youth and the inadequacy of social opportunities for all those who are talented. It is difficult especially for white, working-class young men, who indeed do not have an easy time of it either. Hence the affirmative action backlash—it does not seem fair to these men that society and employers make space for women and minorities when they do not have enough opportunities themselves.

ogists, seeking to refute the notion that patriarchy was universally found among humans, searched for its presumed opposite, matriarchy. Disappointment followed, as each example of matriarchy turned out to be either mythical (the Amazons), disputed, or to have inconsistent patterns of female power. Matrilineal societies in which women's important roles in kinship systems are easily recognized nevertheless usually have men in important power roles as political leaders. Matrilineal kinship systems do not prevent women's subordination or female circumcision. Societies that emphasized goddess cults may have had very important and revered roles for women, however, and some writers have interpreted these as matriarchies.

Eventually, anthropologists have had to conclude that if matriarchies ever existed, the evidence that they mirrored patriarchies, that is, senior women ruling and dominating men in their families and society, is slim. But in any case the truly profound opposite of patriarchy is not a matriarchy but a society that is based on gender equality. Several writers have embraced this model, alternately looking to the hunting and gathering and horticultural precursors of agricultural patriarchal civilizations (and their twentieth-century cousins, the marginalized hunter-gatherers who managed to pursue a somewhat parallel adaptation long enough to be observed by anthropologists in recent times) for examples of "different but not unequal" roles between the sexes (e.g., Leacock 1972) or to the apparently peaceful, goddess-worshiping ancient peoples who seemed to emphasize partnerships instead of conflicts in their values (e.g., *The Chalice and the Blade,* Eisler 1987, and Gimbutas 1989).

It is reasonable to believe that if female circumcision contributes to the oppression of women, it will be found only in the societies in which the oppression of women is established. But because the subordination of women and girls is so common, there is bound to be a strong correlation between patriarchy (broadly defined) and female circumcision. That does not make it causal, of course, because the vast majority of cultures that do not practice female circumcision are also patriarchal.

Antiquity and Folklore

The difficulty of offering a causal explanation for female circumcision practices is further complicated by its antiquity. Various mythologies are part of this set of speculations, and I have encountered them in oral tradition and in print. For example, Al-Safi states that "Female circumcision with infibulation was practised by ancient arabs [the uncapitalized form often means "nomads" in Sudanese writing] long before islam [sic] to protect the shepherd girls against likely male attacks while they were out unescorted with their grazing sheep" (1970:63). According to another speculative origin story, an ancient pharaoh who was endowed with a small sexual organ demanded that women should be infibulated to better enhance his pleasure (Huelsman 1976:123). From a social scientist's point of view, this is no more believable as the start of a custom that lasted for millennia than is the tale about the origin of clitoridectomy reported by English explorer and "orientalist" Sir Richard Burton (1821–90), who sojourned in Somalia and Sudan during the nineteenth century: "This rite is supposed by Moslems to have been invented by Sarah, who so mutilated Hagar for jealousy and was afterwards ordered by Allah to have herself circumcised. It is now universal . . . and no Arab would marry a girl 'unpurified' by it" (quoted in Brodie 1967:110).

Although the origins of female circumcision practices are unknown, several authors report scattered references to its existence in the Nile Valley at least since the times of the ancient civilizations of Egypt and Sudan (Assaad 1980, Sanderson 1981, Rushwan et al. 1983). In addition, there is widespread presumption among contemporary Nile Valley people who practice infibulation that it originated in the society of the pharaohs, as reflected in the contemporary term "pharaonic circumcision." One study of mummies by Elliot Smith (reported in Sanderson 1981) failed to support this idea because he found no evidence of female circumcision in predynastic or later mummies from Egypt. There are documentary indications, however, that it existed. Sanderson cites a statement from Herodotus that Egyptians, Phoenicians, Hittites, and Ethiopians practiced female excision five hundred years before the birth of Christ. She also notes that "Aramaics have described excision in Egypt in the second century B.C. A Greek papyrus in the British Museum dated 163 B.C. refers to the 'circumcision' of girls at the age when they received their dowries in Egypt at Memphis. Strabo described 'Pharaonic circumcision' in 23 B.C. amongst the Danakils of Ethiopia and in Egypt. He noted it at Antiphilus, which was situated at about a hundred miles south of the present site of Massawa. He also described excision in the first century A.D. in Egypt" (Sanderson 1981:27).

Meinardus speculated that in ancient Egypt circumcision was related to the Pharaonic belief in the bisexuality of the gods; humans were thought to reflect this in their anatomies, with the feminine "soul" of the man being situated in the prepuce and the masculine "soul" of the woman being in the clitoris. Male circumcision and female clitoridectomy and labia removal are thus needed for one to become fully a man or fully a woman (quoted in Assaad 1980:4). That circumcision operations establish unambiguous gender identity is an idea widespread in circumcising cultures (see Chapter 2). Even if we were able to nail down the origins at a specific location and even if we were able to bring evidence to bear on the speculations of what it meant to thinkers like Meinardus, we would still need to understand why it is preserved by peoples living today. The preservation across the centuries is documented for several locales (Sanderson 1981:26–28), but because so little is written on the specifics of the practices noted, it is difficult for scholars to conclude whether there was a single origin for both infibulation and milder forms that then spread or whether there were many similar practices that influenced one another over the centuries of migrations and contacts.

In the Nile Valley, it appears certain that the practices predated and survived the spread of Christianity to the ruling groups of Nile Valley kingdoms in Sudan in the sixth century C.E. Waves of Arab migration came later, initially nomadic groups who began to intermarry with the indigenous Nile Valley peoples. Later, Arab identity was strengthened when Islamic teachers and Sufis successfully spread the new religion in northern Sudan, where it became the dominant religion by about 1500 C.E. and the language of its sacred texts eventually became the *lingua franca*.

In Sudan, pharaonic circumcision, along with other pre-Islamic or non-Islamic beliefs and practices, was successfully syncretized into the Sudanese Islamic belief system. These practices were incorporated in such a way that they acquired meaning that was consonant with Islamic beliefs. Indeed, the ability to absorb and incorporate preexisting beliefs and practices, at least for some generations, is one of the characteristics of both Islam and Christianity that has allowed many people to convert without immediate dramatic change to their cultures. Today, however, some of the accepted practices have come under criticism by reformers claiming to speak for a more "authentic" and orthodox Islam, including *zar* spirit possession practices (discussed further in Chapter 3), folk rituals for agricultural fertility or curing, and even the visits to tombs of venerated holy men. The spread of Islam carried with it the use of amulets and quasi-magical practices and the belief in the special status of descendants of holy men, all of which are still found in Sudan and elsewhere today, but some have almost had to go underground as the Islamist movement has challenged them.

But although pharaonic circumcision is considered one of those preexisting practices syncretized into Islam, there is reason to believe that some Arabs, too, may have practiced some form of female circumcision in ancient times. During my short period in Saudi Arabia in 1990, I learned that the older generations in certain areas of the country had practiced some form of female circumcision in recent decades, but that people now considered it un-Islamic and the practice was dying out. However, given the fact that long-distance trade and enslavement of peoples resulted in movement across the Hijaz for many centuries, surely Arabs were aware of the practices. Indeed, that the question should have arisen for the Prophet Mohammed (according to the Hadith traditions, discussed below) indicates that this was so. Indeed, one Sudanese writer, Ahmed Al-Safi, draws upon the work of the noted Sudanese linguistic and literary scholar Abdalla al Tayib to note that a "mention in early Islamic verse suggests that at least in so far as the Sudan is concerned the custom [of pharaonic circumcision] could have been derived from Arabia" (Al-Safi 1970:63).

Custom

In the Nile Valley and especially in Sudan, over the centuries the practices have remained or become deeply embedded in local cultures, and the symbolic significance as a marker of socially approved female fertility plays an important role in individuals' repetition of the custom in the way of life that Janice Boddy documented in rural northern Sudan (Boddy 1989).

To call female circumcision practices "customs" is not, however, a sufficient explanation for their persistence. Yet much of the writing on this topic has not gone much further than to call the practices "customary," which is an oversimplification of complex meanings that is sometimes deeply resented by writers from these societies. For example, Nahid Toubia wrote that "the implicit and explicit message [is] that it is something we inherited from an untraceable past which has no rational meaning and lies within the realm of untouchable sensitivity of traditional people" (Toubia 1981:4).

A more meaningful analysis results if we take the time to understand how female circumcision fits with the complex sociocultural arrangements of women's subordination in a patriarchal society. For it is in most cases women themselves who are the strongest advocates for the preservation of the practices and who in fact carry out the operations, and this simply does not make sense without understanding the economic, social, and political constraints of their lives.

Where women must derive their social status and economic security from their roles as wives and mothers, we can anticipate that the rules of marriageability will be carefully followed. Even if, as is the case for a broad spectrum of circumcising groups in Africa, women have significant roles in subsistence production, wage employment, trade, production of commodities, and family work, economic well-being and even survival may require the efforts of a large family production unit that can take advantage of different environmental and economic niches and allow its members to weather the vicissitudes of the economy. A husband and children are necessary to a woman's economic security for many reasons. There may be limitations or barriers to access to land, cattle, grazing rights, or cash income without a husband. There may be control of production that reinforces economic dependency. There may be a need for physical defense. But in any case, children contribute their labor at an early age to family production, especially in rural areas, making a large family not a drain on resources (as is the experience in industrial countries) but a boon to family prosperity in the short term.

Further, since the majority of people in most circumcising societies have no provisions for old age security other than reliance on family members and kin group loyalties, anything that interferes with a woman's ability to reproduce in a socially acceptable way and to keep her relationship with her children as they grow up into competent adults would undercut her economic security. A childless woman might face a future of poverty or dependency in one of the undesirable social roles such as childless widow or old maid aunt or cousin, entitled to live with kin, but with no one to look out for her interests and provide her with more than the bare necessities.

Where female virginity at marriage is considered vitally important, as in Sudan, even rumors that question a girl's morality may be sufficient to harm a family's honor and effectiveness in a community and bar her from marriage. In this context, clitoridectomy and infibulation serve a clear and compelling purpose: they guarantee virginity, morality, marriageability, and the hope of old age security, all in one decisive action taken when she is too young to object. Any girl known to have been properly circumcised in the pharaonic manner can be assumed to be a virgin and marriageable, since there are usually a number of older women to bear witness to the thoroughness of the infibulation. People can therefore assume that there is both an attenuation of the girl's sexuality (because of the clitoridectomy) and a barrier to penetration (because of the infibulation), so even if she had had the opportunity, they can assume she will not have engaged in premarital sex. But for a girl who has not been properly infibulated, as in the case in which her parents might have chosen to follow contemporary ideas about having only a milder form such as sunna circumcision, doubts can be raised about her virginity and her morality, leaving her vulnerable to being passed over in marriage.

I argue that attempts to formulate policies or activate programs against female circumcision must recognize the significance of the linkage between the operations and the social and economic goal of maintaining the reputations and marriageability of daughters under patriarchal economic arrangements. To that assertion, I must also add the need to consider social class, ethnic relations issues, and the particular structures resulting from economic development strategies, as well as the current political struggles in each of the social contexts. Examples are the Islamist movement in Egypt and Sudan, rapid alteration of traditional cultural life in Kenya and Uganda, rapid urbanization in the countries of West Africa, and of course wars and conflict wherever they are occurring.

In short, there is more to this issue than meets the eye. By no means is female circumcision a single phenomenon with a single purpose such as "controlling women" or "suppressing female sexuality." To the extent that those occur, they are important to analyze, but often the control of women is not the core reason or conscious purpose for female genital cutting. Conscious reasons as well as the effective functions of the practices must both be addressed. The oppression or subordination of women, their poverty, and their restricted opportunities are a more fundamental issue to address if we wish to understand people's willingness to continue to participate in these practices and the obstacles that reformers must face. "Patriarchy" is too simple an explanation. Understanding the historical, sociocultural, and economic context is vital to the analysis, and of course this book cannot provide an analysis of all contexts in which forms of these practices occur. It is an exciting development, however, that more scholars are now addressing these issues in their research (see contributors to Shell-Duncan and Hernlund, 2000), offering deeper understandings than have been presented in the activist literature that too often unfortunately seems to denounce the women and men of poor countries as unreflective and cruel parents.

The themes that are developed in the chapters that follow are intended to provide a fuller and more well-rounded consideration of the factors at work and the challenges that lie ahead.

Chapter 2
Ritual and Meaning

The most common question on the subject of female circumcision is "Why do they do it?" In asking the question, we are trying to understand how anyone could submit their child to a painful and harmful practice that seems to offer nothing positive. It is a question about manifest functions, what people believe to be their reasons, and what they hope female circumcision will accomplish for them and their daughters. But analysts often also rely on the effects (or latent functions) as explanation, even if these are not consciously intended.

The result is a confusing mixture of explanations. For example, one of the fairly common ideas is that female circumcision plays a role in establishing gender identity and symbolically marking the difference between the sexes. Also, the operations often define or enhance ethnic identity. In some cases it is said to reinforce aesthetic preferences. The rituals associated with the operations sometimes mark status transitions and constitute rites of passage. Their goal may be enforcement of religious expectations or socially defined moral behavior. Or the operations may be intended to suppress sexuality.

Writers using the theoretical perspective of functionalism in anthropology routinely offered such resulting functions as explanation for social practice. But that perspective has been critiqued for its tendency to presume that cultures are essentially stable and unchanging and for its failure to account for the differences within a cultural system that contribute to the dynamics of sociocultural change. Contemporary anthropologists have actively critiqued that theoretical perspective, and yet functionalism continues to permeate much writing on "the other." Peoples and cultures are seen as static, except as a result of outside influences. In the writings on female circumcision, the functionalist perspective has contributed to the view that it is ancient and unchanging, serving purposes such as those mentioned above (maintenance of ethnic identity and gender roles, etc.), which cannot change without fundamental disruption in the social fabric. Cultural relativist perspectives are often assumed to adhere to this static perspective.

The general and various interpretations of the latent functions do not completely answer the human question of what motivates a parent or family to carry out the practice, allowing them to cause or witness a daughter's pain. Nor do these interpretations clarify the sociocultural obstacles to discontinuance that might be found in the different situations. "Why do they do it?" remains a key question.

To thoroughly answer the question would require examination of scores of cultural beliefs and value systems because there are different primary reasons given in different cultures. Indeed, each region or culturally identified group is likely to have more than one explanation for any practice. Thus within groups that share a culture or religious tradition, a parent deciding on an operation for his or her daughter or a woman choosing to have herself reinfibulated may select reasons from among those available that make the most sense in that situation. Because of this individual variation in meaning assigned, there can be no simple catalog of reasons given by separate groups.

A good example of this variation is found in the survey research done by Rushwan and colleagues in Sudan. Reporting on a sample of 1,804 female and 1,787 male respondents, the authors found that answers to the question of why female circumcision was practiced (where more than one reason could be given) varied a great deal. The majority of men (59 percent) said it was because of "religious demand," but only 14 percent of women gave that reason. The most frequent reason women gave was that it was a "good tradition" (42 percent), but only 28 percent of men gave that reason. Substantial numbers of men (28 percent) and women (19 percent) said it promoted cleanliness, while relatively few thought it promoted fertility (1 percent of women and 2 percent of men). Surprisingly, only about one-tenth explicitly mentioned protecting virginity and preventing immorality (10 percent of women, 11 percent of men), and even fewer said it "increases chances of marriage" (9 percent of women and 4 percent of men). Quite a few (13 percent of women and 21 percent of men) mentioned the increase in the pleasure of the husband as a reason (Rushwan et al. 1983:92–93).

Data like these are difficult to interpret because those who did not mention a particular reason as their first or second reason nevertheless may have agreed with that reason as well. Most respondents just mentioned their first choice reason. That there were so many different first choices is instructive: The *why* of female circumcision is not a simple matter, even in a single society. As Rushwan and colleagues have noted, "Respondents hard put to clarify their support for a practice so obviously 'right' as FC often resorted to some vague reference to tradition." When asked about pharaonic circumcision, "tradition" was even more likely to be their response: 64 percent of women and 69 percent of men (Rushwan et al. 1983:93).

Similar results are reported for Somalia in a study by Dirie and Lindmark (1991), with religion playing a major role in people's justifications for female circumcision. Allowing respondents just one choice of reason to justify female circumcision, they found that of the 290 female interviewees in their survey (of medium to high socioeconomic status), 70 percent stated "religion," 20 percent said "to remain virgin in order to get married," and 10 percent said "tradition" (Dirie and Lindmark 1991:583). The three reasons are not fundamentally different, however, as infibulation creates a barrier that preserves virginity, which Muslims consider the will of God and therefore religious.

Yet the belief that God demands circumcision is quite different in consequence from a belief that it merely enhances cleanliness. Quite different discussions would need to take place for change to be considered.

It is not very helpful merely to invoke tradition as the reason, even if that is what respondents to a survey might tell you. It makes it sound as if people are unthinkingly succumbing to some generalized tradition or custom without reflection. I would contend that such is seldom the case. I challenge the notion that practitioners are "prisoners of ritual," as Lightfoot-Klein's book title suggested. A more nuanced understanding is needed to understand how families use female circumcision to achieve more complex ends.

A Morning in Abdal Galil

"Get away! What's the matter with you? You're like a bunch of animals!" One of the older women slapped the wire netting that formed the window screen, then stomped outside to continue to chase the small throng of laughing, curious children away from where they were trying to get a peek inside.

She rounded the corner of the rather nicely built rectangular adobe brick house and accosted the boys and girls at the window with her high-pitched, agitated voice: "Move it! See this switch? Let's go!" She smacked the ground threateningly with her long, thin stick, the sort commonly used to prod a wayward donkey or goat.

Predictably, the children scattered. One of the older, more sensible boys standing nearby took up a position where he could keep the others away for a while. The woman returned to her duties inside the house where the circumcisions were to take place.

I was there at the invitation of Besaina, the midwife of the village of Abdal Galil (pronounced AB-dal ja-LEEL). I had arrived in the village

Young women with elderly woman spinning cotton, Abdal Galil village, Sudan.

only a few days before, planning to spend several weeks doing participant observation as part of the study I was doing for the Sudanese Ministry of Social Affairs on the utilization of health and social services in Gezira Province. My research assistants had already carried out interviews in a sample of villages and at schools and clinics we had selected throughout the region. But as an anthropologist, I knew the findings would not be complete without looking at the sociocultural context of people's decisions to use or not use the government services. We also needed to include information on the alternatives to these services that drew upon people's traditional ways of meeting their educational and medical treatment needs.

A colleague at the University of Khartoum convinced me to include Abdal Galil village as the site of the more ethnographic piece of the study, one that would be useful both for the Ministry of Social Affairs study and for my dissertation on health services and health in Sudan's irrigation schemes (Gruenbaum 1982). Thus began my long association with Abdal Galil. Gezira Province was the site of the most extensive irrigated agricultural scheme in the world at that time, a feat made possible by the abundant water of the Blue Nile, fertile soil, ample sunlight, and extremely flat land that gently sloped to the north, allowing for gravity-fed irrigation canals. During the period when Sudan was under the control of the British, pilot projects were conducted and a massive dam, a network of canals, and an infrastructure of railroads, roads, and management offices were constructed, imposing new social and economic arrangements on the people of the area, including some population migration to provide additional labor.

My colleague Ibrahim Hassan Abdal Galil, then director of the Economic and Social Research Council of Sudan's National Council for Research, thought this village would be particularly appropriate for study because it was a fairly old village (about one hundred years old) with a strong tradition of education and religious observance and it was led by an influential family of which Ibrahim was a member. His father had been a prominent leader in the trade union the farmers had formed during the colonial days. Others in the family had achieved high levels of education and were prominent in regional and national politics; his brother had been the minister of agriculture for several years. The village founder was Ibrahim's grandfather, Abdal Galil Hassan, who had gathered kin and supporters at a new well site to build their homes, following a dispute in the nearby village where they had been living near the end of the nineteenth century. The new village had flourished under his and his sons' leadership, attracting educated religious scholars to teach the children of the region at a *mahad*, or school for the study of the Qur'an and religion, literacy, and mathematics. Families housed children of distant kin who came as students. Although it was boys who studied there in its early years, Abdal Galil and his family were early supporters of education for girls, donating money to the famed "father of girls' education," Babikr Bedri. Bedri founded the school in Omdurman (across the Nile from Khartoum) that has become the foremost women's university in the country, Ahfad University. When the government began providing teachers to teach a government curriculum, the inhabitants of Abdal Galil raised money to build a school for girls shortly after they built one for boys.

Abdal Galil offered an ideal situation for research. The village had electricity (as only about half of the villages of the irrigated area did), clean well water in a tall water tank that fed the local taps in homes of the better-off families of farmers, and a fairly good dirt road. There was a clinic that was much superior to the one-person "dressing stations" found in many places. Abdal Galil's clinic was a "health center" that boasted a trained medical assistant, a lab technician, clerical staff, cleaning staff, and even a health visitor, whose duty was to supervise the midwives of the surrounding villages.

My research assistant and I were invited to stay at the home of Ibrahim's widowed, elderly mother, which afforded a respectable niche and easy entree for two women on their own among strangers. Hajja Fatma welcomed us with gracious hospitality. The title *hajja* recognized that she had gone on the Muslim pilgrimage to Mecca. My assistant, a researcher from the Ministry of Social Affairs named Awatif Al-Imam, was unmarried, and although she was educated, employed, and the daughter of liberal parents who did not disapprove of her pursuit of a career that necessitated rural research, this respectable and reasonably comfortable living arrangement was valued. We were both used to Sudanese urban middle-class lifestyles (with electricity, telephones, refrigeration, plumbing, and cold-water showers), so the latrine without a door (requiring a discreet cough as one approached in case someone else was already there) and the sometimes muddy and poorly lit paths of the village took some getting used to. Hajja Fatima offered us beds on a screened porch, fine for the warm nights. She had a refrigerator, so we could drink cold water after a hot morning of visiting and interviewing, and we did not need to cook for ourselves.

The house was well located, just a short distance from the mosque at the center of the settlement. The lofty minaret — from which the call to prayer was chanted at the five prayer times of the day — was visible from a great distance and served to orient me to our house. After hearing about the village midwife from the clinic staff, I met her in our neighborhood.

Besaina was an extremely capable and confident woman, and I liked her immediately. A widow with five children, she was a farmer who held claim on a ten-acre tenancy in the irrigation scheme. She had made the difficult decision some ten years before to spend an entire year living away from her family to undergo the government's midwifery training in a distant town. Literacy was the prerequisite for the training (Besaina had had a few years of elementary school), which consisted of courses and ample direct experience under the supervision of a health visitor with advanced nurse-midwifery training. The class of thirty-six students went to many villages to attend births, and each student had to do twenty deliveries by herself before she could be certified.

So that prospective midwives would apply themselves to their studies and not forget what they had learned, the government's midwifery training schools did not allow students to go home for the entire twelve-month period. Their children could be brought for visits only on Fridays, and those who attended schools at some distance from their homes seldom saw their families.

Despite the hardship, Besaina was very pleased to have had the training, as she could earn additional income and her role had earned her respect in Abdal Galil and the neighboring villages. She earned a reputation for never having any problem deliveries because she referred difficult births to the nearby hospital early and she had done several successful breech deliveries. When I first met her in the 1970s, however, Besaina's government salary was the equivalent of only thirty dollars a month, a very small sum even by local standards. The midwives had been passed over when government raises were set that year; she explained that the government believes that the additional payments and gifts midwives receive from clients provide adequate income. But those sources are not much. At that time she reported such payments to be very small — about five dollars for a circumcision and eight to fifteen dollars for a birth. She was also expected — and was willing — to perform services for free if a family could not afford to pay. Families usually also gave the midwife gifts on both occasions, usually soap, perhaps perfume or incense, and some of the meat if an animal was sacrificed for a celebration.

Once certified as a government midwife, Besaina had been issued some basic equipment she kept in a metal box she carried with her when she went to see clients. Midwives were entitled to ask for supplies at the health clinics, but she told me they usually did not have what she needed, so she bought her supplies in the market in town: razors, disinfectant, antibiotic powder, a plastic mat, and xylocaine to inject for local anesthesia. One day she described her shopping list to me, and the total came to about seven dollars for antibiotic powder, a plastic sheet, and local anesthetic. "Vacation is here," she laughed, "and it's time for circumcisions."

Indeed, within a few days I was invited to join her at a circumcision. "But isn't it forbidden by the government?" I asked, wondering if that mattered to her.

"Yes, but it's what the people want. The health visitor [her supervisor] never told me not to do circumcisions. If she had, I wouldn't have done it. But she didn't." Evidently, the relationship with the health visitor was positive; she had supplied Besaina with gauze and surgical thread, useful for both circumcisions and births, and was available to do deliveries and follow-ups when Besaina needed to be away for a few days. Abdal Galil village fit the pattern I had encountered elsewhere — there was no government enforcement of the ban on female circumcision.

Besaina had done only about six circumcisions in the village that year. The West Africans (the Hausa, discussed again below) in the laborers' quarter of the village do not circumcise (*masheen sakit, zey intu*, roughly, "they go untouched, like you foreigners") and seldom summoned her for childbirth except for very difficult cases. Besaina was responsible for several villages, but one of the larger ones had sent off a young woman for training that year, so there would soon be more help.

The day of the circumcision, Besaina sent for me early in the morning, around seven o'clock, and I joined her at the home of one of the farming families, near the edge of the village adjacent to the dirt road that ran along the canal on the north side of the village.

"Sit right next to me so you can see everything," she instructed me. I scooted my small stool, a *bumber* made of ropes woven on a wood frame, across the packed dirt floor to be closer to where she sat, next to a bed of similar construction placed near the window. The light was good. She prepared her instruments on a small table to one side, placing a new razor, hypodermic needle, a curved suture needle, suturing thread, and a small scissors in a large blue and white enameled metal bowl. A kettle of water was heating on a low charcoal stove outside so she could sterilize these instruments with boiling water when the time came.

Meanwhile the other arrangements for the circumcisions progressed. The plan was to circumcise three children the same day, all members of one extended family (two sisters and their male cousin), thereby allowing the families to share the cost of the celebrations. The boy had been taken by car very early in the morning to the rural hospital about four kilometers away in the town of Mesellemiya to be circumcised by a doctor. He was back by around 8 A.M. Greeted with ululations, he walked slowly to a bed where he could recover. The girls stood nearby, able to see him arrive and lie down.

Then it was their turn. Their mother brought both the girls to the door of the house. The two wore colorful new dresses for the occasion, and the special protective ornaments (*jirtig*) and the family's gold jewelry were ready for them to wear during their recuperation. The girls looked recently bathed, and their hair was freshly plaited and dotted with a little henna paste. The henna and jirtig are commonly used in relation to *mushahara* customs intended to prevent excessive blood loss or the harm that may be caused by spirits (*jinn*). The mushahara beliefs and practices were not as ardently held in Abdal Galil as in the northern Nile Valley region of Sudan, where Janice Boddy did her research (see 1989, especially chapters 2 and 3), perhaps because the inhabitants of Abdal Galil had a stronger association with more orthodox Islamic institutions and longer experience with formal schooling and bureaucratic government institutions. Beliefs in *zar* spirits and the need for quasi-magical protections were very deeply held by many of the residents of Abdal Galil, however, and even for those less concerned, the use of jirtig was routine for circumcision.

By the time of the boy's arrival, about ten women — kinswomen and neighbors — had taken up places in the room, ready to assist and witness the event. There were three beds along the walls of the room, in addition to the one positioned to catch the maximum light from the window, each covered with an ordinary clean cotton sheet and a cotton pillow.

The girls were the center of attention and the subject of conversation, but there was no formal ritual or special sequence of events prior to the cutting, except for the midwife's preparations. Both girls knew that this was their special day and that they would be circumcised, but they did not seem particularly fearful, knowing little of the details of what they were about to experience.

A rather animated discussion developed when the mother of the girls vacillated about her decision to allow both girls to be circumcised. The older girl was six, and doing her circumcision now would allow her to heal before it was time to start school. But the younger appeared to be not much over four.

The mother held the hand of the little one. "Maybe we should wait. She's so young."

Immediately Besaina and the other women offered a torrent of reassurance about the decision to circumcise: It's better to do it early, they don't remember as much, she'll be healed long before school, she's already prepared. The midwife admonished the mother gently but firmly: Don't worry so much, it will be over soon. It's better to just do it, and if she's younger it's better.

The things that happen to children, I was often told, are not so serious because, as the saying goes, "Tekbara, tensa," "You grow up and you forget." I wondered, though, if this sort of experience could be so easily forgotten. Later, when I asked adult women about their circumcisions, it was usually recalled vividly, though most did not dwell on the pain or fear except to laugh about it. Circumcision's psychological effects are surely complicated.

In the end, the mother agreed. They did the younger girl first, so she would be less afraid, I surmised. After the boiling water was poured over the instruments in a bowl and allowed to work for a few minutes, the girl was positioned on the oilcloth cover the midwife had spread on the bed with her dress raised out of the way. The midwife, seated on her stool at the foot of the bed, washed her hands with soap, rinsing them under a stream of water poured by another woman from a pitcher. The girl was told to lie still and not worry, but she started to squirm as soon as the women took hold of her arms and legs. They spread her legs so the midwife could do her work.

After cleansing the area to be cut, Besaina prepared the xylocaine injection and administered it slowly and carefully into the labia and clitoris. The girl cried out at the prick of the needle and cried as she felt the pain of the tissues swelling as the medication entered. Besaina repeatedly injected adjacent areas, while the girl struggled and the women tried their best to calm her.

"Ma'leysh, ma'leysh," they said, trying to soothe her with the comforting phrase for "never mind, it's okay." They held her tightly and as a leg slipped loose and flailed toward me, I caught it and found myself participating in holding her as steady as possible so that Besaina could finish the injections. She waited a few minutes while the anesthesia took effect, then took the razor blade and began cutting, first the clitoris and its hood, then downward to remove the inner labia. The women ululated loudly with the first cut, announcing joyfully to those outside that the circumcision was underway. The girl no longer struggled because she could not feel the cutting.

The midwife worked carefully, making sure I could see her expert technique. She dropped the cut tissue into the bowl on the floor beneath where she worked. The bleeding was not as much as I expected, and Besaina daubed the area with clean gauze when necessary. The nearer women watched, giving advice and encouragement to be sure to take enough off. The girl's mother did not watch, sitting instead with the other girl slightly away from the scene. After cutting a little tissue off the labia majora, Besaina dropped the razor blade back into the bowl of hot water and pulled out the suture needle. She threaded it and began closing the wounds, exerting pressure to stem the bleeding when needed. She stitched carefully with the black suture thread, checking that the tissues met well so the wound would heal easily and the scar would be smooth.

The stitching looked tight, which seemed to stop any bleeding. Besaina dropped the needle into the bowl, then washed the wound, daubed it with gauze, and sprinkled it liberally with antibiotic powder. The women congratulated the little girl as they moved her to one of the side beds and the midwife prepared for the second circumcision. Her mother sat beside her while the other girl was taken to the center bed.

The older girl was admonished to be brave, and she seemed determined to withstand the pain stoically. But as the second operation proceeded, she too could not keep completely still or quiet. But again, ululations drowned her moaning, and her circumcision was completed efficiently.

Once the three children were settled in their beds and Besaina had washed the oilcloth, using soap and warm water, someone took away the bowl of wastes where the blood, cut flesh, and rinse water had collected. Furnishings were returned to their proper places. Besaina instructed the mothers to use "Aspro" (the individually packaged aspirin tablets usually available in even the smallest corner shops) for pain, and said she would check on the girls in a few days. Meanwhile they should send for her if there were any problems.

Within a short time, visitors began dropping by in ones and twos—both men and women—to congratulate each child individually. I noticed several slipping "a little something" under the pillows. I should have known better, after that party in Khartoum, to keep a few such coins or twenty-five-piaster notes in my pockets so I could do a better job of participant observation—though perhaps I had already participated too much. The greetings were affectionate, sympathetic, and encouraging. The mothers stayed near their children for some time, and they and other family members were also congratulated.

The children lay quietly after the procedures, though each evidently had some pain as the anesthesia wore off in the subsequent hours. Most of the activity moved out into the courtyard in the shade of the house where food was being prepared. Like most other celebratory occasions, everyone in the neighborhood, and even from more distant areas, was welcome to come and offer congratulations and share in the celebration. As for any important life event in the communities of Sudan, it is important to show up, even if only briefly at some point during the day or as soon as possible afterward. No invitation is needed, and failure to participate can be taken as evidence of weak or unfriendly relationships. While it is particularly urgent to visit after a death—upon hearing of it, one is supposed to drop everything and immediately proceed to the home of the deceased and stay as long as possible to help with the preparations for burial or to mourn with the family—congratulatory visits are expected for all manner of good fortune as well. Circumcisions, graduations, returns from hospitalizations, and arrivals of long-absent kin require visits within a day or two after one hears about the event. This is a general expectation in northern and central Sudan, even in the cities, where in addition to visiting neighbors one might have to travel some distance to visit relatives, old schoolmates, or co-workers, but it is particularly strong in villages, where the bonds of neighborliness, family relationship, and shared work relationships so thoroughly overlap.

On this occasion, the families had prepared a breakfast for the visitors, some of whom had been out in the fields working in the early morning hours. Between nine and ten was the usual time for a break for a meal in Sudan, whether city or country. As small groups of men or women gathered on *angareebs, bumbers,* or plastic-string chairs in the shade of the house and engaged in conversations, a pitcher was offered for them to pour water over their hands before eating. The kinswomen and neighbors who had gathered to help out prepared trays of food and presented them on low tables to each cluster of people. To mark the special occasion, they served a spiced stew that I particularly liked; it was made of onions and yogurt, was flavored with dried meat, and was served with both the round flat loaves of wheat bread and the thin, pancakelike sheets of *kisra,* the traditional sourdough made from sorghum or wheat. Using my right hand, I broke off a piece of the folded kisra and dipped it in the stew, then placed the whole piece in my mouth at once. Early in my time in Sudan I had learned this technique well, after having committed the faux pas of dipping a large chunk of bread in the common bowl, biting off that part, and dipping the same piece in again and again. Eventually I noticed everyone else had stopped eating that dish. One of our friends later explained the proper method — after putting your mouth on the bread it does not go back in the common bowl.

As usual, glasses of heavily sweetened spiced tea were brought around on enamel trays to those who had finished eating. Over the course of an hour or two, dozens of people were served, and I remember people commenting that it was a very successful day for the family.

So, this was the ritual. Children dressed up with special ornaments and new clothes, a surgical procedure, ululations, small gifts and congratulations, a gathering of people for breakfast. No mystery, no religious figures present, no chanting or manipulation of sacred objects, no patriarchal authority figure overseeing and dictating the sequence of events. Yet there lay three children, their bodies altered for life, their families approving the modification of their anatomies in ways that risked their health and might possibly restrict their sexuality and, in the case of the girls, complicate future childbirth, all for the sake of cherished values.

The procedure itself offered few clues to the "why?" But it was clear that parents are involved in making many choices about the timing, financial commitments, and social statements they are making with this rite. To what extent the actions are based on other factors such as religion, rites of passage, suppression of women, enforcement of morality, and deprivation of sexuality requires further exploration.

Circumcision in the Monotheistic Religious Traditions

Most Christians I know are shocked to think about female circumcision and cannot imagine believing God would want it. Most Jews consider only male circumcision to be commanded by God. Most theologians in the Islamic faith consider female circumcision to be completely unnecessary and argue it is contrary to true Islam. And yet followers of all three of these major monotheistic religions have at times practiced female circumcision and considered their practices sanctioned, or at least not prohibited, by God.

When I first began to learn about female circumcision in 1974 in Sudan, I was unaware that others besides Muslims and followers of some of the traditional African religions did ritual genital cutting. At that time, there had been few scholarly efforts to explain the reasons for the practices beyond the idea of transition rites. But that did not seem to apply in Sudan. Because of the pattern of occurrence, mostly in areas where people practiced Islam rather than traditional African religions, it seemed reasonable to explore the connection female circumcision had to people's religious beliefs.

I soon learned otherwise when a young Sudanese woman from a Coptic Christian family told me that her older sisters had been circumcised and that it was common among the Coptic Christians. Christian kingdoms had existed in the Nile Valley as early as the 500s C.E., and as Islam spread to Egypt and Sudan in the subsequent centuries, Christianity survived as a minority religion, accepted or tolerated by Muslims as a respectable religion. Later, during the British colonial period, missionary efforts resulted in the establishment of other communities of Christians among the non-Muslim people of Sudan. But the Copts and their Christianity were deeply rooted in the Nile Valley cultures.

Relations among the Copts and Muslims were generally respectful in the past, and prior to the conflicts following the creation of the state of Israel, Jews too had been an accepted community in Nile Valley society. The Muslim term "People of the Book" recognizes that Christians and Jews are followers of the same God they worship and of the earliest books of teaching of the Judeo-Christian-Islamic tradition. In this Muslim view, Jews and Christians err theologically in different ways — most significantly by not having heeded the teachings of the Prophet Mohammed, who is considered God's final prophet to the people of the earth. But Muslims generally recognize that pious Jews and Christians are nonetheless obedient to many of God's commands. Therefore Jews and Christians are not in the same negative category as atheists and pagan peoples, unless they are apostate Muslims who have converted to Christianity or Judaism by rejecting Islam. In the Nile Valley context, the three monotheistic religions shared much, including both male and female circumcision.

The relationship among the teachings of these monotheistic religious traditions provides a good starting point for examining the reasons for circumcision practices, especially if we begin with looking at male circumcision.

Male circumcision, for both Muslims and Jews in Sudan and elsewhere, is believed to be required by God, an obligation of believers. Christian theology generally interprets male circumcision to be an Old Testament rule that is no longer an obligation of believers, though in many countries (especially the United States, but not so much in Europe) it is widely practiced. Christians in Europe and North America, though, seldom identify religion as their reason for perpetuating male circumcision. The most common justifications people give for circumcising their sons, in my experience, have been that male circumcision promotes good hygiene and prevents medical problems, makes the child look like his dad, and will prevent future embarrassment in the locker room by conforming to the cultural norms. Commonly, Americans believe the pain caused to the infant is not remembered or that the infant does not feel pain the same way an older child would, despite testimony to the contrary by medical personnel close to these operations. Others cite hygienic considerations because circumcision makes it easier to keep the penis clean.

In short, the American justifications for male circumcision are custom, promoting identification with parental norms, aesthetic preference, health beliefs, and conformity, with an additional justification by Jews and Muslims based on religion. In recent years, physicians' organizations have challenged the tradition, recognizing the occasional risks and the evident pain, advising against performing the operation as a routine procedure, and allowing but not recommending it. Infections are rare with proper care, but the occasional accident of cutting too much and the risk of burns from electrocautery accidents are sufficiently problematic to cause concern. If too much of the foreskin is removed, there can be erectile problems later in life. The risks associated with not circumcising are less serious and can usually be avoided by good hygiene practices (bathing and regular foreskin retraction to prevent adhesions).

Since religious justifications for male circumcision have been important to Jews and Muslims and served as a historical customary foundation for Christians, it is not surprising that non-Muslims who learn that the practice of female circumcision is common in certain predominantly Muslim countries like Sudan and Egypt have assumed that it is based on

Islamic beliefs. But as with any religious tradition, we must differentiate between the practices of believers, what they believe to be true religion, and the differing interpretations of theologians and scholars. Muslims themselves often assert that female circumcision has a religious linkage, as in the case of the Mandinga people of Guinea-Bissau in West Africa, who consider female circumcision a rite of "purification" that establishes a woman's Muslim identity and readiness to pray in the proper way (Johnson, in press).

Muslim believers in rural Sudan vary in their attitudes and practices toward female circumcision, and most who practice female circumcision believe that it, like male circumcision, is expected of them as Muslims. An oft-recited saw in Sudan (and elsewhere) is that "Islam is not just a religion, but a way of life." With that view, virtually any customary act, particularly those with moral weight and symbolic significance, must be redefined by Muslims in relation to religious beliefs. Also, because Muslims place strong value on respect for one's parents, people can easily conclude that practices learned from their parents are part of their religion. It was not until my more recent research in Sudanese villages in 1989 and 1992 that I encountered some of the rural women questioning whether they were doing the proper form of female circumcision under Islam; earlier it was assumed that whichever form they practiced was consonant with their religion.

But the question of proper Islamic circumcision has been discussed among learned Muslims and theologians for decades and perhaps centuries. A fascinating example of such discussion is included in a pamphlet published in English and Arabic in 1945 in Sudan entitled *Female Circumcision in the Anglo-Egyptian Sudan* (Pridie et al. 1945). The pamphlet was commissioned by the British governor-general of the Sudan (who ruled under the unusual form of colonialism practiced in Sudan known as the Anglo-Egyptian Condominium Government) in preparation for a discussion to be held at the Northern Sudan Advisory Council. It was intended to send a strong message against female circumcision, particularly the pharaonic form, and to stimulate a movement against it among the "enlightened" educated Sudanese. The central argument, signed by nine staff members of the Sudan Medical Service (including both Sudanese and British, all males), asserted that the progress of the Sudanese people could not continue unless the practice was discontinued, and they provided anatomical information, description of the operation, the medical risks, and arguments against all possible rationales for the practice. But to strengthen the effect of the arguments, endorsing forewords were included from three prominent Sudanese religious and political leaders, including the then mufti of the Sudan, Shaykh Ahmed El

Taher, who offered his "authoritative Shari'a opinion" on the medical authorities' piece.

Shaykh Ahmed El Taher cited several opinions and commentaries from different schools of Shari'a thought (i.e., opinions of religious leaders about interpretations of Islamic law), including one that concluded it was probable that male circumcision was "a Sunna," or religious obligation based on the traditions of the Prophet Mohammed and that "female circumcision was merely preferable" — permitted by Islam but not required. While Muslim commentators have consistently interpreted certain verses of the Qur'an as making male circumcision obligatory (as one of the "commands" that Abraham fulfilled and that all Muslim males must adhere to as "a definite tradition as well as an attribute of the faith, which should not be ignored by men" (according to El Taher, in Pridie et al. 1945:2), it should also be noted that one of the terms used even in the religious discussion is "purity." The Prophet Mohammed is supposed to have said that circumcision is one of five things that should be done to achieve purity. Although El Taher reported no consensus on what purity meant, the Sudanese term "Tahur" connotes purification, is used for both male and female circumcision, and could therefore strengthen the religious association. Further, the term "sunna circumcision" (tahur al-sunna), used for the less drastic form of the cutting, includes the very term "sunna" ordinarily used for religious obligation. Although El Taher's purpose was clearly to discourage pharaonic circumcision, by naming sunna circumcision to be a proper Islamic practice, a form of female circumcision was effectively confirmed as associated with religion, even perhaps as a religious obligation.

Around 1940, the previous mufti of Sudan had issued a *fatwa* (also *fetwa*), or religious pronouncement, against the severe pharaonic circumcisions. The 1945 Pridie et al. publication appeared shortly before the date of the legislation that made it a crime to perform female circumcisions (see Chapter 8). Similarly, in Egypt the religious scholars had had many debates on the matter of female circumcision, and a fatwa was issued in 1950 that was quoted by Fadilat Allam Bey Nassar, the grand mufti, in 1951: "Female circumcision is an Islamic practice mentioned in the tradition of the Prophet, and sanctioned by Imams and Jurists, in spite of the difference on whether it is a duty or a *sunna* [tradition]. We support the practice as *sunna* and sanction it in view of its effect on attenuating the sexual desire in women and directing it to the desirable moderation" (quoted in Assaad 1980:5).

Nevertheless, scholars and theologians of the Islamic faith deny that female circumcision in any form is expected of Muslim believers (see, for example, Kassamali 1998:43–44). Indeed, they argue that because it is not Islamic, it should not be practiced by Muslims. The strongest argument is that the sacred text of Islam, the Qur'an, which is considered the direct word of God, contains no reference to female circumcision in any form. But Muslims who believe that female circumcision is advocated or at least permitted in their religion can justify it on the basis of Hadith, reports about actions and sayings attributed to the Prophet Mohammed in his lifetime. As the one whom Muslims believe to be the messenger of God, the final Prophet, his actions and sayings are considered excellent guides to pious living, offering guidance on matters not specifically covered by the revelations recorded in the Qur'an. During his lifetime, believers in the Muslim community often asked him, as God's chosen Prophet, for clarification of God's will on disputed matters not specifically addressed in the Qur'an. Since his actions and pronouncements were considered authoritative, followers reviewed and recited them in the years after his death.

For Muslims, there are several problems with the use of Hadith as authoritative sources. Because these reports were initially passed down through oral tradition, often not written down until decades after the incidents reported, they no doubt acquired some distortions of memory and may have been colored by political issues of later times.[1] To judge the authenticity, Muslim scholars considered the reputations of the tellers and the likelihood that the transmission to others was not tainted by other factors. Some incidents are recorded in different written works, which if based on separate lines of transmission would strengthen their authenticity, making some Hadith more authoritative than others.

"Reduce, but do not destroy," is what the Prophet is supposed to have told a midwife who was doing circumcision in the early Muslim community. In Shaykh Ahmed El Taher's commentary mentioned above (Pridie et al. 1945:2–3), however, the various versions given of the quotation illustrate the difficulty of deriving interpretations from Hadith:

Do not go deep. That is enjoyable to the woman and is preferable to the husband.
Do not go deep. It is more illuminating to the face and more enjoyable to the husband.
Circumcise but do not go deep, this is more illuminating to the face and more enjoyable to the husband.

Although any one of these statements is useful in arguing against pharaonic circumcision in that they quote the Prophet Mohammed as being

[1] The importance of such contexts is stressed by Fatima Mernissi in *The Veil and the Male Elite*. She offers a feminist interpretation of women's rights in Islam that uses the historical and political contexts of revelations and traditions to understand them (1991).

opposed to deep excision, they leave people uncertain about whether he was actively encouraging some form of female circumcision or not. In conversations in Sudan, I found that one interpretation was that the Prophet Mohammed was expressing disapproval of the severity of female circumcision practices in Arab society prior to the rise of Islam (the time period termed the Jahiliya) and recommending mitigation of it. By not requiring total rejection, the Prophet seemed to allow for continuation of the less severe forms. Shaykh El Taher's commentary supported this theory, quoting interpretations that describe female circumcision as "an embellishment," "preferable," and "commendable," all of which, as he concludes, "do not imply obligation."

Another interpretation was that the Prophet was actually advocating female circumcision. This is Shaykh El Taher's conclusion: "The Prophet meant that slight excision would serve to illuminate the face and improve the complexion, in addition to being more conducive to pleasure because the skin expands with the penis and helps to increase satisfaction [for the male] in coitus." It is difficult, however, to imagine any possible connection between clitoridectomy and "the complexion" of the face.

In either interpretation, it is clear that the more destructive pharaonic circumcision was discouraged and something less severe came to be termed sunna circumcision in recognition of this recommendation of the Prophet. For those who wish to preserve some form of the practices, the saying provides support. For those who seek to eliminate all forms of female circumcision, the interpretation that expresses disapproval is emphasized, claiming that it is proper Islam to go even further in rejecting Jahiliya practices.

The potential for religious disputes on this matter is clear because there is no single agreed-upon authoritative view. Noor Kassamali's comment is apt: "The debate regarding FGC [female genital cutting] among them [i.e., the *ulema*, or learned scholars of Islam, most of whom are men] is rife with disagreements and contradictory opinions" (1998:43). Indeed, the pronouncements and contradictions have persisted, as the brouhaha in Egypt in the mid-1990s demonstrated. Kassamali's account summarizes it well: "In October 1994, the mufti of Egypt . . . publicly declared that the Qur'an does not have any stipulations regarding FGC. He went on to assert that the hadith . . . attributed to the Prophet were unreliable and that there was no evidence to suggest that the Prophet had ordered his own daughters to undergo any type of FGC. . . . However, within days, Shaykh Gad al-Haq Ali of al-Azhar [University] issued a fatwa (religious ruling) that 'female circumcision is a part of the legal body of Islam and is a laudable practice that does honor to the women'" (1998:43).

I recently invited an Egyptian professor to give a guest lecture in my anthropology/women's studies class on women and Islam. I knew that because he was a pious Muslim who had lived in the United States for some years he wanted to be sure the students would have a more positive understanding of women's roles in Islam than they would have from media stereotypes, and I wanted the students to have the opportunity to interact with a strong advocate for Islam as part of their educational experience. I welcomed his offer to give his perspective on the female circumcision issue. The students had done some reading, and I had lectured on the topic myself already; I expected that he would declare it is not Islamic. But my class (which included two American Muslim women) and I were not prepared for his opinion: he concluded that it is "optional, but on the side of recommended" in Islam, based on the Hadith. It was desirable, he explained, because of the need to reduce female sexual desire in the event of polygyny, in which case a wife would not be able to have sex as often as her husband. My students, predictably, were not prepared to accept polygyny, particularly because the previous week's Middle Eastern speaker had said she would be very angry if her husband wanted a second wife. But our speaker was convinced that polygyny is really a good thing in certain situations, lest single, divorced, or widowed women be tempted to have sexual relations outside of marriage.

But despite these religious interpretations and his reasoning related to sex drives of women and men, our speaker had also concluded that neither polygyny nor circumcision is desirable in the United States, and he does not intend to circumcise his daughters. Polygyny is not an option in the United States and in his view women's sex drives tend to be less than those of men in any case, so to promote marital harmony he believes it is better not to reduce them further.

After class, the one student who had been raised as a Muslim in the United States and had studied Islam in depth told me, "That's the first time I ever heard anyone say it was Islamic!" Within the next few days she checked with several other religious teachers to confirm her view that his interpretation was not correct.

Clearly, religious pronouncements and interpretations, lacking direct Qur'anic references, are not adequate to change practices because the fertile human mind looks for logical reasons as well as doctrinal views and draws upon cultural heritage as well. But the religious exchanges deserve attention and can be put to good use by activists seeking change.

Identity

Female circumcision, like many other cultural rituals associated with establishing or strengthening identity, derives some of its power and tenacity from its symbolic value in identity formation. Male circumcision (and other body-altering practices such as subincision and ordeals of scarring) has carried the symbolism of a variety of meanings — maleness, age status such as incipient adulthood or adult manhood, membership in an ethnic or religious community. But male circumcision can also be fairly neutral, as it is for most American men — an operation performed in infancy signifying nothing more than social conformity. Only the uncircumcised are likely to be concerned about the "meaning" of their condition, if it has any meaning at all.

Female circumcision conveys meaning in a similar range of ways in different cultural contexts. Age status, marriageability, gender identity, social status, ethnicity, and even moral quality can be socially established, strengthened, or weakened in the eyes of others by an individual female's circumcision status and type of operation. The contextual variation is as stunning as the temptation by outsiders to overgeneralize. To assume that the meaning in one context is general to all is mistaken, however, as can be seen by the examination of several examples from different cultural contexts. I leave the discussion of ethnic identity to Chapter 4, but examples from Maasai, Gikuyu, Gambia, the Nile Valley in northern Sudan, and West African immigrants to Sudan can be used to illustrate the variation in symbolic significance for the other identity and status issues.

Gender Definition

Gender identity issues are evident in many cultures, where removal of "malelike" or "masculine" parts ("the masculine organ," writes Assaad of the Egyptian view of the clitoris [1980:4]) is often given as one of the reasons for excision of the protruding clitoris and other tissues. Boddy notes this interpretation in Sudan (1989), where removal of the parts considered masculine and the construction of smooth scar tissue is seen as feminizing, producing enclosure. As mentioned earlier, Assaad (1980) quotes Meinardus (1967), who interprets the removal of malelike parts from women and femalelike parts from men as reflective of gender definition in ancient Egypt. Talle (1992), Van der Kwaak (1992, quoted in M. Johnson, in press), and Helander mention that for Somalis, the removal of "hard" male parts of the female makes a woman feminine. By removing the clitoris, the Gikuyu in Kenya believe they are removing the ambiguity of gender: "status and gender became crystalized" (Davison 1989: 201). Gosselin (in press) describes a similar conceptualization in the West African country of Mali.

In short, for a broad spectrum of cultures in the countries most affected by female genital cutting, it appears that to be a true woman, one must be physically altered: "Excision is practiced to clearly distinguish the sex of the person. A boy is 'female' by virtue of his foreskin; a girl is 'male' by virtue of her clitoris" (Assaad 1980:4).

Even when they have given the subject a great deal of thought, it is difficult for noncircumcising outsiders to understand what is virtually mandatory alteration in some societies. As I discovered in a conversation with a Sudanese neighbor the year I lived in the city of Wad Medani, I clearly continued to see such alterations as anomalies to be explained, not as the norm. My neighbor, who had recently given birth, told me about her reinfibulation (letting me know that a tight reinfibulation would be pleasing to her husband, and husbands who are pleased when they resume intercourse are sometimes generous with gold jewelry). She asked me whether we reinfibulate in the United States, and I told her, "No. We leave women 'natural,' with no circumcision at all."

She paused thoughtfully before her reply, "This is 'natural' for us."

The clitoris and labia, in cultural contexts in which they are considered "male parts," are viewed as something that must be removed, lest they produce ambiguity of gender. Inhorn and Buss (1993) mention the idea found among some people in Egypt that an uncut clitoris will eventually lengthen into a male phallus. Having such masculine parts come in contact with the baby at birth is thought to cause harm to the child, an idea not unique to Egypt.

For northern Sudanese, the "masculine parts" (the clitoris and labia) are considered not only masculine but indeed ugly on a girl and must be removed, just as the foreskin is considered "female" on a boy and must be removed before manhood to eliminate gender ambiguity (see also Assaad 1980:4).

Going further, those who advocate pharaonic circumcision find the smooth, infibulated vulva highly feminine and aesthetically pleasing (Boddy 1989, El Dareer 1982, Hayes 1975). The women Janice Boddy interviewed in 1984 were quite explicit about this. They denounced sunna by comparing an open and a closed mouth: "Which is better," they asked her, "an ugly opening or a dignified closure?"

Closure, smoothness, and boundaries are themes Boddy explores in great detail in her book *Wombs and Alien Spirits* (1989), offering an important example of the ways in which body aesthetics, social organization, and morality are intertwined. As Boddy has analyzed it, "Genital surgery accomplishes the social definition of a child's sex. . . . It completes and purifies a child's natural sexual identity by removing physical traits deemed appropriate to his or her opposite: the clitoris and other external genitalia in the case of females, the prepuce or covering of the penis in the case of males" (Boddy 1989:58). Female circumcision thereby both eliminates "any vestiges of maleness" and associates females with enclosure, socially defined propriety and purity, and the gender-appropriate areas of adult roles — interiors of houses for women and the exterior, public sphere for men. For the more gender-segregated communities of Sudan, such as the village of Hofriyat where Boddy's research was carried out, the time of circumcision marks a transition to the start of gender segregation and the observance of increasingly greater feminine propriety, to eventually result in the modesty and deference expected of the adult woman in her social relations with most men. This is not terribly consistent in other areas of Sudan, where for some girls (as in my examples from Abdal Galil) circumcision precedes starting school, but the elementary school years include boys and girls together in some villages.

It would be a mistake to overgeneralize the symbolism of eliminating maleness and achieving enclosure and propriety to all circumcising cultural settings. Nevertheless, the profundity of the Sudanese woman's observation of circumcision being "natural" is instructive. If the very meaning of what it is to be "a natural woman" can be embedded in female circumcision, tenacity to the practices and resistance to change is predictable.

Transitions in Life Stages

For some cultures such as the Maasai, the practice of female circumcision emphasizes the transition in age status from girlhood to marriageable age. Maasai is the term for several Maa-speaking peoples of East Africa, especially the cattle-keeping people who live mostly in Kenya. For the most part, Maasai are followers of their own traditional religious beliefs, placing high value on the well-being (*enkishon*) associated with a successful life defined by the achievement of material wealth, marriage (preferably several wives for a man), and many descendants. As an old woman said in the film *Maasai Women,* seeing your offspring and grandchildren survive and be circumcised is an important part of that well-being (Llewellyn-Davies 1983).

For Maasai girls, circumcision does not come as early as for Sudanese girls. Usually it is not until a marriage has been arranged for a girl sometime during her teen years that the circumcision is scheduled. Several weeks later, once she has healed, she completes the transition to womanhood with marriage. Her female kin shave her head, she gives her beads and ornaments to her sisters and friends, and then she leaves home to join her new family. (The film *Maasai Women* gives a detailed portrayal of the transition rites associated with marriage.) This period of her life is clearly a significant transition, and circumcision is a prerequisite.

For the Gikuyu people of Kenya, a complex initiation ritual that includes female circumcision (*Irua*) has traditionally constituted a similar transition associated with approaching womanhood. But it was traditionally done in groups, and those circumcised in the same year formed an age-set (*riika*). According to Jean Davison's older informants, the strong bond that developed during the Irua rituals continued "as a form of mutual aid throughout the lifespan" (1989:17). These circumcisions, at least for members of the older generations who grew up in the first half of the twentieth century, took place when a girl was in her teens, prior to the age of marriage, and according to Wanjiku, Davison's oldest informant (born about 1910), they occurred preferably before first menstruation. First menstruation, of course, was probably significantly later (mid-teens) in the early part of the century than among well-fed urban peoples of the late twentieth century.

For the Gikuyu, circumcision was a true initiation process that included lessons in proper behavior; one of Davison's informants stated that the ritual included "learning how to behave around the elders and how to act with different age groups" (1989:23). One of Davison's interviewees, Wanoi, described the irua as "like being given a degree for going from childhood to womanhood." Uncircumcised girls lacked a degree of respect that could only be achieved by undergoing irua. To refuse irua in times past meant one might be beaten or abused, and a girl refusing it "would not have anybody visiting her home looking for her to marry. But the minute you got circumcised, no one would stand in your way—you were ready to marry" (Davison 1989:149).

But in many cultures, as we have seen, the cutting is performed at such an early age that it cannot be construed as a transition to womanhood, but only an end to being a little girl and becoming an older girl with more responsibilities. In Nigeria, circumcision (clitoridectomy or partial clitoridectomy) may be done in concert with decorative scarification and tattooing by a male barber when a girl is just three or four years old, as depicted in the film by the Inter-African Committee called *Female Circumcision: Beliefs and Misbeliefs* (1992; review in Gruenbaum 1994).

Considering the ages of the girls circumcised in my Sudanese examples and the practices of Egypt, Nigeria, Eritrea, Somalia, and other countries, it is clear that it is inaccurate to consider female genital cutting a rite of passage to adulthood. In Rose Oldfield Hayes's article, she reminds us of John G. Kennedy's criticism of "those who attempt to identify all genital mutilations as rites of passage," which seems to be an effort to make this practice fit their theories (Hayes 1975:621). More accurate would be the statement that female rites of passage and age transitions often utilize body alteration and marking, including female genital cutting and other forms of body decoration and alteration.

Body alteration practices such as tattooing, ear, nose, and lip piercing for the insertion of ornaments, decorative facial and body scarification, and scars that encode tribal/ethnic/clan affiliation, as well as the various genital alterations of males and females constitute a significant part of many rites of passage. They often mark visibly the new status or reinforce group affiliation (see also Chapter 4) or are intended for supernatural protection. But the body alterations that are part of these rites, like other body alterations that have little or no ritual import, derive additional meaning from their aesthetic objective.

Aesthetics of Body Alteration

Body alteration and mutilation are well-known and time-honored human practices. This affinity for marking the body shows no signs of disappearing in human societies, as the current ubiquity of tattoos and body piercings in Western culture attests. Aesthetics is often one of the more difficult aspects of ethnocentrism to overcome, particularly when it relates to the human body. "Ethnic" or "primitive" artistic expressions have been incorporated by both the "free spirits" and New Age mentalities that seek to transcend the limitations of late capitalist industrial societies and have also been incorporated into contemporary urban industrial design in a way that seems to capture and own the "otherness" of world cultural diversity.

Acceptance of the body-altering aesthetics of "the other," however, is somewhat more complex and, in my view, an extremely profound opportunity for the development of human consciousness in the era of globalization and grappling with the rest of the human crowd on the planet. It is not easy for humans, in my experience, to overcome their sense of revulsion at what they have learned to consider ugly or disgusting, nor is it easy to give up what they consider beautiful. But aesthetics also is not static, and the desire for unique and new expressions drives the movements of fashion and style in every culture. Two potent examples of the process of aesthetic change are Price's study of changes in calabash carving designs, patchwork sewing, and embroidery among the Saramaka Maroons of Suriname (1984) and Drewal and Drewal's examination of dances, songs, costumes, and masks of Gelede performance in West Africa (1983).

When it comes to changes in the aesthetics of the body, one only need consider from one's own cultural perspective the dramatic changes in hair styles that take place as each generation defines its parents' hairstyles as geeky, ugly, and in need of a more dramatic challenge and individualized expression acceptable to the styles of one's own generations. The punk spikes that used up many bottles of Elmer's glue in my own home during critical years of one family member's transition to adulthood and development of personal identity were a clear answer to the flat-tops and wrestler-shaved head in the various high school pictures of his father.

This desire for change, though, sometimes reaches to cultural symbols with deep roots, sometimes grabs cute imports, often to play with (rather than merely emulate) their supposed meaning: the Statue of Liberty hairstyle in blue on an American teen, the addition of deelie-bobbers to the sculpted cattle-horn hairstyle of a Dinka youth, and Americans adopting "corn rows" and elaborations of that style.

But all such creative impulses in personal appearance, despite their intention to individualize, provoke, or make statements, are ultimately subject to some group approval. While it may be satisfying to hear one's mother say, "Yuck, why did you want to pierce your *tongue?*" there also needs to be the circle of friends who consider it cool, bold, "far out" (as my generation called it), moving away from the mainstream crowd one is rejecting, challenging, or playing with. The nonconformity must conform to certain principles and meet the judgment of approved arbiters of taste. The contemporary urban phenomenon, especially popular in Europe and North America, of pursuing elements of ancient culture and "primitive" imagery to enhance body adornment and alteration (which clearly has both aesthetic and sexual stimulation goals) is certainly a phenomenon in need of further anthropological investigation. The book *Modern Primitives: An Investigation of Contemporary Adornment and Ritual* (Vale and Juno, eds., 1989), offers a discomforting glimpse of the subculture of imitative ritual (including that of sadomasochistic and other sexual practices) and creative application of human rituals and body alteration practices for aesthetic or erotic intent. Seeking pleasure and creative expression, people have sought tattoos and scarification in styles of specific cultures, have pierced labia and other sexually stimulating areas, have cut and altered the shape of sexual organs, and have developed clubs with rituals to support and celebrate body alterations (see also Mascia-Lees and Sharpe, eds., 1992; Sanders 1989).

While much of this might be considered sufficiently "deviant" to warrant dismissal from this discussion,[2] it offers a useful comparison to the aesthetically motivated cosmetic surgeries and procedures that seem to have greater social acceptance (though by no means unanimous support) in Western cultures. Is the popularity of face lifts, liposuction, laser skin removal, breast implants, hair removal, nose alterations, and other cosmetic surgery in the affluent classes in the West significantly different from the popularity of multiple piercing and extensive tattooing? Adherents of either set of practices claim beauty and self-expression as their

---

[2] Anthropologists rarely use a term like "deviant," steeped as we are in the wide variety of human cultural diversity and reluctant to suggest prima facie disapproval. The term can be taken to indicate a practice of a small subculture rather than a majority of a society or ethnic group.

primary motivations, and analysts note that both sets involve conformity to cultural and subcultural ideals.

The human desire to shape and decorate the body to accomplish a culture's aesthetic ideals is part of what is at work in the case of female circumcision practices. If one has grown up with an understanding of a generally practiced alteration as normal and other manifestations as abnormal, it is not difficult to predict that aesthetic norms will follow and that the altered state will be considered more beautiful than the unaltered. For those who practice infibulation, the resulting vulva is something they are used to and it therefore seems beautiful, even if people outside the experience find it repulsive. As mentioned above, smoothness and being enclosed were culturally valued and considered beautiful by the women Janice Boddy studied (1982). From that perspective a vulva without infibulation seems ugly and male.

Can that view change? Can individual and cultural preferences be altered so that something that was previously considered ugly comes to be considered acceptable or even beautiful? Abandonment of the body alteration of infibulation represents a fairly dramatic change in body aesthetics; I anticipate that such change efforts may require fostering new aesthetic values for female beauty.

One example of a successful process of aesthetic change in a circumcising culture was the change in women's facial scarification practices in Sudan in the most recent decades. Deep facial scars cut in girlhood were the norm for women in older generations; marking patterns were given the names of tribal groups, indicating membership. Other facial scars were meant to resemble birds or other symbols for protection and luck. But some time ago, a popular singer put out a song about the beauty of the unscarred face, a pure face. The song caught on far and wide, and it is said that it accelerated the discontinuation of facial scarring. Tribal identity had already lost much of its importance in northern Sudan. As people settled in new areas, migrated to jobs or educational opportunities in other areas, and strengthened their national and religious, rather than tribal, identities, the scarring had already become less meaningful. The highly poetic imagery of song, glorifying the maidenly beauty of the pure, unscarred face, was apparently just the thing to carry the trend forward. Today, even in very rural areas, almost no young women have the deep facial scars, only small decorative or protective cuts over the cheekbones are common.

In 1989, though, I noticed quite a few girls with a small, dark spot somewhere on their faces. It turned out to be a beauty fad of preadolescent girls, who created tattooed beauty marks called "sun spots." These same girls rejected the idea of having their lips darkened with the blue tattoos that many of their mothers had. I personally had never found the

Kenana women in Garia Wahid, some with traditional facial scars.

blue lips at all beautiful, but the older Sudanese women did. Clearly, facial aesthetics can change a great deal in a generation or two. This change can be particularly accelerated when media get involved — radio conveying music and songs, magazines with makeup ads, slender models promoting a different body shape, and where television has spread, dramatic interest in new body images and styles.

But because the vulva is hidden, these means of promoting cosmetic/aesthetic imagery will not be appropriate. Across the countries where the Interafrican Committee (see Chapter 8) is working on change, women's discussion groups and public health educators use plastic models of female anatomy that can begin to provide another model of normal appearance. But for the unaltered vulva to be considered beautiful, in the way that many women speak of the infibulated vulva, will probably be a process of change that takes somewhat longer, perhaps requiring a more subtle message conveyed by poetry, music, or art.

In this chapter, I have considered just a few of the areas of meaning on which the female circumcision practices of the various cultures impinge. But the most profound meaning of these practices is that which speaks to sexual morality and marriage, the subject of the next chapter.

Chapter 3
Marriage and Morality

Virginity at marriage is vitally important in many of the circumcising cultures, as is marital fidelity.[1] But of course the significance of virginity extends to many noncircumcising patriarchal cultures as well. Even in the United States, where virginity at marriage is less and less the case, it is still considered the ideal by many people and gestured at symbolically in the traditional white wedding dress and veil. Proof of virginity is celebrated in some cultures. One vivid example occurs in Elizabeth Fernea and Marilyn Gaunt's film about Morocco, *Some Women of Marrakech,* when the celebrants at a wedding wait outside during the consummation on the wedding night and then parade the bloodied cloths through the streets of the neighborhood (1981).

Such community displays of morality are not limited to Muslim cultures but have also been practiced in other circum-Mediterranean settings, including Catholic ones. Examination of the bloodied sheet is not usually considered necessary in Sudan and would indeed be very difficult because the first successful intercourse is often delayed because of the difficulties created by the severity of many brides' infibulations. El Dareer notes that for "some tribes" in Western Sudan the relatives do wait outside the "marriage room" to see the cloth spotted with blood, called the cloth of honor (*tobe al sharaf*), which may be hung outside on top of the house (1982:41). This both denotes the bride's virginity and demonstrates a successful test of the groom's virility. In such Western Sudanese traditions, "If the bridegroom finds his bride to be good and tight, he will give her mother a cow or money. If he does not, which implies that she has had previous sexual experience, the outcome depends on the groom. Either he prefers to keep this secret and gives the cow or money to his mother-in-law anyway, or he refuses and everyone will know the

---

[1] Some of the examples used in this chapter were previously summarized in Gruenbaum 1996. Pseudonyms are used for most of the individuals discussed.

truth. . . . If he declares that his wife is too tight, then this will be a credit to the bride, and her family, especially if she needs to be decircumcised" (El Dareer 1982:41–42). In that situation, the husband will need to give the bride more money, and people will say "her husband admitted it" (El Dareer 1982:42).

But although most Sudanese do not require such exhibits, virginity is vital for the majority Muslim population, and a girl found not to be a virgin on her wedding night risks immediate divorce and brings great shame on her family. That is not to say that premarital sex never occurs or always results in disaster; indeed there are cases where families have managed to conceal daughters' pregnancies and find ways for them to later marry. But it does create problems.

The importance of virginity is tied to Islamic prohibitions on sexual relationships outside of marriage, prohibitions that are taken very seriously indeed. Socially, as has been observed for many countries, the prohibition is most strongly enforced with respect to women's behavior. While pious men also adhere to it, the consequences for violations by men are not as heavily sanctioned from a social perspective. Nevertheless, it is worth noting that for many Muslims adherence to virginity is not merely traditional or socially required but also considered a religious obligation.

Honor

Although sexual misconduct is prohibited for both sexes in Islam, misconduct by women is more strongly sanctioned, an attitude related to the great importance placed on honor and decency (*sharaf, 'ird*) in Muslim societies and how valued qualities are maintained (see Abu-Lughod 1993; Bodman and Tohidi, ed., 1998; Hale 1996; Boddy 1989). Honor is thought of as a quality that can be lost and is very difficult to regain once lost. Honor connotes dignity and high moral status. To maintain it, one must have decency with respect to sexual behavior.

Maintaining honor and decency is not merely a personal responsibility in Muslim societies but is usually understood to be based on the behavior of members of one's family as well as oneself. In his research on Sudanese concepts of ethics, Nordenstam found that the responsibility for maintaining the honor of a family rests mainly with the men, but that the "*sharaf* of the family depends mainly on the conduct of the members of the family in sexual matters, and especially on the conduct of the female members of the family" (1968:94). Women are presumed to be weak in the areas of emotion, and therefore it is the men of the family, primarily, who must be responsible for protecting the honor of the family. And to preserve the decency of one's female relatives "means above all to protect them from extramarital sexual intercourse" (Nordenstam 1968: 195). Social customs such as veiling, chaperoning, seclusion/segregation, and male authority to grant or withhold permission for the activities of female kin — customs that vary dramatically in their practice from one culture or community to another — can all be understood as means for maintaining the honor of the family.

Janice Boddy found that residents of the Nile Valley research community in northern Sudan linked circumcision explicitly to honor. She notes that people saw a "need for circumcision to curb and socialize their sexual desires, lest a woman should, even unwittingly, bring irreparable shame to her family through misbehavior" (1989:53). Whether circumcision actually has a deterrent effect on female sexual behavior is another matter, but it was believed to contribute to the all-important preservation of honor through the preservation of virginity.

Thus, although virginity and sexual propriety are religious commands, it is the ethical values that structure the daily practices that assure adherence to those commands. Avoidance of that which is forbidden is facilitated by following a habit of positive actions or structured behavior guided by values like honor and decency and the fear of loss of honor.

Female circumcision can serve as a key mechanism for ensuring that girls arrive at their marriage beds untouched, thereby preserving family honor. For groups that practice pharaonic circumcision, the circumcision itself is taken as proof that the young woman must be a virgin. The common explanation is that the infibulated vulva forms a "natural" barrier of flesh, making penetration nearly impossible, a difficulty many a newly married couple must deal with in the days, weeks, or months of attempted consummation. One older married woman in Abdal Galil laughingly described to me her intense fear of the wedding night. As a young adolescent bride, she had cried when her new husband came into the bedroom, and she wanted to hide under the bed. She curled up in a ball on the bed every time her new husband approached her, refusing to let him touch her, despite his promises to be gentle. Eventually she was persuaded, but, according to her story, it took a couple of days.

In addition to the pharaonic circumcision's barrier of scar tissue, the removal of the sensitive clitoris is believed to reduce the girl's sexual desires, so as to reduce the temptation to seek sexual experience inappropriately prior to marriage. Some also add that reduced desire will similarly help to promote fidelity during marriage because sex is likely to be less appealing and illicit sex therefore less of a temptation.

Neither effect, though, could actually stop a girl from having sex before marriage, although penetration is less likely. Even if she does engage in intercourse and damages her infibulation, she can hide the fact by being sewn shut again. As a strictly observant Muslim woman physician (see Chapter 7) told me, infibulation is in a way "more dangerous in terms of morality" because it can give the appearance of morality.

Yet infibulation is one important means of effecting control over women's and girls' sexuality and their virginity prior to marriage, one that is perhaps less restrictive in some ways than the seclusion, segregation, and strict dress codes used in some societies. When combined with some restrictions on activities, it can provide a powerful set of virginity guarantors (Hicks 1993:76).

Premarital chastity is clearly associated symbolically with female circumcision because the term "tahur" (purification) is also linguistically associated with chastity (Boddy 1989:55). While it is only the pharaonic circumcision that provides an actual barrier to penetration, both sunna and pharaonic circumcision are symbolically linked to virginity.

But for pharaonic circumcision, the symbol and the reality are closely linked, as an oft-quoted observation by researcher Rose Oldfield Hayes reflects: "In Sudan, virgins are made, not born" (1975:622). Virginity is both socially constructed and physically constructed by infibulation. As Hicks comments, drawing on reports from several societies, "infibulation is considered to both create and guarantee virginity" (1993:76). A family that does not arrange for pharaonic circumcision would seem to be abdicating its responsibility to guarantee a daughter's virginity. To avoid shame and dishonor to the family, the daughter must be circumcised, closed with the scar of infibulation.

In her research, however, Boddy noted that there was a marked difference in how men and women spoke about the role of infibulations. Men mentioned prevention of promiscuity more often, but Boddy found that "while the operation restrains female sexuality, this is not the purpose avowed it by women" (1989:55). Instead, women emphasized the clean, smooth, and pure body that results from circumcision as being a prerequisite and preparation for marriage and reproduction, preparing a girl's body for womanhood and thereby conferring "the right to bear children" (1989:55).

According to Boddy's argument, although they are taking an action that seems intended to promote chastity by reducing sexual desire, or at least reducing sexual sensations (and with significant frequency it probably does the latter), women are not in fact aiming at that goal. Instead, they are asserting their social indispensability not as partners of husbands but as reproducers, the mothers of sons and thereby socially important people, cofounders of lineages. By being a *haboba* (grandmother) with male descendants, a woman is more likely to have old age security (Gruenbaum 1982) in the form of economic support, respect, and a place of honor in the community, and even the spiritual well-being of having the permission and financial support to complete the pilgrimage (*Hajj*) to Mecca. As the mother of successful sons who had married and given her many grandchildren, Ibrahim Hassan Abdal Galil's mother held such a position in Abdal Galil village, recognized in the honorific titles before her given name: she was "*Haboba Hajja* (grandmother pilgrim) Fatma."

From a Western cultural perspective, the idea that chastity can be promoted by a barrier to penetration seems archaic. The medieval chastity belts in which wives of Crusaders were supposed to be locked during their husbands' years-long absences (the key hidden in the trust of a faithful servant) offer the image of unsafe conditions and potentially unfaithful wives, as well as the ownership of women's bodies against which centuries of women's rights movements have struggled.

The concept of guaranteeing individuals' chastity against their will (assuming their will might at some point violate the moral norms of the society) offends contemporary Western sensibilities in a way that deserves further consideration. Much of Western philosophy focuses on moral philosophy, the duties of a just person, while Judeo-Christian theology, which is entwined with Western philosophy, has concentrated on the righteous behaviors expected of individuals. Individual behavior and responsibility are paramount in this cultural perspective. From this Western view, female circumcision is hardly an adequate route to chastity because it does nothing to enhance the girl's desire to be moral, but rather is an apparent attempt to substitute for morality.

That view was evident in the British-inspired pamphlet discussed in Chapter 2, in which Pridie et al. (1945) offer refutations from a Western cultural perspective of the various reasons people give for practicing female circumcision. It is apparent that the writers viewed their opinion as rational, modern, and enlightened, and they did not reflect on the potential for it to be seen as ethnocentric, although this may be implicit in the inclusion of several educated Sudanese coauthors from among Ministry of Health staff. The rhetoric of modernism and enlightened thinking was, and continues to be, strong among educated Sudanese, even those who reject other aspects of Western thought or the Christian religion. The authors of the pamphlet state: "If it is to promote chastity then such chastity is not a virtue when the individual is not herself responsible. Virtue is a much higher attribute which can only be implanted by proper moral education and then be maintained by the individual's own conscious effort and self-chosen conduct" (p. 6). The authors of the pamphlet thus seem to say that what is in the mind of the individual is paramount. And they further argue: "If the operation is performed to prevent pregnancy out of wedlock then it can only promote loose living"

(p. 6). Again, the virtue, as they see it, is in the intended behavior of the individual. Obeying moral rules under duress is not valued.

Shared Responsibility for Morality

A different approach to morality and obedience to rules set by the deity is more highly valued in African and Middle Eastern cultures than in the West. While individual believers in Islam are clearly expected, as individuals, to obey God, the idea that they should be on their own without the assistance of a community is alien. It is up to the community to provide the conditions that help the individual conform to God's will. Neglecting that responsibility is itself a violation of God's expectations of the righteous.

Rules about chaperoning, segregation of the sexes in some areas of social life, and veiling can all be understood as part of this responsibility. In another film by Elizabeth Fernea, *A Veiled Revolution,* a young Egyptian woman who has chosen to wear the more modest form of dress known as *hegab* or "Islamic dress" — in her case, a loose-fitting long dress with long sleeves and a head-covering that conceals the hair and neck but not her face — describes the reasons she believes it is God's will that she dress modestly. In addition to the Qur'anic instructions to dress modestly and the saying in the Hadith that leads to the interpretation that modest dress requires long sleeves and thorough hair covering, the young woman in the film believes that a logical fulfillment of her responsibility toward others is to prevent them from transgressing God's moral rules. She compares dressing in a revealing way to putting a plate of apples in front of a group of hungry people and then telling them "Don't eat." That would be unkind, thwarting their natural appetites. Similarly, the logic goes, men and women alike are endowed by God with sexual appetites, intended for use in marriage, and it is the duty of women to reduce men's temptation to sin by covering themselves when outside the family to prevent or mitigate inappropriate sexual desire.

This is not to say that Muslim societies or Islam as an ideal do not hold individuals accountable for moral behavior. In fact, that responsibility was alluded to in the October 1994 declarations of the mufti of Egypt mentioned earlier. Declaring female circumcision unnecessary for Muslims, he stated that "a young girl's modesty does not stem from 'circumcision' but rather from a good religious and moral education" (Shaykh Muhammad Sayyid Tantawi, quoted in Kassamali 1998:43), although it should be noted this declaration was subsequently challenged by another religious authority, who favored female circumcision as part of Islamic legal tradition. Still, although individual responsibility for morality is encouraged, there is strong social and theological support for the notion that Muslims share a responsibility to protect and contribute to the morality of the community. Cultural concepts of honor and shame fit well with this orientation.

While it may seem unfair that women should dress uncomfortably to take responsibility for men's moral behavior, some of the Muslims with whom I have discussed this are quick to point out that pious men have a similar duty to dress modestly so as not to tempt women. The traditional attire of Arab men — the long-sleeved, flowing jalabiya and a head-covering — is certainly modest, and even if a man wears trousers and a shirt, they should be loose-fitting and of nonprovocative colors. Pious Muslims would generally accept the idea that they bear some duty to help others fulfill their moral obligations, even if that means restricting their own freedoms or those of their family members. Appearances play a significant role in maintaining honor. From the perspective of those with a fairly strict interpretation of Islamic dress codes, to appear in public unsuitably dressed suggests not only that one might have loose morals, but also that one clearly does not embrace the communal moral responsibility to protect the morals of others. More tolerant attitudes can be applied to outsiders. Foreigners and followers of Judaism and Christianity need not meet the same standards of communal responsibility (although this is indeed a problem for minority groups within a country in which the government has become dominated by Islamists who advocate applying Islamic law to everyone).

Can female circumcision be understood as providing a similar expression of communal responsibility for the morals of others? For some of its practitioners, female circumcision, particularly infibulation, has precisely that function. If they don't want their sons and daughters to risk premarital sex, it is the duty of parents to ensure that the girls of the community are infibulated because the natural drives with which God has endowed them for use later could lead to error.

In this way of thinking, the early marriage of girls (even before the first menstruation) is similarly desirable to prevent inappropriate use of sexuality. Also, one Sudanese man I interviewed commented that marrying a wife when she is really young allows you "to care for her and train her so she will listen to you," resulting in the requisite degree of cooperation and obedience expected of a Muslim wife in rural Sudan.[2]

---

[2] "Obedience," as a woman in Garia Wahid told me, does not mean simply doing whatever one is told. A woman must still learn to behave in a responsible and respectful manner. Not going out against a husband's wishes, for example, is obedience, but it is also a sensible way to preserve good relations in the family. "Didn't your husband give you permission to come to Sudan?" she asked me. "Would you have come if he was against it?"

Most of the adult village women in the rural villages of my research had themselves been married in their early to mid-teens, and while not uniformly enthusiastic about the idea of early marriage, many of them noted that early marriage was preferable to taking the risk of premarital sex or pregnancy. Among many of these families, however, the preference for early marriage was beginning to weaken, particularly when educational opportunities for girls were available. But even then, teachers complained that girls were sometimes taken out of school before finishing the sixth grade (around age twelve or thirteen) in order to be married. Even as late as 1992, when middle-class, urban, and educated families quite commonly preferred that girls complete high school (if they had the opportunity) or reach a similar age before marriage, I frequently met young village women who had married as early as age twelve to fourteen and had babies soon after.

And does infibulation, together with early marriage, work to prevent inappropriate sex? Do young girls and boys really avoid sex if the girls are infibulated? Or does it result in the "loose living" feared by Pridie and colleagues? A historical study of the development of the government's midwifery service in Sudan claimed that a "side-effect of the complicated sex relations caused by Pharaonic circumcision seems to have been a prospering of prostitution" and syphilis (Torsvik 1983:29), preserving the system of family honor but requiring a class of women outside that system.

A famous debate centered on the drive for premarital sex was held on the campus of the University of Khartoum sometime around 1970; it was discussed among students and faculty for years afterwards. The debate topic: Is prostitution a social necessity? Those who argued that it was a necessity believed sexual experimentation was inevitable for men. They argued that this other class of women, prostitutes, was needed as an outlet for men's sexuality, lest they cause moral young women to stray. Pious Muslims might well expect both men and women to adhere to the same rules, but the double standard of male and female expectations — that normal young men would seek sex in the years before marriage, but young women should not — was as common there as it was in many other parts of the world.

And there was ample evidence of a sex industry in Sudan in the 1970s. One particularly filthy side street in Khartoum at that time was well known as the entrance to the quarter where prostitutes worked. The street was visible from a major thoroughfare, and one could often see men lining the walls there, waiting their turns. Such quarters were periodically cleared, however, particularly after the declaration of Islamic law in 1983. The prostitutes were either arrested or chased out of the city, only to reappear again later and establish themselves in another neighborhood. Even in rural areas and small towns like Mesellemiya, it was not difficult to learn where illicit alcohol could be found (even before alcohol was prohibited in 1983, illegal brewing and distilling produced popular drinks that required somewhat surreptitious production), and the women who sold it were reputedly sometimes available for illicit sex.

My informants in Khartoum, Wad Medani, and Abdal Galil declared that most prostitutes and illegal brewers were outsiders, either refugees from the then current war in Ethiopia/Eritrea or later the civil war in Sudan that produced thousands of internal refugees in the southern and western areas of the country. Others were members of impoverished minority groups such as the so-called "Fallata" or members of several western Sudanese and West African–originating ethnic groups. All these people could be considered external to the social order of the mainstream Arab-Sudanese, external to the community (despite many of them being Muslim) and thus not subject to the same rules of propriety. But the point is that men's sexual behavior with prostitutes was acknowledged, even though it was viewed with disapproval. When I asked rural women about prostitutes, they were adamant that their husbands should not even think about the possibility, and said that it was really a lower class of men who went. There was also a widespread assumption, however, among both urban and rural people that the majority of men did not arrive at their wedding night totally inexperienced.

It was beyond the scope of my project to investigate the sex work industry, but I was able to visit a couple of these sites in the 1970s and again in 1992 after the Islamist regime had been in power for three years. Thus the existence of prostitution, together with the fact that young men generally have traveled to market towns and may have been alone for long periods away from parents, makes it a reasonable hypothesis that a "double standard" persists. Although discouraged from doing so, boys are acknowledged to be likely to stray from premarital celibacy. Girls are expected not to. Indeed, as Hicks comments, the ideal of virginity is in fact enhanced by the existence of prostitution (1993:77).

Premarital Sex

Infibulation in a sense proves a girl has not had intercourse. If her infibulation is intact, it hardly matters whether the hymen is. There it is, proof that she has not had intercourse. Reformers are quick to point out, however, that it is not really proof at all. A girl whose infibulation is torn or cut can have it repaired, they would argue, if she can find a discreet midwife or doctor. But generally, the infibulated vulva is considered proof enough of virginity. In a village or neighborhood, a girl known to have been infibulated when small can be presumed to be a virgin and therefore marriageable later on.

Village informants who claimed that there was no sex before marriage and no risk of premarital pregnancies were giving me the idealized version of their culture. In fact, there were exceptions, and premarital pregnancies, although rarer than in the United States, had occurred in the previous generation as well as more recently. Although stories circulate that a father might kill his daughter if she got pregnant before marriage, that seemed to be more of a moral tale used as a warning to children than something that anyone could give a concrete example of. There have been instances cited of such murders, but once such a tale is established in oral tradition, it takes on the status of folklore and it is hard to distinguish fact from fiction. Did the Muslim father in Khartoum really throw his daughter off a bridge into the Nile after she eloped with a Christian? I heard the story from people who had no idea when or where this incident took place and had not seen it in news media. They had just "heard about it from someone." It had become the sort of tale (told as true, whether fictional or factual) recounted to reinforce a moral lesson, what Alan Dundes calls "urban folklore."

While it is indeed considered a terribly shameful situation if a girl becomes pregnant prior to marriage, it is not unheard of. In fact, although during my first period of fieldwork, people denied it ever happened, when I returned to two villages several years later, I was accorded greater acceptance and got to hear of a few cases that would have been too scandalous to mention when I was there for the first time. In one case, a pregnancy had been hidden by sending the girl far away to stay with distant relatives, who adopted the baby after it was born and sent the young woman home. She later married locally and had children, with apparently no enduring stigma attached. If others knew, they did not make an issue of it.

More tragically, a pregnancy might be hidden at home. Although the girl's pregnancy might be concealed from people outside the family and she might manage to give birth in secret (more likely, it is only the pretense of secret, with the neighbors only whispering the rumor rather than exposing the family to ridicule), the newborn's fate could be infanticide. In the case of one family I was told about, it was death by drowning in an irrigation canal. This infanticide was discussed only very surreptitiously, and it was considered a rather scary matter that might involve spirits. But the lesson of the tale was to underscore the need for virginity at marriage. The attitude that the child of such sin is tainted, a bastard, was particularly strong among many northern Sudanese, both urban and rural, making infanticide conceivable and understandable. It was the pregnancy, not the infanticide, that was the more shameful, although infanticide is illegal.

Infanticide is probably as rare in Sudan as it is in the United States because Islam has explicit teachings against it.[3] The ending of female infanticide, which was said to have been practiced in the Jahiliya period before Islam, is often pointed to by Muslims as one of the advances for women that emerged from God's revelations to the Prophet Mohammed. But any case of infanticide in Sudan is likely to be related to the intense fear of the damage to family honor this situation presents. For a woman to rear the infant could only result in severe social stigma and ostracism (see also Fleuhr-Lobban 1994:74).

The disdain for the "child without a father" is so strong that it commonly leads to the abandonment of such infants. In the 1970s, I had the opportunity to visit an orphanage in Khartoum with two friends, a Sudanese and an American. The orphanage was where many such abandoned children ended up. The women hired as caretakers were mostly "Fellata" and foreign women, while the supervisory staff were educated Arab-Sudanese. We observed the smallest babies being fed bottles, two of them in each cot, not even being cradled in the arms of an adult. The toddlers, starved for contact and affection, pulled at us and climbed on our laps when they could. Although dressed appropriately and well fed, the children seemed to crave adult attention and cuddling, which we did not see the adults giving them. As we moved to the rooms with the older children, we noticed a shift — all the children were male. The explanation was that all the girls had been "adopted" by that age. While legal adoption is not possible in Islamic family law (see Fleuhr-Lobban 1994: 75), children can be accepted into a permanent foster arrangement often called adoption. Yet in a society with strong preference for sons, boys were not adopted but left to grow to adulthood as socially displaced persons with no kin. The girls, our Sudanese companion explained, were often adopted because they could work around the house. Later, a girl might find a chance to marry; there's always someone who needs a wife, and such a girl would presumably be grateful for any opportunity. The boys, though, could never expect a family to treat them as a true son who would get assistance with the costs of marriage or a place of respect in a kin network — they were illegitimate. And non-Muslims were not permitted to adopt these children.

That orphanage visit was one of the saddest days I spent in Khartoum. The enthusiasm for children and family that I had seen as the fabric of Sudanese social life had a painful boundary. But understanding the existence of that boundary helps to explain the high value placed on virginity.

---

[3] Michelle Oberman's research on "modern American infanticide" illustrates that it is a recurrent phenomenon for young women with inadequate social and emotional supports (Oberman 1998). Although these women are treated as criminals, they are frequently also victims.

Marriage

If virginity is vital to maintaining the respectability and morality of girls so that they will be marriageable and if circumcision is perceived as protecting virginity, we can begin to understand why circumcision might be considered vitally important to marriage. But why is marriage so important to Sudanese women? In many cases it is arranged marriage or marriage to a cousin, rather than the product of romantic involvement. There is often little privacy or independence at the beginning of marriage, and one might even be a co-wife, sharing one's husband with another woman. For an innovative parent considering not circumcising (or at least not infibulating), would it be worth the risk of making one's daughter unmarriageable by refusing to circumcise her?

It is because marriage and reproduction are vital to a woman's economic security and social status that circumcision is unlikely to be given up purely because of medical risks (Gruenbaum 1982b). The social risks of not circumcising are still too great because marriage is vital to achieving status and security in a situation in which there are few alternatives for women, and circumcision is vital to the definition of marriageability.

The economic relations of rural Sudan, like many other places in the region, strongly favor males. For pastoralists in regions of northern Sudan such as the Baggara (Cunnison 1966) and the Kabbabish (Asad 1970), livestock ownership is in the hands of men and patrilineages. A woman gains the use of animals for milking and their other products through her ties as a wife. Although she will always have retreat rights to her father's family in the event of divorce (even if the role of dependent divorcee is not a desirable one), it is her role as a wife and mother that offers her significant economic security in the use of animals and in the access to the loyal support of her children, especially important later in life. Her relationship to her children is strengthened and preserved in a successful marriage, which women strongly desire, lest divorce lead to separation from one's children in their formative years. Although Islamic inheritance rules require females to receive shares of their parents' wealth, in rural Sudan is it not uncommon that in practice women cannot exercise this right and waive it to benefit their brothers. In farming areas, although women can and do assert their land rights (but practices are not uniform), much farmland has similarly tended to be in the control of men much more often than women, for even if the inheritance rules are followed, a male heir receives twice the share of a female. Another way that fathers sometimes manage to elude Islamic inheritance rules (examples are offered by O'Brien's research in Northern Kordofan, 1980) is to give gifts of land to favored sons before they die. If a daughter is married off to someone in a distant village, she can still inherit family land, but in practice her brothers will farm the land and she will receive just a small portion of the harvest. Endogamy is highly valued in northern Sudanese Muslim ethnic groups (especially marrying the son or daughter of one's father's brother), which has the effect of keeping wealth in the hands of the kin group.

For village women without access to high school education, there are few opportunities for employment. Quite simply, there is no other way to provide for one's old age or to achieve a place of respect in society but to found a family. Eventually, if you are fortunate, you will have adult sons who are loyal to you and can be expected to support you, respect you, send you on the pilgrimage to Mecca, and provide you with daughters-in-law and grandchildren to help with the chores and bring you status and joy in life. Even for those women fortunate enough to have received an education — and in Abdal Galil there are several because of the village founders' early commitment to attracting religious teachers, building public schools when that became possible, and establishing coeducational opportunities — employment is no guarantee of social respect or long-term security. Without a national social security system, there is no safety net for old age, illness, or job loss, and without kin in other lines of work, the vagaries of the inflationary economic situation (the reality of life in the 1990s) can be devastating.

In short, the complex of symbolic and religious values surrounding female morality are reinforced by the economic imperatives on women's lives, making challenges or attempts at modification and reinterpretation risky for parents, even those inclined to change. Will a young woman be unmarriageable if she is not circumcised or if her parents opt for a less severe form? This is a central question in the process of change (see also Chapter 7) because marriageability is so vital to women's lives. And it is quite reasonable to fear this change, particularly in light of the economic trends of the last few years. Labor migration to wealthy oil-producing countries such as Saudi Arabia has dramatically benefited some families, resulting in inflation in the cost of marriage, while inflation at home (particularly steep after the Islamist government came to power in 1989 and escalated the civil war) has eroded the value of workers' salaries. Farmers find that despite increases in the sales prices of their crops, they are still struggling as they see prices for the things they must buy outpace them. In Abdal Galil, the disparity between the going rate for a marriage and the funds most families have available to cover such costs for their sons has had the effect of delaying marriages.

In fact, in a dramatic departure from the early marriage patterns of the past, young women in their mid-twenties, even with the desirable attribute of an education, were finding themselves unmarried and without suitors in the 1990s. Worried parents were willing to accept a son-in-law with little money rather than risk their daughter becoming too old. One mother told me that to protect a hard-up potential son-in-law from embarrassment, "If people ask, I would tell them he had given a lot of money [in bridewealth, or *mahr*]."[4]

My friend Halima was in such a situation in 1989, when she was twenty-eight. Educated and employed in a low-paying job at a school in the village, she lived with her parents, helped care for her younger brothers and sisters, and worked on the farm when needed. Her parents were clearly worried that it might soon be too late for her to find a husband. "He just would need to provide a room or furnishings for a room, that's all," her father Musa told me.

But right next door, his brother-in-law's son, aged thirty-eight, was getting ready to be married. He had to prepare a set of gifts for the bride, locally called the *shanta* (suitcase), including dresses, tobes, handbags, shoes, perfume and incense, soap, toothpaste, combs, and lingerie. Although ten of each of the main items was considered desirable in Abdal Galil, less affluent young men were only expected to produce two of each and these were not expected to be costly. The shanta that Musa's nephew had prepared was praised politely by those of us visiting that day, despite its obvious economy. Yet with only three of each of the main items, the cost still came to around LS 30,000 (roughly $300 then), a staggering sum when compared with the low salaries afforded by employment. In addition, there would be expenses for the sheep and provisions for the bride's family for the feast, the actual cash bridewealth *mahr* (sometimes *mal*), buses and entertainment for the party, the honeymoon trip, and other items. The group helping me estimate the total costs quickly came up with an amount in excess of LS 60,000 ($600 at that time) over the cost of

---

[4] The problem of inflation of marriage costs was widespread in the early 1990s. Some villages had responded by holding meetings at the mosque in which fathers made a pact to limit bridewealth to some token amount for any marriages within their village, thereby making it honorable to give little. Another solution, somewhat controversial, was government-sponsored group weddings (*zowaj juma'i*). As these were described to me, dozens of couples from a region were registered as desiring to marry, and the government sent busses to the villages to transport them to a site where dignitaries — in one case in 1991 Iranian political leader Rafsanjani and his wife, President Omer el Hassan and his wife, and the governor of Gezira province — witnessed the ceremony, which was followed by a meal. This was intended to save the costs of the wedding celebration at home and heighten the importance of the occasion, despite the lack of bridewealth. The government contributed LS 10,000 (about $100 then) and two beds to get each couple started. Although some disapproved, many people in the villages were very happy about it. "It's plain sugar!" said one man. To further encourage marriage, the government was making available building plots for newlyweds in some towns. With an educational system that already could not accommodate everyone, educators worried that the shortages of classrooms and teachers would be further heightened by the anticipated baby boom to follow.

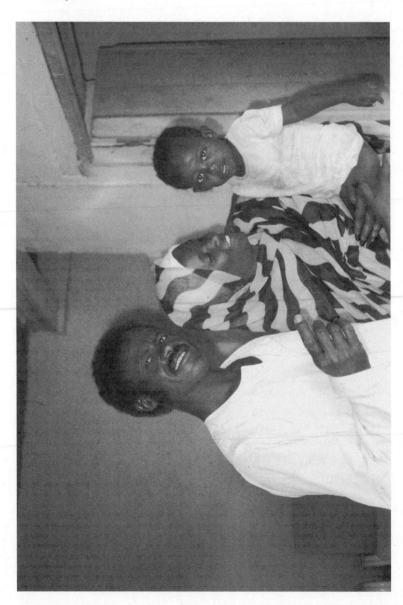

Halima Musa, with her husband and son, Abdal Galil village.

the shanta. The groom told me he was hoping for the contribution of LS 10,000 from the government, but he would rely on his kin for help with the costs.

In Halima's case there was a happy outcome in that one of her cousins of modest means came forward and was accepted. He, like Halima, was employed, but in a distant village where he had to stay six days a week. Neither of them earned enough to support themselves or establish independence. But Halima's parents rearranged the sleeping areas so that the young married couple could have a room of their own in the family's brick compound. The room had a dirt floor, like most in the village, but the ceiling fan, screened windows, painted walls, furniture (wardrobe, beds, and dresser), adjacent veranda and a corner of the yard, made for a quite comfortable place for a young couple, even though of course others had access to it and slept there when the young husband was away at his job.

During my stay in Abdal Galil that year, I slept under the stars in that yard as Halima's guest when her husband was away, on a bed a few steps from the one she shared with her little son, Ghotayba. Born before my research visit in 1992, he was a happy child (something they told me is the desired effect of laughing into the hole where the placenta is buried with dates, sorghum, and coffee beans after a birth). At any rate, he brought joy to everyone in the household, especially ancient Medina, the great-grandmother. Another married sister had left for Oman with her two small children a couple of years before, when her husband got a job as a teacher. When they visited, they brought home several appliances and luxury items — a blender, new tobes for the women and jalabiyas for the men, and a television.

In such circumstances of marriage becoming too costly, anything that might add a barrier to marriage — such as having taken the risk not to circumcise, leaving one's daughter's virginity open to question, would certainly be unwise, and parents knew that. But despite the importance of marriage and the risk that rejecting or modifying circumcision would heighten the risk for daughters' long-term security, some families were challenging circumcision anyway, as two cases from Abdal Galil highlight — Suad's family and Sittana's.[5]

Suad's Family

The first thing I noticed about Suad's *hosh* was its size. The hosh is the yard around a house, enclosed by a wall for privacy, giving the family an outdoor living area. In her case, it was vast. There was room for a chicken coop, goats, parking for the car, a couple of trees and some flowering

---

[5] "Suad" and "Sittana" are pseudonyms.

plants, and a vegetable garden. Most of the space, though, was bare ground, and some of it to the east and south of the house, toward the fields, was simply marked off by piles of bricks that had not yet been crafted into a wall. Suad and her husband had staked a claim on a truly suburban-size lot, perhaps an acre, a marked contrast to the cramped quarters of the central part of the village, where spaces around the homes of the founders had been filled over the years with new houses as each member of the family married. The original section of land set aside for other than agricultural uses when the irrigation project was laid out in the 1920s had seemed vast and highly adequate for future population growth when I first saw the village back in the 1970s. This had enabled the village leaders to add the intermediate level schools for girls and boys and set aside a large plot for the health center. As growth and affluence encouraged several families to begin moving to the edges of the village in the 1980s, they staked out larger claims. In the 1970s, some of the edges of the village had been occupied by transient laborers, but such people now had camps in the fields. The Village Council had control of allocations, and it was clear that the affluent who wanted to build modern large houses, particularly those closely connected to the central families, were receiving the larger holdings. In fact, in recent years all the land has been divided up among the Arab-Sudanese people of the village, including allocations to some nonresidents who have migrated to Khartoum but plan to retire to the home area.

Such generous real estate allocations were in marked contrast to the increasingly cramped quarters of the village's growing population of the Hausa minority group. During the late 1920s, the British brought members of the Hausa group in from West Africa as laborers for the cotton enterprise in the irrigation scheme (Duffield 1988; O'Brien 1984, 1986; O'Brien and Ali 1984). The present-day Hausa were for the most part born in Abdal Galil. The immigrant generations — those who held the dream of someday going back home — have died by now. Not being entitled to tenancies in the irrigation scheme (which were originally given out only to the indigenous landowners whose land was used for the irrigation project and their clients and kin), most Hausa work as day laborers and sharecroppers with no land rights in the irrigation scheme and only a small living area in the village. The old shaykh of the Hausa in Abdal Galil, whom I interviewed in the 1970s, believed they would go back to Nigeria someday, so they did not bother with educating their children other than encouraging the boys to take lessons on the Qur'an from one of the old men. But his son, the new leader, whom I interviewed in 1989 and 1992, says they cannot go back, even though the Nigerian Embassy held a meeting to inform them they could if they wished. "How could I leave my aging mother and my children and grandchildren here? And if we all went, where would we go? We've never been there, and we don't know anyone there," Lebo Mohammed Saani told me.

The Hausa formed a castelike group in Suad's village. Both the Arab-Sudanese and the Hausa themselves reinforced their separation by not intermarrying, and the Hausa have maintained their language, a separate mosque, and, significantly, separate customs with respect to female circumcision. The social disdain for them is quickly evident in conversations with Arab-Sudanese in Abdal Galil, many of whom would like to see them relocated outside the village. Suad told me emphatically, "This isn't their country. We won't give them any more land." In fact, people on the Arab-Sudanese side of the village were amazed that I went to visit the Hausa and laughed heartily when I referred to the Hausa quarter as being "part of Abdal Galil."[6]

Although not the cause of their inferior status, Hausa female circumcision practices come under criticism from the Arab-Sudanese, who say the Hausa do not practice female circumcision, "not even sunna!" Some Hausa claimed that they did in fact take a tiny bit of the clitoris or prepuce, which they called "sunna." The Hausa consider it a symbol of a man's success if he can support his wife in seclusion, making it unnecessary for her to work in the fields or do domestic labor in the homes of the more affluent Arab-Sudanese, and this seclusion is also called "sunna." High fertility is common, and the freeze on access to building land makes the future seem grim for this group.

Both Suad and her husband are teachers, members of the Abdal Galil founding family, the community's elite. They have benefited from this status in getting education, connections, employment in Abdal Galil, and land, but it has not been without effort and enterprise that they are able to live in a comfortable large house with their children and one of Suad's brothers.

Both husband and wife have a sophisticated outlook and urban experience; thus it did not surprise me to learn during my 1989 visit that Suad and her husband had taken the step, back when their girls were small, of breaking with the Arab-Sudanese tradition of pharaonic circumcision. Not wanting their daughters to be infibulated, they decided Besaina should not be the midwife to do their circumcisions. They did not reject

[6] Many surveys and reports in Sudan routinely exclude "Fellata" neighborhoods and populations, based on the social mythology that they are transitory pilgrim populations on their way to Mecca, who will someday leave. While this may have been the case in the past, the stability of these populations is evident, and the discrimination they experience as an oppressed minority group deserves further research.

circumcision entirely, though, so they arranged for a health visitor to give their daughters only an intermediate form of circumcision, "some stitching, but not all the way." At the time, they did not make a big issue of their innovation because it was rather rare and probably also because it was still socially unacceptable in the village. But by 1989, the subject of change was widespread in Abdal Galil, and they could openly advocate that the minimal intermediate form was better than the pharaonic one. In fact, Suad's husband, Hussein, mentioned to me approvingly that he knew a doctor in the provincial capital, Wad Medani, who had left his daughters totally uncircumcised (*sai*).

Hussein, like our friend Mohammed in Khartoum, was not alone in being a father concerned about the form of his daughters' circumcisions. Reformist men can play important roles if they become involved in influencing the fates of their sisters and daughters and in making it known that they would prefer to marry an uncircumcised woman. But many men do not take such an active interest, viewing the whole subject as a matter for women to handle.

Sittana's Family

In the second family, there was a definite generation gap in the women's opinions about female circumcision. The older woman, Sittana, was an extremely interesting woman I had gotten to know in the 1970s because of her *zar* spirit possession. In those days, she held a zar "clinic" (*shefakhana*) on Fridays and Sundays, and her daughter Laila, then a teenager, had helped by making and serving coffee to her clients and running errands. At the clinic sessions, which were similar to the zar coffee parties described by Kenyon (1991), women gathered from nearby villages for visits to Sittana while she was in the persona of her possessing zar spirit, Janubi, whose name means "southerner," a term denoting a male from a southern Sudanese ethnic group. Unlike the more lively drumming and trancing at major "zar parties," where possessing spirits are invited to descend on the adherents under the guidance of a *shaykha* who can maintain some control of the situation, these coffee "clinics" struck me as serving primarily a support group or community mental health function for women. The more active trancing was not permitted in Abdal Galil village, where so grand a mosque stood and where so many pious families resided. But these quieter gatherings allowed women an opportunity to discuss their physical and social ills with a sympathetic group and with someone who could offer hope from a supernatural source. This assertion requires some explanation, however, about zar and Sittana's case.

Sittana's involvement with the zar spirit possession practices began during her reproductive years, when she experienced particularly vivid dreams immediately prior to a miscarriage. In these dreams she was overtaken by thirst and went to find water in the town of Sinnar, the city near the dam that supplies the Blue Nile waters for the Gezira Irrigated Scheme where her village is located. She turned on a tap, and the spirit Janubi hit her on the back with a can and she started to bleed. She woke up bleeding, in the early stages of a miscarriage. Even with medical treatment, she was unable to save her pregnancy, but the message from Janubi in subsequent dreams was clear: Janubi expected her to acknowledge being possessed.

But Sittana was a stubborn woman and refused to allow the spirit to control her. Then in her next pregnancy she became extremely ill. Despite medical treatment, she ended up at home in bed, disoriented, and so ill that a zar practitioner (shaykha) was called in from the provincial capital to diagnose her and perform ceremonies. Warned that she might miscarry if she sat for the ceremonies, she sat anyway, for three days. The shaykha diagnosed her as possessed and told her that the spirit wanted her to hold clinics to treat the sick and that he offered protection for the pregnancy if she followed his demands. She continued to resist and did not lose the baby, but after another four and a half years of suffering headaches, pains, and frequent illnesses, she finally gave in and started doing clinics as Janubi demanded. After that, she told me, she was well, "*al hamdu lillah*" (praise to God); the phrase reinforced her Muslim piety and recognition of God's sovereignty, even though she needed a spirit's help to achieve health.

The zar practices are widespread in the countries of northeast Africa, including Egypt, Somalia, Eritrea, Sudan, and Ethiopia. Referred to as a "cult" by some writers, who are perhaps echoing Anthony F. C. Wallace's use of that term to mean a form of religious organization, zar should not be assumed to be a cult in the common understanding of that term. Indeed, although its practice is characterized by specialized activities and gatherings of devotees who believe in the spirits, Muslims who practice it do not consider it to be divergent from Islam. Indeed, many Sudanese Muslims believe the practice of zar enhances their piety — although orthodox theologians disagree — and even those who do not accept the practices as desirable or pious may nevertheless consider the spirits to be real and dangerous. Zar is closely related to other spirit-connected practices in West Africa and Central Africa, but as it is practiced among Muslims in northeast Africa it has some distinctive characteristics.[7]

---

[7] For a set of studies on a wide range of zar and other spirit-possession practices, see Lewis, Al-Safi, and Hurreiz, eds., 1991; for the most significant in-depth study of Sudanese zar, see Janice Boddy 1989. Other research and analysis of zar that have been particularly

My first encounter with Sittana in 1977 had been a memorable one. Having arrived in the village for research a few days before, I went with Awatif al-Imam, my research assistant and collaborator, who was a university-educated employee of the Ministry of Social Affairs, to observe one of Sittana's twice-weekly clinics. These clinics were held every Friday and Sunday at her home next door to the Health Center from late morning until evening, and anyone was welcome, though it seemed that only Arab-Sudanese women and a visiting anthropologist attended.

We entered a small, dimly lit room, apparently a storage room with a few sacks, boxes, and tins on the dirt floor. As our eyes adjusted, we could see that several women and girls were already there, sitting on mats or low stools or boxes. Awatif and I each offered the customary ten-piaster coin, placing it in front of Sittana on a mat, and took seats across the room. Sittana sat on a mat at the end of the room farthest from the door. She had several canisters and small boxes on her left. Incense, strongly dominated by sandalwood, was wafting from the small charcoal censer to which she added flakes of incense mixture from one of the tins from time to time. Because her spirit was male, she was dressed in a variant of men's clothing — a tattered old jalabiya and a colorful scarf wrapped like a man's turban on her head — and wore several leather pouches and amulets around her neck.

Sittana was in trance, it appeared, so the usual ebullient friendly greetings and handshaking seemed inappropriate. We greeted her very simply and sat down quietly in the back. Soon her daughter appeared with tiny cups of spiced, sweetened coffee for us on a tin tray. As the conversations resumed after our entrance, we found that the women were talking about a number of topics — health problems, difficulty finding a husband for the daughter of one, headaches that kept another from getting her work done, a niece's infertility — mostly problems of a social, psychological, or stress-linked nature, so typical of women's concerns.

From time to time, Janubi uttered a string of nonsense syllables that were rather similar-sounding to the glossolalia outbursts of Christian Pentacostalists and in this case were purported to be *Rutana,* an Arabic term for unintelligible languages such as those of southern Sudan. Clearly that was supposed to be Janubi speaking. Other times, Janubi/Sittana spoke in Arabic, in a somewhat labored, masculine voice, with angular gestures, and sometimes she rolled her eyes. She asked questions, left some odd silences, and gave advice, to which others listened carefully.

Nobody seemed in any hurry to go anywhere. The atmosphere added

---

useful in studying gender role implications are found in the work of Kenyon 1991; Constantinides 1978; Hale 1987, 1996; Samia El Hadi El Nagar 1987; Morsy 1991, 1993; and Grotberg 1990.

to my feeling that the consultations with the spirit were not the only reason for visiting Janubi. Here one could get advice on one's problems, listen to the problems of others, give and receive sympathy, and get to know others who might serve as an additional social support network in daily life. Sittana's daughter brought in a second round of coffee.

Still relatively new at fieldwork and respectful of cultural differences as dramatic as spirit possession beliefs, I planned to do nothing more than observe. But Janubi initiated consultations with Awatif and me. I was obviously a foreigner because of my face and dress — a print-fabric jalabiya with braid trim and no tobe was a bit odd — so Janubi/Sittana started with me. She asked my name, where I lived, and if I was married. I told her I was an American, was married, was living in Khartoum, and had come to do research in Abdal Galil.

"How long married?"

"Seven years."

"Where are your children?"

"I don't have any children yet."

There were probably a few quiet clucks of pity in the room because my situation would have been nothing short of a disaster to a village woman. Seven years of barrenness was too much to endure, enough to make even a devoted husband consider divorce, or at least taking a second wife. This infertility must arise from a major physical problem, they would assume, perhaps of supernatural origin. It's not that no one knew about birth control methods, though indeed they were not in frequent use. But no woman in her right mind would use birth control to delay the birth of a first child.

Janubi pondered. I didn't know whether to try to explain. "No babies died? No stillbirths?"

"No. I — "

She waved me silent and stared at me with narrowed eyes. "I know what your problem is. There is an *'ard* in your House of Birth [uterus]. I can help you."

No reply was called for because Sittana was just making a diagnosis, Awatif explained to me quietly. If I wished her to solve the problem — the actions of an earth spirit were blocking my uterus and preventing conception, she believed — I would have to come back later and pay a great deal more, probably several Sudanese pounds, to receive a treatment that would probably involve such things as special amulets and incense.

I did not volunteer that I was just then four months pregnant. It was no secret, but somehow it seemed like it would be rude to challenge her diagnosis right there in front of her other clients, and my condition did not show in my voluminous long dress. Although the women I had met in my neighborhood already knew, some of the women in the room were from other villages in the area, and it is possible the news had not traveled so terribly fast. After all, pregnancy is a rather unremarkable state for women in Sudan and unlikely to create as much interest as my hair, my clothing, or my accented speech. If Sittana knew, apparently Janubi (her dissociated trance state) did not. Anyway, as a respectful researcher I did not want to rock the boat or seem to be exposing her as a charlatan.

Not so with Awatif. She decided to participate boldly and assertively, perhaps disliking my choice to let these rural women continue in their "superstitious" beliefs rather than challenging Janubi. Fabricating a story, Awatif joined in: "Janubi, I want my husband back. Can you help me?"

Sittana/Janubi shot back immediately, "You're not married! You have no husband!"

"Yes, I do. We were married only a short time," she elaborated, "and then he went off to Egypt and did not come back." She went on at length, adding details to the story: She has written letters again and again, but he won't come back. She thinks he's involved with another woman. The family is not helping.

Janubi listened thoughtfully but adamantly refused to believe that this young professional woman had ever been married. "No, you're not married. You're a girl. You're not telling the truth."

Awatif was tough and persistent. Then with a slight smirk she pleaded, "It's the truth and I need your help! Can't you get him back?"

The other women were attentive as the two argued back and forth, but no one took sides. It was a standoff. I was aghast and embarrassed. Eventually Awatif stopped, but I felt responsible because it was I who had initiated this visit, never dreaming that this Sudanese researcher's values as to proper participant observation etiquette would so thoroughly differ from my own.

But it would have been equally inappropriate to have interrupted her. What I had witnessed, I later realized, was an episode in a cultural "argument" among Sudanese women of different backgrounds. Awatif, with her education and cosmopolitan, enlightened outlook, was playing a role in undermining what she saw as superstition and old wives' tales. Although not directly attacking their beliefs, she presumably did not want to allow her countrywomen to be fooled by this woman Sittana. And I suspect she was not particularly happy about some foreign anthropologist in the mix, taking notes on the exotic beliefs of the Other.

Later, when I got to know Awatif better, I realized how important it was to her to maintain Sudan's good image and how she disliked foreign misapprehensions. On a visit to her hometown to meet her family, I once observed her ironing some clothes with a charcoal iron. Before going to Sudan, I had never seen anything but electric irons. Naively, perhaps, I didn't even realize there had been a charcoal precursor. Shaped rather similarly to an electric iron, its two layers are hinged to insert burning coals and then it is locked shut, allowing ventilation through decorative holes. The heat is adjusted by means of swinging it gently now and then to increase air flow to the coals. Steam is produced by spraying or sprinkling water on the clothes before ironing, a technique I had learned from my grandmother before steam irons were invented.

Naively, I had not realized that people without electricity would bother to iron clothes. Awatif was shocked when I admitted my ignorance, scoffing, "Did you think we were so uncouth that we would want to go around with wrinkled clothes?" Indeed, later on an elderly Kenana woman who had grown up in a very rural and isolated area told me that even in the days before the advent of charcoal irons, they tried to smooth their clothes. All they could do was pass a warm pan full of coals over them: "We didn't know anything then; we were like animals." Far from animals, I thought, because they cared to look their best, despite technological impediments that I personally would not have tried to surmount.

Awatif's disdain for Janubi and zar seemed to be about national pride — she saw zar as marginal and atypical, and she probably attacked Sittana's credibility to sow seeds of doubt in an effort to "enlighten the women" (as other Sudanese have suggested). Awatif herself chose education and employment as the route to improving women's situation, not zar and its small rewards and moral support.

The day of the visit to the zar clinic, I waited until we had left to ask Awatif why she had lied. She laughed and did not answer. Silence and avoidance are the culturally appropriate responses to uncomfortable questions in Sudan. She pretended not to hear when I tried to pursue the matter.

Four days later, on a day when there was no "clinic," Awatif and I visited Sittana at her house to interview her about her life and her involvement in zar. We talked for nearly an hour before Awatif asked her if she remembered our visit to Janubi on Friday.

"Not really. I usually can't remember anything that happens when Janubi descends on me."

When I returned to Abdal Galil in 1989, I found Sittana still possessed but no longer holding the clinics. She was limping badly on a damaged leg: "Janubi did it," she said. In the year or so since I had last seen her, she had fallen in the heavy mud that pervades the village after a rain, and the fall resulted in a compound fracture to her leg. While she convalesced, she discontinued the clinics, and the leg continued to cause her difficulty walking. In 1992 she told me that she and her spirit were locked in an argument. He wanted her to resume the clinics or he would refuse to let her heal; she insisted that he heal her leg first and then she would resume the clinics. Both were intransigent.

Sittana's argument with her spirit directly paralleled a major dilemma of contemporary Sudanese society. Zar had come under heavy criticism in the Islamic religious resurgence of the 1980s and 1990s, and many Muslims were attempting to suppress or discredit zar as a non-Islamic practice that Sudanese should discontinue. But that does not mean Muslims could not believe that spirits existed and be frightened by them. Just by talking about her spirit possession in answer to my questions, Sittana began to feel the possession and speak in Rutana. My companion on the visit, a pious young woman from Ekhlas's family, became alarmed when the spirit seemed to descend on Sittana. She recited several times the Muslim statement of faith, "There is no god, but God" (*la illaha illa lah*), a phrase often used as an exclamation or invoked as protection.

Although I have not emphasized zar as a form of resistance, it is clear from the work of Boddy (1989), Lewis (1991), Constantinides (1982), Hale (1996), Morsy (1993), and others that women's ability to use zar practices and the demands of their spirits to extract resources and indulgences from husbands and other family members is a means of resisting some of the manifestations of patriarchal power in their lives. The social and psychological supports analysts have identified also should be recognized as a form of resistance (Abu-Lughod 1990, Gruenbaum 1998, Lock and Kaufert 1998). The current challenge to social acceptability of spirit possession rituals effectively undermines one of the ways women have defended themselves from the power of patriarchal relations.

But Sittana is not a radical. She does not articulate challenges to women's traditional roles and duties in the home, despite her own employment and her desire for her daughter to be educated. And when it comes to female circumcision, she is quite conservative.

Sittana's daughter Laila, in her twenties in 1992, had rejected pharaonic circumcision. Knowing that the midwife Besaina's circumcisions would be radical, Laila arranged to have her young daughter circumcised by a midwife she invited from a nearby town. The circumcision was an intermediate form. Although Sittana was present during the surgery, apparently she did not position herself to see the actual cutting. It was not until a couple of weeks later, she said, that she realized that only a small amount of tissue had been removed from her granddaughter. Sittana wanted to have it redone. But Laila, a determined young woman, refused to consider it, and she was quite confident her mother would not dare interfere.

Sittana sighed. There was not much she could do. But she picked up a small great-niece whom she had been given to care for after the girl's parents divorced and cuddled her. When the time came, Sittana told me, *this* girl would be given a proper pharaonic circumcision.

Part of Laila's confidence that she could resist her mother's desire to have her daughter's circumcision redone stems from a change in attitudes in the Gezira village that is beginning to take hold, a change attributable to discussions stimulated by educated community members and the work of the medical assistant at the clinic (see Chapter 7). People were becoming more aware of the serious health risks of the surgeries, and discussions sparked by the growing desire to learn more about the proper interpretation of Islamic doctrines led some people to conclude that the pharaonic form of circumcision should be abandoned in favor of sunna or nothing.

Migration experiences also contributed to the local debates, as in the case of Besaina, the village midwife mentioned above. When I interviewed her in 1989, this midwife, who had been doing nothing but pharaonic before, informed me that she had decided to discontinue pharaonic surgeries and do only sunna. The medical assistant's influence was apparent in her rationale (see Chapter 7), but so, too, was the fact that she had become more religious. Increasing religiosity is not uncommon for older women, and the growing Islamic resurgence in the region was no doubt also a factor, as was the migration of her eldest son. He had gone to work in Saudi Arabia, where he was influenced by the conservative Saudi (Wahibist) religious interpretations, and he also was able to accumulate enough wealth to send his mother on the pilgrimage to Mecca. So by 1989 she had begun to listen to arguments that pharaonic circumcision was not Islamic.

Dramatic changes have occurred in villages like Abdal Galil since the 1970s, some of which have significantly impacted local ideas about female circumcision, moving the community in the direction of reform. But what is unlikely to change rapidly here is the intense importance of marriage and the strongly held values on morality. Unless circumcision can be carefully detached from such concerns, as the religious discussions are starting to do, people will be less likely to feel at liberty to discontinue circumcision.

I leave the topic of polygyny to Chapter 6.

Chapter 4
Ethnicity

Female circumcision practices are deeply entwined with ethnic identity wherever they are found. Understanding this should provide an important insight into the tenacity of the practice and people's resistance to change efforts, and it can help to explain why the practices may even spread in certain situations.

In *The River Between* by Kenyan novelist Ngugi wa Thiong'o, an adolescent Gikuyu girl, Muthoni, makes the decision to undergo circumcision in defiance of her preacher father, an ardent Christian convert who has rejected the rite as sinful. Her sister reminds her:

> "Father will not allow it. . . . The missionaries do not like the circumcision of girls. Father has been saying so. Besides, Jesus told us it was wrong and sinful."
> "I know. But I want to be circumcised. . . . I—I want to be a woman. I want to be a real girl, a real woman, knowing all the ways of the hills and the ridges. . . . The white man's God does not quite satisfy me. I want, I need something more." (Ngugi 1965:25–26)

Although still embracing Christianity, Muthoni wants to become a woman and achieve beauty in her community as her Gikuyu ethnic heritage has defined it. Ngugi thus portrays her, and later other characters, in a struggle to engage in change without loss of the rootedness of ethnic identity. This young girl, by her choice to be circumcised, is implicitly questioning the new ways that have been adopted uncritically, yet she does not reject the new religion. It is not just a matter of tradition, but a desire to look critically at the new as well as the old and to value what is solidly rooted in identity and heritage. The novelist thereby raises complex questions about what it takes to be a woman and a full member of this ethnic community, especially when one has adopted a new religion.

Similarly, the Gikuyu women described by Jean Davison in *Voices from Mutira* (1989) find that the changes occurring in female circumcision practices—many members of the younger generations are giving up circumcision, and along with it some of the other expectations about morality and sexual restraint—can challenge their own sense of identity as a member of their ethnic group. Davison reports that in Kenya during the 1930s and 1940s, female circumcision was held "as central to the Gikuyu way of life" and a "symbol of ethnic pride pitted against colonial domination" (1989:23). But if contemporary encouragements to modify or eliminate the practice are followed, those historic areas of resistance to external influence are undermined. In short, where missionaries and health personnel had tried to stop female circumcision in the past, the current resistance to change efforts may be related not only to the meaning of circumcision within a culture's system of roles and rituals, but also to its symbolism as opposition to colonialism. In the Gikuyu case and doubtless many others, ethnic identity and nationalism paralleled one another. Davison comments that cultural asynchronicity has developed—circumcision no longer has the same meaning (1989:202).

Body Alteration and Ethnic Identity

Body alteration is not uncommon as a part of rituals of transition that recognize a new status (manhood, womanhood) and initiate the formation of a new identity for which the pain and dramatic change help to create a psychological marker. The Dinka and Nuer of southern Sudan use facial scarification for such rites of passage. Other cultures use or have used male circumcision, subincision (in certain Australian aboriginal groups), or other painful or humiliating (but less permanently body altering) practices to mark these transitions.

Because they differ so much from one group to another, it seems plausible that the markings and other bodily changes can and do serve as ethnic markers as well as tests or psychological traumas to heighten the social and emotional effects of the status transition. These markers are prone to have an ideological use and to have an important secondary effect on ethnic identity. For example, to be an initiated Nuer man required forehead scars that were received in a painful ordeal experienced with a group of others during the teenage years, marking arrival of manhood and requiring changes in role and behavior. Those in the younger generation who rejected this, through influences of education and Christianity, occupy an anomalous status as adult men who are still considered boys, termed "bull boys" (Hutchinson 1996). Because they have not undergone this rite, they must make special efforts to be regarded as men (and marriageable), and even their loyalty to their Nuer identity is questioned.

Insofar as the maintenance of ethnic identity is a powerful factor in social dynamics, we can expect that when ethnic (and more generally cultural) authenticity is at issue, female circumcision will tend to be preserved. In addition, in situations where people are in the process of reconceptualizing or altering their ethnicity, ideologically significant symbols such as body alteration may assume added significance, either in resistance to change or as symbols of it.

Differences in circumcision practices by ethnicity sometimes follow the pattern that the more severe female circumcision is practiced by higher status ethnic groups. Not only might this serve to preserve the practice, but it could bolster ethnic identity and the social boundaries associated with ethnic difference in a multicultural society. In a class-stratified society where a particular ethnicity confers privilege, the boundaries of ethnicity may be even more closely guarded and individuals may be defined by their adherence to identifying customary practices, motivating insiders to preserve and assimilators to adopt such defining practices.

Female circumcision continues to serve as such a marker of ethnic, and in some cases class, identity. This pattern is evident from the several examples from differing ethnic groups in Sudan given in this chapter (see also Gruenbaum 1988). Where female circumcision serves as an ethnic or class status marker, this can be expected to constitute another obstacle to change or even a motivation for further spread of the practices. Strong feelings about female circumcision and moral quality are evident in certain situations of interethnic rivalry, as the following examples from Sudan's Rahad River Valley demonstrate.

Focusing first on the ethnic differences within the Muslim, primarily Arabic-speaking, majority population of Sudan, we note that most of these ethnic groups have practiced some form of female circumcision traditionally and consider it part of their own culture. There is considerable variation among them, however, in the types of surgeries and their meanings, symbolism, and ceremonial contexts.

For example, at least two nomadic groups, the Rashaida and the Messeriya, both say they do not infibulate but perform only the sunna because as nomads, they cannot count on finding a midwife for a woman in labor, which of course is essential for an infibulated woman. More recently, some people within these nomadic groups have begun to infibulate, apparently because of influence from contacts with neighboring peoples (El Dareer 1982), but for reasons that have not been adequately researched. Among the Beni Helba, according to El Dareer, the women of the higher status families (the lineage of the *nazir,* a local hereditary leader) were pharaonically circumcised, while other women had sunna circumcisions only; the more drastic operations were thus associated with higher social standing.

A small minority of Sudanese Muslim ethnic groups, including the Fur and the Kinin in the far west, do not traditionally circumcise. This western region was one of the last areas of Sudan to come under colonial domination because it was the site of a powerful Islamic kingdom. The Kinin are said to refuse to circumcise for religious reasons, believing that true Muslims should not do it, but their refusal has resulted in the disdain of their non-Kinin neighbors. Also they have trouble getting trained midwives to settle in their area because midwives, dependent on collecting payment for births and circumcisions, find they cannot make an adequate income where no circumcisions are performed. As for the Fur, many have begun to circumcise now, especially those who live in towns. It is interesting to note that the Fur in precolonial times did not circumcise girls, with the exception of one category. According to historian Lidwien Kapteijns, among the nobility clitoridectomy was "fashionable and constituted another element of their claims to be more proper Muslims than the commoners" (1983:17). Similarly, Tubiana notes that for the Zaghawa (Beri) people, who live in Chad and western Sudan, male circumcision was general but "female circumcision is practiced only among the daughters of royal clans" (M.-J. Tubiana 1984:156, quoted in Hicks 1993:230).

The spread of pharaonic circumcision in the western part of Sudan appears to be related to the influx under the colonial administration of a new urban middle class of government officials, police, soldiers, and traders from the Nile Valley whose social and religious practices came to be emulated by local people in the growing urban areas, who were apparently aspiring to a higher class status (Kapteijns 1983:20).

In Sudan there are four categories of ethnic groups that do not follow the infibulation practices: the primarily non-Muslim southern Sudanese; Muslims of West African descent (including the Hausa discussed earlier and other ethnic groups commonly referred to by the pejorative gloss "Fallata"); some of the groups of Ethiopian immigrants and refugees (present in large numbers in the towns and in rural eastern Sudan); and European and North American expatriates (called "Khawajat") and people of Mediterranean origin who hold Sudanese citizenship (e.g., Greek-Sudanese, Lebanese). With the exception of expatriates and Mediterranean groups, who, despite their differences in religion and lack of circumcision, are generally respected for their positions of education and wealth, the other noncircumcising groups are not only ethnically different, but generally occupy lower social statuses. It is not uncommon to hear Arab-Sudanese express dislike or disgust for those who do not circumcise, an attitude which, while certainly not universal, is sufficiently widely held that it reinforces the social class and ethnic boundaries.

Status and the Adoption of Circumcision

Ethnic rivalry and conflict is not new to Sudan. But the forms it has taken in the twentieth century represent growing inequality of access to political and economic resources, which is a fundamental condition that has inflamed the civil war between the central government and a movement supported by numerous minority ethnic groups.

It is not surprising that in such situations of ethnic group inequality, individuals and communities are tempted to assimilate to ethnic groups in better situations by accepting particularly crucial social customs such as female circumcision. A couple of cases serve to illustrate this problem.

In one study in Kordofan, Jay O'Brien found several families of West African origin who had successfully established a new ethnic identity as part of a Joama village; their adaptation included adopting the practice of female genital surgeries (O'Brien 1980). Similar pressures have been noted in other areas, but unfortunately it was not uncommon in Sudanese survey research in the 1970s and 1980s to overlook resident populations that made up the minority groups who were often considered to be "not Sudanese." El Dareer's study of female circumcision in several northern provinces, for example, did not include people of West African origin in the surveys, so it is not clear how widespread the trend may be whereby younger generations of these people have begun to circumcise girls in order to assimilate (1982). The motivation, however, is clearly there because important economic and political rights and opportunities (such as access to tenancies on development projects, citizenship papers, and certain licenses) are often unavailable to "non-Sudanese" groups (see Duffield 1988).

Town-dwelling Nuba, not traditionally circumcisers, have apparently taken up the practice increasingly. El Dareer reported that Nuba in towns "want to be like Arabs," and she was told by a Nuba woman she interviewed that she had been teased by her Arab neighbors until she finally conformed and had herself and her daughters circumcised.

The large southern ethnic groups such as the Dinka and the Nuer have not been interested in adopting the practice in their home areas, as I found during fieldwork there in the 1970s. Even then, however, the practice was not unheard of. Women I interviewed told me about a case of a Dinka woman who had married a northern merchant living in a southern village. Through her contacts with wives of her husband's Arabic-speaking friends, she was told that being circumcised was much better, so she tried it. As the story was told, she found that it deprived her of sexual pleasure, so she warned others not to do it.

What is significant about this example is that it took place in southern Sudan, where Arab-Sudanese are the cultural minority, yet as the dominant majority in the country as a whole they exert an ideological hegemony emanating from the strong religious system of Islam. Followers of Islam, as part of their faith, assert the superiority of Islam over traditional religions, whose practitioners do not claim such superiority. This is reinforced by the economic dominance of the more developed northern Sudan and its wealthy merchant representatives.

What these few examples suggest is that female circumcision is not merely a residual traditional practice, but is in certain situations an important marker of privileged ethnic group status, used ideologically to exclude aspiring lower status groups, who are in turn tempted to adopt it as part of the cultural assimilation necessary to upward mobility. Thus individuals and groups that pursue strategies of assimilation tend to adopt circumcision as a critical cultural marker. Yet for those groups that have not been able to assimilate or have not chosen to attempt to do so, their avoidance of this practice has in some cases become an element of their case for their own moral superiority over their dominators, reinforcing the cultural boundary from the other side.

Kenana and the Zabarma in the Rahad River Valley

A more extended example from my fieldwork in the Rahad area of Sudan shows how this happened and how people have responded over a twenty-year period. Prior to the opening of the Rahad Irrigation Scheme in 1978, there were two villages located about a mile apart on the southwest bank of the Rahad River and about ten miles over a dirt track from the small market town of Mafaza; the villages lay on either side of the boundary between Blue Nile Province and Kassala Province. These two villages were the focus of a study of family farming, economic relations, and labor migration in the 1970s (O'Brien 1980), and my involvement with that project gave me the opportunity to study the patterns of family living in the two villages (Gruenbaum 1979). In these river villages, they practiced rainfall and riverbank cultivation, combined with various other activities such as seasonal agricultural labor migration and herding. The residents of one village were all of the Arabic-speaking Kenana ethnic group. Traditionally pastoral nomads, who had in recent decades found it necessary to cultivate, the Kenana said they were descendants of the Prophet Mohammed. The residents of the other village nearby were Zabarma, a people of West African origin who had been living in Sudan for three or four generations. Most of the inhabitants of the two villages later relocated to the irrigation project, where I was able to continue my research with them in 1989 and 1992 and investigate subsequent developments with respect to circumcision, women's roles, and ethnic relations.

The people of the two villages practiced very different forms of female circumcision, one group practicing very mild sunna and the other very severe infibulation.

To make my point about the role of female circumcision practices in the maintenance of ethnic identity, I want to convey a sense of what life has been like for the people of this area over the past couple of decades, so that the differences in these two ethnic groups will be apparent and their subsequent contacts more meaningful. The story begins for me in 1976 when I first came in contact with these ethnic groups, the Kenana and the Zabarma, that inhabited the two villages.

"Mother Elephant"

It was my husband Jay who first got me involved with the village called Um Fila, or "Mother Elephant." He and one of his graduate students, Salah El-Din El-Shazali, decided to work in Um Fila during Jay's first trip to the Rahad River Valley in the fall of 1976, while he was on a research leave from the University of Khartoum. The name of the village dated back to its founding in the 1930s, when elephants still roamed this far north (13° 30' north latitude).

The project was to focus on the rural economy and seasonal labor migration from this area. In order to include the variable of ethnicity in the study, Jay and Salah decided to study two villages with differing ethnic affiliations. They chose Um Fila (population 426, according to a 1975 census) and its nearest neighbor, Hallali (population 203), only about two kilometers distant. Both villages were primarily farming villages, with cultivation based on rainfall agriculture and some riverbank agriculture, with sorghum as the staple crop.

Jay and Salah set up camp in Um Fila. Although I was teaching that term, I was able to join them for a couple of weeks in the middle of the research. My responsibility in our small team was to observe aspects of family living and the roles of women that could supplement the detailed data Jay and Salah were collecting about family economic decisions.

The inhabitants of the two villages were members of different ethnic groups, speaking different languages, following somewhat different Islamic practices, and not intermarrying. The village of Hallali, upstream from Um Fila, had been settled by the Kenana, a formerly nomadic group that still practiced pastoralism (sheep, goats, and camels) as an additional economic activity along with farming. For them, as for so many of the pastoral nomadic ethnic groups in Sudan, farming was considered unpleasant; the necessity of settlement and farming would only be undertaken as the result of hard times, dwindling herds, or other misfortune. According to local history, the group had settled in the area only about forty years before, and they still managed to continue herding by sending the animals of a group of kin to the *khala* (wilderness grazing areas) for several weeks at a time with one or more of the young men while the others stayed to farm. The Kenana had an additional economic activity in their annual migration to irrigated cotton projects in their region, where they picked cotton for wages to supplement their farm and pastoral production.

The Kenana considered themselves true "Arabs." Not only did they speak Arabic and continue to identify as nomads (for which the common Sudanese term is 'arab), but they claimed descent from the Prophet Mohammed and origination on the Arabian peninsula. As the Prophet's descendants, they could claim a measure of moral superiority over other groups. Unlike the groups of Arabic-speaking peoples who had intermarried with the local people in the past generations (who, according to historians, mingled in large numbers over many generations with non-Arabic-speaking peoples and in the process Arabized and Islamized Sudan), the Kenana had practiced endogamy properly according to some of my informants so that "even our mothers are Arabs," as one of the women told me. Even so, they also claimed to have been in Sudan for so many generations that they were the real Sudanese, unlike their immigrant neighbors in Um Fila.

The residents of Um Fila, by contrast, call themselves Zabarma, a Songhai-related ethnic group originating in the area of Niger and Mali in West Africa. The community's oral history claims that they have been living in Sudan since the end of the nineteenth century, with subsequent relocations taking them progressively further east, to the present site in the Rahad River Valley in about 1930. Like many other West African–originating immigrants, the impetus toward eastward migration was partly a result of the effort to make a pilgrimage to Mecca to fulfill the obligation of their Islamic faith. But to regard them as only pilgrims who are just passing through is incorrect, even though it is an explanation regularly given by Arabic-speaking Sudanese who do not consider West African–originating peoples to be legitimate citizens. In the case of this particular group of Zabarma, up to three generations had already been born in the same village, so they were truly stable.

In the 1970s, when they were first surveyed in a Sudanese demographic research project, the Zabarma families in Um Fila all considered themselves to be members of a single clan. Since endogamy is the preferred marriage practice, outsiders marrying into the community were so rare that very few of the adults were from groups other than Zabarma.

The trip to the camp in Um Fila demonstrated to me the harshness of the environment. Although Um Fila was only about 150 miles from Khartoum, the last 50 miles was a rutted dirt track. In some places, there was not one main track, but several separate tracks cross country. Khayrat, our university driver (who doubled as a superb and resourceful cook), seemed to relish the challenge of such terrain, speeding the aging Landrover to jump depressions and charting new courses across flat, open spaces. In the absence of seatbelts, Khayrat's utterance of "b'ism al-lahi" ("in the name of God") before the most risky maneuvers was our only protection. It took some getting used to, but I eventually resigned myself to the will of al-Lah and trust in Khayrat's love of life to see us through.

On another drive to Um Fila that Jay and Salah made with Khayrat as their driver, the Landrover conked out more than once. Each time this happened they were very worried, surrounded as they were by expanses of dry savanna grassland and occasional acacia forests. In the daytime, the sun was blazing and the temperature was probably over 100 degrees, while at night the dry air turned uncomfortably chilly. Although as usual they had water along, getting help was quite another matter, as the area was sparsely populated and the tracks were not well traveled.

When the Landrover first stopped, Khayrat's explorations under the hood revealed the problem: the distributor. There had been a problem with it before Jay and Salah left Khartoum, and the university mechanics were supposed to have repaired it. Apparently all they had done was to wad up a piece of foil and stuff it in where the connection was needed. This spelled disaster to Jay. If they didn't have spare parts in Khartoum, they surely would not find them out in the countryside.

Self-taught in ingenuity, Khayrat asked Jay for his pack of Benson and Hedges, pulled out the foil lining of the cigarette pack, folded it carefully, and made the same repair the university mechanics had. "B'ism al-lahi," he said as he turned the key. The engine started and the group thanked God. It probably would have made sense to turn back to the nearest city for help, but instead, they continued on to Um Fila, Khayrat confidently repeating the same repair at each of the subsequent breakdowns.

When I first arrived at the research camp in Um Fila I was not surprised to find it was spare. Jay and Salah had decided not to intrude into village space. Instead, they had set up one of the university's old white tents (looking like a relic of the colonial period, which it probably was) next to a tree some two hundred yards from the nearest house. A goatskin bag we had filled with clean water from the deep-bore well five miles away was hung on the tree to serve as our water supply so we would not have to drink from the river. The goatskin looked very scenic and all, but the water tasted funny, so we used a big plastic barrel of well water for our main supply. Jay and Salah had gotten help from the village men to build a six-by-eight-foot *rakuba*, a shelter of wooden poles covered with straw, as an extension to the tent to provide more shade. Supplies were locked in a large trunk inside the tent. Our furnishings were the simple wood and rope beds called *angareeb*, cotton mattresses, a couple of metal tables, two or three folding canvas director's chairs, straw mats, a charcoal burner made of an old five-gallon tin, and an assortment of pots and pans. By day, the tent was too hot, and at night it was airless and full of mosquitoes. The rakuba offered protection from the sun — though it was by no means cool — and a degree of privacy for washing and changing if you hung a sheet across the doorway. When not out doing research, we mostly sat outside in any shade we could find, and at night we slept under the stars, wrapped in Chinese red cotton blankets from the market in Khartoum.

As soon as Khayrat had prepared a meal and we had all had some tea, Jay and Salah took me to meet the shaykh (the local leader) and look around the village. The houses looked like larger versions of our rakuba, except that they were round and had sturdy conical thatched roofs. Although such roofs could keep rain out fairly well, the walls were not plastered with mud as the homes along the Nile were. The cold night winds could easily penetrate these walls. The clusters of houses in each compound, or *hosh*, were hidden behind high grass fences supported by posts and protected from hungry goats by well-placed thorn branches. It all seemed very private, very closed. But in front of most of the compounds was a small house. This was the "men's house," (referred to as a *khalwa* in this village) where the men of the household did their indoor work, spent their leisure time, and received their guests. Not all of the families had that extra house, but men without one could spend time with their wives inside or with their neighbors, most of whom were relatives anyway.

We spoke briefly with the shaykh in front of his house, but as he was on his way to the mosque to pray, we said we would visit later. The "mosque" was really a *masjid,* or designated prayer place, and looked like a slightly larger, rectangular version of the thatched houses. It had no minaret, as those in the cities, so the call to prayer was chanted standing on the ground. We saw a number of other men walking toward it, but Salah advised against getting involved in extensive greetings because I was along. The men were focused on prayer, and they would need more time for what might turn out to be the extended greetings of meeting Jay's wife.

The last houses of the village were close to the riverbank. The sight of all that water in the midst of the dry, hot land was breathtaking. Narrow forests lined the high banks on both sides, providing cool shade and a natural source of firewood, building materials, and forage for goats and camels. In places where the banks were not too steep, *jeruf* (riverbank gardens) were laid out, surrounded by stacks of thorn branches. The tomato plants, melons, squash, and other vegetables nearest the water level were smallest, while higher rows, planted when the river was full, had had more time to grow. Crops could grow to maturity with just the residual moisture in the soil, providing fresh vegetables for weeks and a surplus to store, sell, or trade. A man was hoeing, probably a farmer from the village of Sherifa a quarter mile down on the opposite bank, and a boy stood on the bank watching the sheep and goats in his charge descend to drink. Farther on, I could make out several women carrying large tins of water on their heads, climbing the steep path to Sherifa.

We walked farther along the river, savoring the cool of the shade and the singing of the birds. A blue-gray fishing bird swooped down to the water, and small, dull-colored chirping birds like sparrows flitted through the branches. On another day we spotted a monkey near this spot.

Out of sight of Um Fila, Jay and I decided to wade into the wonderfully cool water — Jay up to his waist. At this season, the water was still moving swiftly enough that the usual water-borne diseases should not be much of a problem. Getting wet while fully clothed wasn't a problem here, where the heat and dry air quickly dried you. Salah could not be coaxed to join us, however — probably because I was there. When I wasn't around, he and Jay cooled off here daily.

In the cool of the evening, several of the village men dropped by our camp in twos or threes to welcome the men back, meet me, and stay for an evening's conversation. Khayrat kept the kettle of tea hot and Jay, Salah, and I took turns spooning three or four teaspoons of sugar into each small glass, pouring, stirring, and serving. One man quipped that the tea tasted better since Jay's wife had arrived. I laughed and insisted, "No, it was Khayrat who made the tea. Men can make tea just as well as women, can't they?"

"No, no," they disagreed laughingly, teasing Jay and Salah about the bachelor cuisine they had to endure from Khayrat. "That's why we need wives, to cook for us and give us children."

Salah joined in the laughter at first. But then he got that dreamy look on his face that meant he was thinking about Sara back in Khartoum. "My wife — when I get married — will be my companion, too. She'll be someone I can talk to about my work." He sighed.

The men listening shook their heads in amazement, chuckling at the naïveté of youth and these radical ideas from the city.

In the absence of a latrine, I had to plan ahead. Before it got completely dark, I walked off in the direction of the bushes a couple of hundred yards away, where I could not be seen if I crouched down. I carried a bottle of water, even though I intended to use the wad of toilet paper in my pocket — no one asks where you are going or tries to join you if you carry the water everyone uses to wash themselves after performing their bodily functions. The cracking clay soil of this region is deeply fissured during the dry season and the hot sun quickly dries out anything left on the surface, so the fact that an entire village uses the land in this way does not result in any accumulation of wastes, particularly because people walk so far to be out of sight of the houses.

As darkness fell, Jay lit the lantern. From the back of the Landrover, Salah unloaded a small, rough piece of plywood painted black — a blackboard they had borrowed from the shaykh — and some chalk, paper, and pencils. Several of the men had asked Jay to teach them to read and write, which was ironic because, for all Jay's education, the "Ustaz" from the University could not write Arabic, only speak it. But he "supervised" (as they evidently preferred) while Salah the student became their teacher. None of them had ever had the chance to go to school, although most of the men had received some limited Qur'anic lessons in childhood and knew the letters and could write their names.[1] It was a moving sight, these middle-aged farmers, one of whom had arrived riding high on a camel, seated on mats on the ground, studiously copying the letters and words Salah wrote for them. They also recited the alphabet with him: "Alif, ba, ta, tha, jim, ha . . . "Although they could make mental calculations about yields, crop sales, and earnings from seasonal jobs, they wanted to be able to do such things as read the receipts to make sure they were not being cheated. Most could not read or write much more than their own names. Before they left that evening, Salah wrote down some words for each of them to practice copying.

Meeting the men of the village was easy because they spoke Arabic, could be encountered as they moved along the main paths to the fields or other destinations, and socialized with Jay and Salah. But according to Zabarma traditions, women were expected to be much more secluded. Although not confined to their compounds, they nonetheless did not go out much unless on a specific errand like fetching water from the river or visiting kinswomen and neighbors. When they did go out, they were careful to avoid the main paths through the village. Whenever they spotted a man ahead of them, they simply took an alternate route. Walking around with Salah and Jay, I could not expect to meet women; indeed Jay and Salah had not met any of the women yet either. Sometimes they would see a woman in the distance, ahead of them on the path, but as soon as she saw them, she would take a detour or step inside a fenced courtyard. When they visited men to do interviews, Jay and Salah were always received in the men's houses, never inside the courtyards where the women spent most of their time. In addition, although my Arabic was still not as developed as I wanted it to be for doing research, the women of this village, unlike their husbands, were said to know very little Arabic.

On our second evening a man named Adam was the last to leave. At 52, Adam was the proud father of eight children, all from his one wife (who then had twins the following year). Adam and Jay had developed a special friendship. Jay had started calling him "Uncle Adam," which pleased

[1] Rote learning was the method of instruction, and although the Qur'an might be memorized that way, they did not necessarily master reading or writing as a result.

Adam a great deal. Now I had joined the family. "Ellen, tomorrow you must come and greet my wife and drink some coffee with her," Adam said, as he was leaving.

"Send my greetings to her," I replied.

The next day I set out alone for Adam's home. Jay had said I would recognize his hosh (house and courtyard) as it was somewhat squarer than most, had no khalwa, and was just north of the village corral. Adam was home, working under the shade of his *neem* tree. His smallest daughter was sitting on his lap while he fashioned a leg for a stool with a small hatchet. Furniture-making, using wood from the forest and strips of hides from village slaughters, was his second occupation and provided extra cash for the clothes, sugar, tea, and other commodities his family needed. The other small children laughed excitedly to see me approach and ran to tell their mother. With a warm smile, Adam invited me in and led me to his wife.

Amna was working in the kitchen, a dilapidated structure that probably had been their main house some years before; now they had a sturdier one on the other side of the tree. She rose from the low stool, pulled her tobe over her head, wiped her hands on a cloth, and shook my hand.

I greeted her in Arabic, with a full formal greeting, prepared for the usual exchange of blessings, inquiries after health and children, and more greetings. She replied with a simple "Salaam, salaam" (peace) and a shy smile. I offered another blessing, "Baraka fikum," but again she just said "Salaam."

I greeted one of the daughters. "What's your name?" She stared at me blankly, then giggled as I repeated the question. I looked to Amna, "Doesn't she want to tell me?" I asked, speaking slowly. Amna said nothing, then told the girl something in Zabarma, motioning for her to bring me something to sit on. Amna returned to her fire. She was making *kisra,* the thin, pancakelike bread made from a sort of sourdough batter made from ground sorghum. I noticed the grindstone near the door. According to what I knew from Geraldine Mary Culwick's research on Sudanese nutrition (1951), I realized that it would take Amna more than two hours a day to pound and grind enough grain to feed a family this size using this traditional food-processing method.

I pulled the stool closer, to watch. Evidently she only spoke Zabarma. "Can I watch you make kisra?" I asked, knowing that even sounds without meaning convey more than silence.

"Yes, kisra," she replied. At least we shared that word. I watched as she poked another piece of firewood — a dry branch — under the large metal rectangle that served as her griddle, then wiped its surface with a cloth dipped in grease from a can by her side.

Using a small gourd ladle, she poured a long arc of batter across the top of the griddle. Working quickly, she dipped a straight-edged reed into a bowl of water and used it to spread the batter back and forth across the griddle until she had fashioned a large, thin layer a little larger than the size of a cookie sheet. She let it bake until the edges began to brown a little and start to curl upward so she could grasp them with her hand, first loosening any sticking edge by scraping the griddle with an overturned tin can. She lifted the entire paper-thin sheet off in one piece, and added it to a stack on the tray beside her to cool. A small burned edge that had stuck to the griddle was wiped off and tossed across the room where a scavenging chicken quickly found it. Amna then poured out another scoop of batter.

The heat was intense so close to the griddle, so I moved back several feet. "It's too hot for me close to the fire," I said in Arabic, adding a more communicative gesture of wiping my brow, rolling my eyes, and exhaling.

She smiled, "Yes." Adam came in to see how we were doing. I asked him how to say hello in Zabarma. Amna seemed pleased when I tried out "Nee-GA-ban" in her direction. She replied with a musical "Banee sami," which I repeated several times. She seemed to enjoy the role of teacher and corrected my pronunciation. The children thought this hilarious and came closer, finally deciding to be friendly.

I asked Adam the children's names, and they giggled when I repeated them. He took me to see the inside of their house. The only source of bright light was the doorway, and at first it was too dark to see further inside, but as my eyes adjusted to the dim light that filtered through the straw walls I could make out the simple furnishings. There were two large beds and one smaller one made of ropes strung across hand-hewn wood frames Adam had made himself. Each bed was covered with a straw mat, and one had a thin cotton-stuffed mattress as well. The parents generally sleep inside. Girls and smaller children sleep inside, too, sharing beds or mats on the floor. Older boys take their mats outside or sleep in their own or a relative's khalwa.

At the back of the house was a wooden storage chest on legs, and beside it was a sort of counter or table where a few household supplies, glasses, and bowls were kept. I noticed the shiny tin oatmeal can with a tight-fitting lid that Jay had given Adam the previous night after the others had left. Good strong containers, sealed enough to keep the ants and other insects out of your sugar and other supplies, were hard to come by in the village, so Jay and I had collected as many empty containers as we could in Khartoum and brought them to the village. We had filled some with coffee beans or cinnamon bark as small gifts.

Ropes were strung across the rafters, and their spare clothing and a couple of sheets were hung over these. Tools were tucked in the edge of the roof, and a bowl with a lid was suspended in a basketry hanger. "Dog medicine," he said, "*dawa kalib.*" Being interested in folk medical treatments, I asked for more information.

"What do you use it to cure? Can I see it?"

Laughing at my misunderstanding, Adam pulled down the bowl to show me its contents. It looked like strips of beef jerky. "It's *sharmut,*" he said, "sun-dried meat. The dogs would steal it if they could. Whenever we have food we want to keep, we hang it from one of these dawa kalib things to prevent the dogs from getting it." The word for medicine can mean prevention, I realized.

Adam called to Amna in Zabarma, apparently asking her if she was ready to make the coffee. Not wanting to trouble a busy woman to stop and make coffee, I said, "Thanks anyway, I had some earlier. It's not necessary; I should be going." But Adam said, "No, you must have some. It's no trouble, we always have a cup at this time of day. You must taste Amna's coffee, she'll use the cinnamon you brought." Of course I stayed.

On the way to rejoin Amna in the kitchen, Adam pointed out the shelter where the donkey was kept, the place where their goats were tied at night, the little straw teepee-like chicken house into which the children had to chase the chickens each night to protect them from predators. Outside the main fence was a large thorn fence enclosure where during the rainy season they had grown corn, okra, greens, and other vegetables, and *karkadeh*—the hibiscus flowers that are dried and then brewed to make a flavorful, sweet tea, drunk hot or cool. It was amazing to me how few things they had that they had not made or grown themselves.

Adam and Amna seemed a happy couple. They had married when she was very young—only nine, Adam told us. But people did not always know ages accurately, nor did marriage always mean immediate wifely responsibilities, and as one would expect, she had not borne children for the first several years of marriage. Adam said he was happy with one wife and had no plans to take another. "If you have two, there's always jealousy and fighting," he said. "I prefer a peaceful life." Amna was about thirty-nine now; I wondered if he would change his mind as she got older and stopped having babies.

While I drank my coffee, Amna folded the cooled sheets of kisra into the multilayered "leaves" that are arranged on a tray around bowls of food at mealtime. She piled a large quantity of them on a clean enamel tray, covered them with a colorful basketry cover that was large, round and flat, and lifted it to the head of one of her daughters. In Zabarma, Adam instructed her to take it somewhere, pointing in the direction of our camp.

The new greetings in the Zabarma language were helpful in my attempts to meet people. While I was walking around the village, children who spotted me usually ran inside to report my movements to their mothers. Occasionally I noticed a woman peeking back at me from a doorway, but the first few retreated shyly. Then I met Khadija. A short, smiling elf of an old woman leaned her head out a doorway. When our eyes met, she smiled and came out for a closer look. "Nee-GA-ban!" I called out.

"Banee sami!" she replied. She strode quickly toward me on her short legs and offered a delighted, "Ka-DAY-ban."

My "In-da-GOOM-ni" didn't come out quite right, but she laughed and repeated it for me correctly as she pulled me into the courtyard of her married daughter, whom she was visiting. I still had no idea what I was saying, but producing the syllables and voice patterns of greeting was enough. Her enthusiasm for my visit put the other women present at ease, even though they eyed my long red jalabiya as if I were strangely dressed.

Khadija, it turned out, had married in from a different clan. In her younger days, she had spent some time in one of the towns in the region and had even been as far away as Wad Medani. Although she had married a distant relative here in Um Fila, she still traveled occasionally to visit kin in town. The most cosmopolitan woman in the village, she spoke enough Arabic for us to communicate. She had an odd accent, switching m's and n's in some words and often neglecting feminine endings or plural forms. I made a lot of those mistakes myself, so we quickly got used to each other's idiosyncratic Arabic. As an elderly woman with two grown and married children (and a number of grandchildren), she had the time to spend with me explaining things and providing a little translation.

The same day I met Khadija, she took me for a brief visit to an older woman who was ill; she lived in another house in the compound. I noticed that this woman was wearing just a tobe of indigo homespun cotton, without a dress underneath, and loose, boxerlike undershorts. Before the days of sewing machines, the length of woven cloth called a tobe was a complete garment in itself, artfully wrapped to provide modest cover, but liable to slip out of place when one did chores. Still, I was surprised to see someone dressed this way in the modest Muslim north, but of course the courtyards were very private.

Khadija took my hand and led me out of the courtyard, calling our good-byes. "Let's go to my house and have some coffee," she said. She cupped her right jaw in her hand and explained that she had terrible pain in her tooth. The only thing that could make it feel better was coffee.

"Have you been to a dentist?" I asked, knowing it was very unlikely. The nearest one was probably in Wad Medani, and the government had too few to treat everyone, so people often had to pay to see someone during private clinic hours in the evening. But even a medical assistant at a government clinic in a regional town might be able to help.

"I'm a coward," she said. She told me an itinerant "doctor" had passed through the area the previous year doing extractions and injections for a small fee, but she had refused to go, hoping the tooth would get better. But it didn't.

It took only a couple of minutes to reach her house on the southeast edge of the village. We entered the large courtyard through the main gate next to her husband's khalwa. There were five well-built round houses arranged in a circle, which meant five married women lived here. Hers was the second to the left of the gate as you entered, with the other two nearest the gate belonging to her two co-wives. The houses on the far side were those of her son Nur's two wives, Hawa and Kalthoum, two women I will discuss again in relation to polygyny. A shelter and enclosure for a donkey were located near the back entrance to the hosh on the side facing the forest and river. On their trips to fetch water or firewood, the women could come and go through the back entrance without being observed by men. Men customarily did not enter the hoshes of anyone but their closest relatives and would not do so unannounced, so women could be assured of privacy in the compound. Still, they wore their tobes when outside the house itself.

Khadija was the senior wife. Khadija called out a greeting to the wife next door but went straight to her own house to get her coffee equipment. She had no cooking fire going, so she carried them over to Saadatu's house and went in. "Nee-ga-ban."

"Banee-sami." Saadatu sat on a stool in front of the hearth just inside the door, stirring a pot of stew with a wooden paddle in rapid rotations by rolling its long straight handle between her palms. This was the final touch, apparently, as she put the lid on the cast iron pot and moved it to the side where it would stay warm until needed. Khadija put her handful of green coffee beans in the small toasting pan, discarding a couple of pebbles, and shook them back and forth over the glowing charcoal until they were black and fragrant.

Saadatu's toddler climbed in Khadija's lap to watch her pound the toasted coffee beans and spices. She cooed at him and gave him a kiss before continuing the pounding in the small mortar. The rhythm was solid, but by hitting the sides of the mortar lightly with the pestle on the upward strokes, she jazzed it up, laughing when I started to move my head and neck with the beat as if dancing.

The third wife joined us, bringing with her a tray of kisra and a covered bowl. A goat tried to follow her in, but one of the little boys chased it out. She noticed some dirty glasses and spoons, so she washed them in a shallow pan and stacked them on a tray to dry.

I had not expected such cooperation and friendliness among co-wives. Ideally, Islam allows polygyny only if the husband can treat each of his wives equally, but I knew that in practice this was difficult, and throughout the Muslim world competitiveness among co-wives was well known. Khadija's family, she claimed, had smooth relations because they adhered to the Islamic rules carefully, their husband spending equal amounts of money on each wife and following a strict pattern of rotation. Each night the husband slept in the house of one of his wives, and she cooked for him that day. The next night would be a different wife, and the following night the third. Although each wife did some cooking every day—because she always had herself and her children to feed—the wife cooking for the husband would make the most elaborate stew, preferably one with meat, spices, and a vegetable like pumpkin or okra. She might also make a small side dish. She or a co-wife would make kisra to go with it, or some days they just ate a sort of sorghum porridge (known as *asida* or *lugma*) with the stew. The other wives cooked simpler stews or soups. When it was time for the main meal—around two o'clock—each brought some of whatever she had cooked to the house of the wife whose day it was so they could all eat together and have some variety. Small children were fed something, but the women and older girls usually waited until the husband, and any guests he might have, had eaten.

When the husband was ready to eat, he sent a child to his wife, and she arranged the food on the tray and sent it back with the child. Men usually gathered with other men at mealtime—perhaps four or five in one man's khalwa one day and somewhere else another day—and shared the dishes their wives had prepared. The wife whose food was to thus be on display, as her husband's contribution to a men's communal meal, had an added incentive to produce particularly tasty, attractive, and plentiful foods, both to enhance his reputation as a successful provider and respected household head and to maintain his respect for her as a good wife. The wife had to carefully monitor the amounts served, and if the husband should send back for seconds—particularly likely if he spontaneously invited guests who were far from their own homes—the wise wife would have saved enough aside.

After I finished my coffee and promised to visit again soon, I hurried back to camp, eager to get to my notebook before I forgot anything.

The picture that emerged of Zabarma life was one of hard work, simple pleasures, and careful adherence to Muslim religious values as the Zabarma understood them. Female seclusion also meant less arduous field labor; men and children did the work of cultivation, and adult women seldom were needed to participate. There was plenty of work to do in the home, however. Women hauled water from the river, carried it long distances from shallow riverbed wells after the river dried up, or pulled water buckets with rough ropes from the deep well. They pounded grain and ground it by hand; their other activities included cooking, cleaning, childcare, handicrafts, and tending to small animals, as well as the social obligations to care for the sick and visit their neighbors. They observed prayers and taught their children to follow the faith.

Female seclusion was stricter for Zabarma than in other Sudanese Muslim communities, to the extent that Zabarma women were careful to avoid encountering men when moving outside the extended family's fenced compounds to fetch water or visit neighbors and kin, and they specialized in work that could be done inside of courtyards, such as pounding and grinding grain, manufacturing household items, child care, and other domestic tasks. Married women sometimes cultivated small plots in or next to the compounds. But one should not conclude that Zabarma women were isolated from men. There was frequent face-to-face contact with husbands, brothers, fathers, sons, and grandfathers, most of whom lived nearby (unless a woman had married in from outside). In my observations, both men and women demonstrated respect for each other, and both sexes showed respect for their parents and older people in general. But there was careful protection of women from much outside contact. A clear illustration of this is that even the women of the village across the river called Sherifa, with whom they shared a well, could not engage in conversation with them because they had no common language. Women did not travel to go to the market, and most had never been to a medical clinic.

Zabarma men clearly had more power to make decisions and grant or withhold permission for the various activities of their wives and children. Fathers controlled their sons' ability to marry through their control of the family treasury, but fathers' control over their married sons and their families was based on the mutual benefit of maintaining the larger production unit (to provide a viable age and sex mix of the various types of workers needed in a production unit), buttressed by ideological supports such as respect for elders. The ability to maintain a large and well-off production unit depended in part on luck — in fathering enough sons spaced appropriately — and on being able to marry second and possibly later wives as each approached the end of her childbearing years, while at the same time keeping married sons satisfied with their income and influence in decision making so that they did not decide to split off and form independent production/consumption units (see Ali and O'Brien 1984; O'Brien 1987; Gruenbaum 1979).

But Zabarma men also took great pride in hard work, piety, sobriety, and fairness, which seemed to balance their power effectively in most cases. Yet despite the relative isolation of the Zabarma women of Um Fila from neighboring ethnic groups, they had adopted the clothing styles and cooking practices of other rural central Sudanese ethnic groups like the Kenana.

But in the 1970s, the Zabarma, for all their quiet pride in their ethnic heritage and religious piety, faced discrimination based on their West African origins. Most Arabic-speaking Sudanese labeled and continue to label the Zabarma as "Fallata," a term derived from the Kanuri word for the Fulani that Sudanese apply to Hausa and Songhai peoples alike. Ethnic prejudice is easily detected in the disparaging comments openly made about Fallata among the majority of people in northern Sudan, and discrimination against those so labeled is practiced in numerous ways, including through obstacles to citizenship, civil rights, and social benefits.

Hallali Village

The Kenana of Hallali shared and continue to share this prejudice, regarding the Zabarma as their social and moral inferiors. The Kenana claim descent from the Prophet Mohammed, a heritage that affords them prestige, regardless of their present economic circumstances or actual religious observances.

Our research with the Kenana back in the 1970s revealed some surprising differences that we thought might undermine their superiority claims. For example, the Kenana family we visited on one of the major holidays did not sacrifice a sheep, as others do if their circumstances allow it, but only a chicken, even though they owned sheep. They were far more lax in their observance of religious obligations like prayer times.

With respect to women's roles, we noted two major differences. Although Kenana women wear modest tobes, they did not provide the fences to screen private life from view but built their houses more in the open, a pattern consonant with nomadic heritage. Although they recognized the propriety of the greater privacy of Zabarma families, they did not emulate it. Also, when the Kenana families traveled seasonally to be employed in the cotton harvest in other areas, both women and men went, and the women worked in the fields (except for new brides and new mothers) and earned their own money. By contrast, if a Zabarma man thought it necessary to add to family income through labor migration, he and his sons would go, not the women.

Contrasting Female Circumcision Practices—Zabarma and Kenana

Although both communities are Muslim, their practices concerning female circumcision are totally different and are interpreted by the two groups as being based on religious as well as ethnic differences. In Um Fila, the Zabarma believe that only the sunna circumcision should be done, and as they described it and showed me on a little girl, they take almost nothing off. Because there is no closure or covering of the opening, childbirth is easier and can be attended by any experienced older woman.

But in Hallali, the Kenana Arabs despised that form of circumcision, considering Zabarma women to be virtually uncircumcised. They insisted on complete pharaonic circumcision with infibulation, despite the difficulties this causes for childbirth and the dependency of all pregnant women on the availability of their village midwife. Both Kenana men and Kenana women disparaged the Zabarma for the impropriety of the "uncircumcised" state of Zabarma women.

Acculturative Influences in the Irrigation Scheme

A social experiment on female circumcision became possible with the construction of the Rahad Irrigation Scheme. Farmers from throughout the region were recruited in 1977–78 to move to the new irrigation scheme as tenant farmers. For the farmers it represented a risk because they had little experience with irrigation and they would have to rely on central management control of their supplies of seed, water, and fertilizer, as well as the marketing of the main crop, cotton. Also, they would have to dismantle their houses and rebuild in a new multiethnic village several miles away, no longer near the cool, wooded banks of the river. But other irrigation schemes (most notably the Gezira) were famous for their success and the dramatic improvements in the standard of living that took place over a few decades, with increased incomes, markets, roads, health services, and schools.

According to the experience of the people in these two villages, applicants for tenancies were asked their "tribe" (*gabila*). If they named a recognized Arab group, they were given a tenancy without further questions. Otherwise, they had to be able to show nationality certificates. Since Kenana was a recognized Sudanese ethnic group, every family from Hallali signed and received a tenancy. The Zabarma were somewhat more reluctant to join because preserving their identity and following their values on women's seclusion had required a degree of separation from the dominant culture. But even those who wished to go found that it was not enough to have been born and raised in Sudan. Many could not produce nationality certificates because they had never had occasion to obtain them, and it was difficult to prove birth or continuous residence where births were not registered. They would have to bring witnesses to appear in a distant town to process paperwork. Only those few who had been able to travel to Mecca on pilgrimages had gone to that trouble and expense. At that time, Sudanese law dictated that a person must be descended in the male line from a recognized Sudanese ethnic group since 1898, the year of British colonial conquest, to have unquestioned citizen-

ship. Others had to prove birth and long residence or residence of sufficient duration to become naturalized. Thus, although the 1960s was a
period when many West Africans were offered the opportunity to take
Sudanese citizenship, many either chose not to since resistance to assimilation was important for many West Africans (Duffield 1988) — or were
unable to overcome the obstacles of illiteracy, lack of connections, or
inadequate resources to carry out the bureaucratic requirements.[2]

Eventually when the Rahad project management could not find
enough tenants, they made additional tenancies available to the Um Fila
families, and about half of them relocated to the project.

Both the Zabarma and the Kenana were assigned to Garia Wahid
(which translates as "Village One") in the Rahad Irrigation Scheme.
Needless to say, the opportunity to move to the Rahad Scheme created a
major disruption in the lives of the families we had worked with in the old
villages. Jay and I first visited the new site in the irrigation scheme while
they were still building their houses in 1978, taking along our small son
born in 1977. People had moved to this new village not only from Um Fila
and Hallali, but also from a couple of other nearby villages. They had
brought with them the poles and thatch from the houses they had dis-
mantled back in their riverbank villages. The rectangular house plots
were assigned in clusters by the family's village of origin, so at least one's
neighbors were familiar. But it was a dismal, flat, treeless plain with the
newly laid-out fields and canals nearby. We wondered how they would
fare in this new place.

Jay was able to get there for a couple more trips in 1979, but I knew it
would probably be a long time before I would get back to these people.
With a small child, and hoping for another, we needed to go home and
establish some roots. Ten years went by.

The New Village: Garia Wahid

"Allam! Come and see it!"

The sun had set quickly as it does in the tropics, going straight down
twelve hours after it had come straight up, spending most of the day high
and hot overhead. The evening always seemed so welcome. In the dark-

---

[2] Many members of the dominant Arab-Sudanese groups state that the West Africans
have had ample opportunity to become equal but have chosen to resist education, etc., as a
way to resist assimilation. They point to examples of successful Hausa individuals as evidence that there is no discrimination. Yet there are numerous examples of antipathy and
hostility toward West Africans that belie the presumed openness to their participation in
society. Legal barriers may have been removed, but the ability of most West Africans to
realize equality continues to be hampered by the heritage of subordinate status as a minority group with low economic status.

Children keep company with a Kenana mother while she prepares straw for mat weaving, Garia Wahid.

ening sky above the conical straw rooftops, the slim crescent moon had appeared, much to the delight of a small group of kids in dusty jalabiyas who ran past me. One of them, a boy named Yousif, skipped uninhibitedly, calling out "The moon! The moon!"

Several women of the Kenana extended family I was staying with during this research trip joined the children outside to enjoy the evening sky, moving a handy *angareeb* (wood-frame rope cot) out from the straw veranda into a more open spot nearby. "Isn't it beautiful? Do you see the crescent moon like this in America, Allam?"

Allam, meaning flag, was a name some parents gave to daughters who were born in 1956, the year of Sudan's independence, when they took down the British Union Jack and proudly put up their own flag. Those who found my name, Ellen, difficult to say called me this more familiar sounding name.

"Of course," I answered, "we see the moon, too. But I've never seen it as beautiful as this." I would have liked to try to explain the difference in its angle—in our northern latitudes it appears tilted, while near the equator their crescent moon is balanced and level, like a bowl for milk. But I knew that would be too much of a challenge. Although they were very bright and knowledgeable about all manner of practical things I had no inkling of, both the men and the women here had not had any formal schooling, had never seen a globe, and were not too sure about the solar system. So this trip I had brought along an inflatable globe that turned out to be a terrific way to explain where California was. Some of the men had asked how many hours I had traveled to get there and didn't seem sure they believed me when I had described the long flights via England. I explained the globe, shining my flashlight on it to show the sunlight of day in Sudan and the shadow of night at the same time in California. Questions flew, and their amazement was evident with the repeated exclamation, "La illaha illa Lah!" "There is no god but God!"

The evenings here were so peaceful, compared to my usual lit-up urban life. Here there was no electricity to run noisy equipment like the swamp coolers in the towns. The dirt road along the canal carried vehicles very infrequently. For a short period each evening, someone might turn on a battery-powered radio for a few minutes to hear the national news, but most of the sounds were quiet activities. A group of men who had gathered on mats in front of the shaykh's house could be heard saying their sunset prayers. "Allahu akbar . . ." A woman shook a small charcoal brazier to loosen the ashes and bring the coals back to life for evening tea. A cow had been brought in from the fields and tethered nearby for the night. Soon we heard the pleasant sounds of rhythmic squirts of milking by hand, ringing into an enamel bowl as level as the crescent moon. The warm milk would be scalded and added to the tea and drunk with sugar—if our household had not yet run out of the month's ration.

I loved these evenings, once I got used to the pitch dark. A kerosene lamp might be lit if needed, but fuel was too precious to waste. A few people had flashlights they tried not to use for more than a brief moment now and then, so as not to use up the precious batteries. So mostly we let our eyes adjust to the starlight as we sat on the angareebs outdoors. The cots would be taken inside the one-room dwellings later on, but there was plenty of time for visiting first. Sleepy children could simply curl up on a corner of a cot, securely nestled near adults.

One or two of the married men often dropped by on these evenings, finding conversation with the *Khawajiya* (me) a good source of entertainment and information. One of them, Hamid, often dropped by to ask about news of Khartoum or life in America. He had the makings of a cultural anthropologist, asking lots of questions. What do you do when people die? What are your weddings like? How many wives do men marry there? I told the story of my brother's recent wedding a dozen times, each time elaborating on some new detail—the church, what the bride and groom wore, the flowers, the food at the reception, who attended, and so on—and getting better and better at my Arabic and at my storytelling skills. The experience gave me an entirely new appreciation of how oral history is preserved and folklore can be elaborated.

Topics ranged widely over farming issues, market prices, and religious beliefs. Heaven and hell, Christianity and Islam, national politics, and kinship relations were all discussed. Women complained about the price of charcoal or the need for the water system to be repaired; Umselima blamed the delays in the needed repairs on the failure of competent leadership by the men in the village council. But in the dark, problems were seldom resolved, just discussed. And then they served the glasses of milky tea.

Soft singing wafted over from across the courtyard. In the dark, I could not see the singer, but the plunking of his *rababa* carried well. A gallon oil can, modified with neck and strings, could be the medium for sweet music, the accompaniment to songs of heartache or joy, under the stars of our lovely sky.

The intervening decade had not changed everything. During my research trips of 1989 and 1992, I found that the social life was still very similar, both in the new village and among the families who stayed in Um Fila, the Zabarma riverbank community about five miles away. Yet although so much seemed the same, a number of significant changes were evident. Garia Wahid had grown to a large village of about five thousand people. It had a school, a clinic, and a market with shops, cafes, a mechanized flour mill, meat sellers, vegetable and fruit vendors, and a bakery. A couple of people owned Toyota pickup trucks. For a fee and with patience one could usually get some transportation to town on a vehicle, which significantly reduced people's sense of isolation. A system for water filtration had been available for a few years, but by 1992 it was no longer functioning and they couldn't get spare parts to fix it. The bakery never had enough bread to meet the demand and ran out of flour before the end of each month. Even if farmers reserved their own grain for baking, the services of the mill were costly and charcoal was not always available at a reasonable price. The school could not accommodate enough of the children. The clinic was usually short of medicine. With this uneven pattern, people felt both better off and worse off.

But the social experiment I spoke of was the result of the new situation of the Zabarma and the Kenana, such different ethnic groups, living in close proximity. There was bound to be intercultural influence.

After the move, Zabarma seclusion practices began to change significantly. In the past, Zabarma women's participation in field labor had been quite limited, but in the irrigation project, women began to work more in the fields, particularly during the cotton harvest, if they did not have small children. Children over the age of seven frequently participated in field labor. The desire for more children for such work has always meant that frequent pregnancy and child rearing are seen as highly important. Thus women's participation in agriculture should not be so extensive as to interfere with these primary activities, but their participation had clearly increased.

By contrast, after moving to the irrigation project, the Kenana women, who were formerly more active, have in many cases reduced their involvement in agricultural work, although they continue to be involved in field labor. Their reasons seem to be connected to husbands' new financial control resulting from the tenancy system. Many complained that though they used to be paid for cotton picking when they were migrant laborers, their husbands now expect them to do it for free on the family tenancy. The income from the tenancy, though, is controlled by the husband. Thus they often choose not to do field labor, preferring to specialize in domestic labor. Women who are tenants or whose husbands are unable to work can be seen doing heavy agricultural work, but able-bodied women, even those without young children, may well choose not to engage in it. Although there are plenty of other tasks to occupy them, the advent of a flour mill and a bakery have lightened the food-processing work considerably.

The social gulf between Zabarma and Kenana women narrowed once they were living in closer proximity. By 1989, after a decade of living as neighbors, I anticipated that the higher status Kenana would have exerted more cultural influence on the lower status Zabarma, even though the superiority beliefs had no reinforcement in wealth distinctions and seemed to be based almost entirely on ethnicity. And as I expected, the Zabarma women had acculturated to Kenana ways in several areas. Most of them had learned Arabic very well and interethnic visiting had become fairly common, whereas it was almost unheard of before. The fact that Zabarma women were participating in agriculture was also very significant because it represented a modification of their seclusion practices. In fact, I observed that unrelated men, even Kenana, were entering the compounds and even the houses of Zabarma women on occasions when others were present, something the Zabarma women I was closest to disapproved of but tolerated.

Yet sensitivity to and even tolerance for certain differences between the groups was noticeable. For example, although Kenana men and women commonly sat together in the same house, the men did not sit with the women if Zabarma women were present, especially if they had been served something to drink. Zabarma women consider it improper to eat or drink in front of men. In mixed groups of women, they articulated these observations, pointing out to me how different their customs had become and yet how they were capable of being sensitive. In separate groups, greater disapproval of the differences was voiced. Zabarma women criticized Kenana women for not praying regularly, and they were proud of their own stricter religious observances and greater deference to husbands.

When it came to female circumcision, though, the two groups remained fairly far apart, and the Kenana remained convinced that their ethnic superiority was manifest in their practice of infibulation. Most of the Kenana women regarded the entire subject as fairly humorous, sexually charged, and a matter that women should not speak of in the presence of men. They continued to believe that infibulation was essential for pleasing the man in sex and accepted the fact that it did nothing for women's pleasure, except perhaps indirectly because giving pleasure to one's husband is basic to femininity. Religion, I was assured repeatedly, had almost nothing to do with it, though they figured sunna circumcision, at least, must be required by Islam.

My queries about the possibility of change and my reports on the health education messages against circumcision current in Khartoum received little interest from the Kenana, who generally believed change in the practices was unlikely. Of the Kenana women I interviewed and observed, only one young seventeen-year-old married woman in her first pregnancy told me she would like to leave her future daughters uncircumcised. One of the few beneficiaries of the educational opportunities of moving to the new project, she — but not her husband — had had a few years of elementary school. She did not think it likely she would be able to

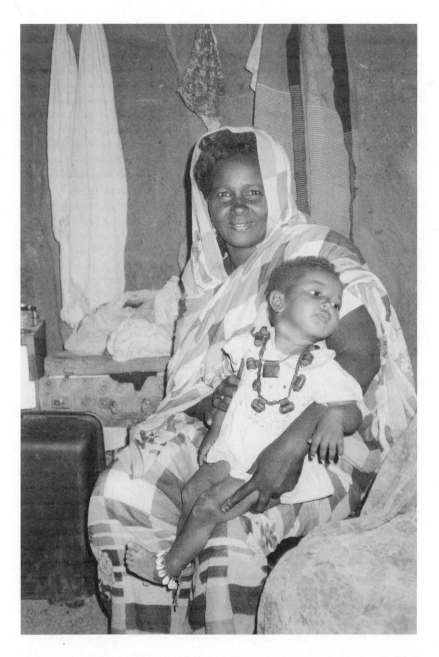

Garia Wahid village midwife, with her child. The child is wearing scented balls and Qur'anic amulet.

carry out the idea of not circumcising, however, because she knew her mother-in-law would never allow her granddaughters to remain uncircumcised.

Pressure and Resistance

Of greater concern than the status quo, however, was the intercultural pressure for Zabarma to adopt infibulation, an innovation against the cultural traditions of their ethnic group. Stories varied, some claiming most Zabarma had embraced infibulation, others claiming they had not. But my persistent interviews were only able to confirm three cases of pharaonic circumcision of Zabarma: two adult women and a girl.

In one of the cases, a Zabarma husband had married a third wife who came from a different village. I knew the senior two wives and their mother-in-law well even before the move to Garia Wahid, so I felt confident of their report. The third wife, for whom this was a second marriage, had been pharaonically circumcised earlier. After a while, the husband persuaded the younger of the two more senior wives to have the infibulation done also, reportedly because he preferred how it felt during sex. The wife who acceded to his wishes later regretted the decision, saying it made both sex and childbirth "*harr*" (hot, painful). She and the senior wife both advocated maintaining the custom of sunna. Although most of the adult Zabarma had no intention of abandoning sunna, despite acculturative pressures to adopt pharaonic circumcision, their daughters nonetheless felt the pressure more keenly.

Zabarma daughters found that their minimal sunna circumcisions were not enough to assure social acceptance from the Kenana girls. They were subjected to mockery and name-calling. The Kenana girls called, "Ya, ghalfa!" (roughly, "hey, unclean!"), the same name that was used to make fun of uncircumcised girls. Some Zabarma mothers reported that their daughters began to respond to this pressure by asking to be circumcised, needling mothers with comments like, "What's the matter, don't we have razor blades like the Arabs?" Under such pressure, according to the non-Zabarma midwife, at lease one Zabarma girl had indeed been infibulated.

I was pleased to hear about cultural resistance evident from the creative responses of some of the Zabarma girls, who invented names to call back at the pharaonically circumcised hecklers. "Ya, mutmura!" they answered, referring to the underground grain storage pits that are opened and closed, opened and closed, just as the scar tissue is (for birth, after which it is reinfibulated). Also, referring to the tissue lost from repeated cutting and sewing as "meat," they are reported to have heckled back with the following: "When you run out of meat, will you buy some in the market?" These taunts were reported to me with great pride by several mothers, who saw their daughters as sticking up for their group's practices. All the Zabarma women I asked favored continuing sunna circumcision, considering it a religious duty to circumcise but preferring the mildest form.

Ethnic superiority and religious piety entered into the debate. Both men and women of the Kenana occasionally said things that indicated their disdain for the physical appearance, hygiene, circumcisions, and ancestry of the Zabarma, in spite of their neighborly behavior toward each other. One of the few explicit insults I heard a Kenana man express about a Zabarma man (but not to his face) referred to the "open" (i.e., uninfibulated) vagina of his mother.

For their part, Zabarma men and women, as followers of the respected sect of Islam known as the Tijaniya, continue to be proud of their greater religious piety. Although the move to the village in the irrigation project where they now live has led to some relaxation of the stricter female seclusion practices they had observed in their old village, women's ideas about the importance of deference to husbands and about daily religious observances made them feel superior in religious piety to Kenana. In light of the Kenana claims of social superiority, this religious pride probably helped the Zabarma women to resist Kenana social pressure to infibulate. In 1992, most Zabarma women were holding firm to their view that sunna circumcision was better than pharaonic, and they considered sunna a religious duty.

The village midwife who regularly served the Kenana and sometimes the Zabarma neighborhoods where I did my research did not advocate sunna circumcision and continued to do pharaonic. Although she was aware of the discussion among health workers of the sunna being preferable, she had not gone through the formal government midwifery training. Because the majority of her clientele preferred the pharaonic circumcisions, she continued to perform them. If she was called upon to deliver a baby for a Zabarma mother, however, she followed their custom and left the mother uninfibulated.

Ethnicity and Circumcision

In this chapter I have given examples to illustrate how ethnic identity is bolstered by the powerfully symbolic action of body alteration. The process of change that is occurring with respect to female circumcision encounters ideological obstacles when ethnicity is at issue because for most people ethnic identity is carefully guarded and markers of it are changed only when there are persuasive incentives. Alternatively, competing identities can at times trump ethnicity, as has already been happening in several countries where the Islamist movement (broadly defined) engages in struggles to define cultural authenticity for Muslims. Islamist reformers seek to discourage Muslim people from practicing certain aspects of their cultures by claiming that Muslims must embrace an authentic Islamic culture — defined variously by the differing interpretations of Islamic teachings. Wailing at funerals, forms of dress, and spirit possession practices have all come into question in Sudan, for example, and while most people stick with their traditions for now, as members of one's community become convinced of the reformers' arguments that these are inauthentic to their Muslim cultural roots, ethnic heritage cannot maintain its sway. As pharaonic circumcision, too, is questioned by Islamists, health educators, and public opinion about what it is to be modern, ethnic ideologies can be expected to lose some of their force. Similarly, as opportunities and pressures to acculturate influence people to rethink their ethnic markers, as in the case of the Zabarma and Kenana, there will be situations when the direction of change is different than expected, as when people experiment with adopting infibulation. Although at times it appears that what is happening is a replacement of one ethnic group's traditions by those of another group that is claiming superiority, we should look for a master narrative (like health, modernity, or "proper Islam") that rises above ethnicity to justify the priority.

The examples in this chapter led me to anticipate that such pressures will cause people to creatively reassess what it means to be a member of a particular ethnic group and also to stretch beyond ethnic identity to larger visions of national, international, or transcultural religious or modernist identities.

Chapter 5
Sexuality

A frequent concern about female circumcision practices is the effect on female sexuality. When the sensitive tissue of the clitoris is lost, when scarring and tightness result from infibulation, it is reasonable to assume that significant changes in female sexual functioning might result. Indeed, this assumption is supported by Koso-Thomas's Sierra Leone study that included the experiences of women who were sexually active prior to undergoing circumcision and then experienced a reduced level of sexual satisfaction after undergoing excision (1987). These data are limited, however, because there are so many problems with the assessment of sexual experience. As Koso-Thomas notes, there had been little or no research on sexuality in African countries (1987:38), and she was unable to be certain that the respondents were clearly reporting what they experienced: "possibly they were unable to identify what it was they did or did not experience" (1987:41).

But is it reasonable to generalize that female sexual response is essentially destroyed in circumcised women? And is the effect the same with different forms of the practices?

Any negative effects of female circumcision on sexuality cannot be assumed to be a significant factor in motivating people to abandon or alter the practices. Indeed, many people intend to attenuate sexual desire with female circumcision, on the assumption that reducing pleasurable sensations will curtail inappropriate behavior, as discussed above (Chapter 2). Either way, negative effects on female sexuality constitute a key issue in the controversy, as people outside the cultures in which circumcision is practiced react strongly to the notion of deprivation of sexuality. Alice Walker and Pratibha Parmar, for example, use the metaphor of "the sexual blinding of women" in the subtitle of their book *Warrior Marks* to convey the notion of destruction of sexuality, a powerful image to their Western readers. Since understanding the relation of the various forms of female circumcision to male sexual pleasure is equally important for understanding change efforts, sexuality issues for both females and males are addressed in this chapter.

The concerns of outsiders about female sexual response are in part the result of ethnocentric perspectives. Concern about the sexual gratification of women in circumcising regions is a logical extension of the sexuality-oriented popular cultures in which many North Americans and Europeans are immersed. During the twentieth century and into the new millennium the United States and European countries have become in certain respects increasingly open about sex, so that even the very young are familiar with sexually provocative images. In advertising, a buxom woman in a slinky dress draped across the front of a new car on a billboard is a common device to attract attention to the car. Some are even more directly advertising commercial sex; a billboard on the interstate displays a bikini-clad woman lying on her side with a come-hither look advertising a "gentleman's club" that features "Girls, girls, girls!" Romantic love and its move to the bedroom are commonly depicted in movies. Teenagers, especially boys but also girls, may brag of "scoring" with the other sex if they succeed (or pretend to succeed) at having intercourse. Particularly in the last forty years of the "playboy" era, sex and sexual gratification are definitely on the agenda in the public arena (see Ehrenreich 1984).

Unfortunately, the openness about sexiness is not necessarily congruent with an openness about sexual health or mutual sexual pleasure and its link to intimacy and love. In fact, the prudishness and hypocrisy of many Western sexual attitudes persists despite the burgeoning of sexual imagery and increased openness about sexual activity. This prudishness is cause not only for much of the confusion and sexual dysfunction among those persuaded by these values, but it also contributes to much social conflict about the "decline" in morals and "decay" of the family characteristic of the "family values" debates of recent decades.

Still, the concern that women in a circumcising region might be deprived of sexual pleasure — something highly emphasized in Euro-American popular culture — does evoke an initial highly ethnocentric reaction. In fact, deprivation of sexuality is a very strong theme in recent oppositional writings on the subject (e.g., Walker and Parmar 1993, Lightfoot-Klein 1989, and Brownworth 1994).

There are two different reasons to question this approach. One is that it is too narrow a view of sexuality, demeaning the significance of sensuality and love and neglecting the psychological components that may impede female sexual response. The second is that it is a false conclusion about the actual sexual sensations circumcised women experience.

During my first period of research in Sudan, most of the Sudanese women I asked whether they enjoyed sex said they did. But I remained unconvinced at that time for a couple of reasons. First, women who had never achieved orgasm might not have any idea whether they had had one or not and might suppose that some other sensation of arousal was an orgasm. Without more probing interview questions, I could not be certain that the "pleasure" they felt was based on orgasmic response. Such probing questions were, however, precluded by the sensitivity to the subject, its marginality to my earlier research projects, and the limitations of my Sudanese Arabic, particularly in my first few years (something that my hand-me-down mimeographed vocabulary in the pink folder was no help with). My sense at that point was that sensuality was what was being enjoyed, stimulated by a melange of incense, perfume, music, poetry, flirtation, and physical and emotional closeness, but not necessarily orgasmic response.

Female Sexual Response

The second reason that I was unconvinced about women's sexual pleasure was that it was my belief that female sexual pleasure required clitoral stimulation. Back in the late 1960s when I had studied Masters and Johnson's 1950s and 1960s laboratory research observations on sexuality in an undergraduate course on human sexuality, I had learned that clitoral stimulation was necessary to achieve female orgasm (Brecher and Brecher 1966). This view was common in the U.S. women's movement, as can be seen in the statement of the Boston Women's Health Book Collective that "In the sixties, sex researchers found that for women *all* orgasms depend at least in part on clitoral stimulation, although some women respond to internal pressure as well" (1984:169). So how could women without clitorises achieve orgasm?

This finding of Masters and Johnson's was a key element in feminist arguments against Sigmund Freud's theories of female sexuality. Freud's idea that there are two distinctly different types of female orgasm — clitoral and vaginal — supported a traditional heterosexual image of female sexuality. Clitoral stimulation, in this view, was the means to clitoral orgasms, the immature or "infantile" orgasms characteristic of childhood masturbation. To achieve full adult sexuality, a woman needed to experience penetration by the male penis to allow for the vaginal stimulation needed for the presumably more satisfying mature vaginal orgasm. In Freud's view, the latter was better than the former, and this seemed to suggest further that to stimulate the clitoris was not particularly desirable in comparison with the alternative of intercourse with a man. In fact, those women who found the vaginal orgasm elusive or could not achieve orgasm without clitoral stimulation, were at risk of feeling inferior if they were aware of Freud's labels, such as "vaginally frigid." Janet

Hyde comments that many women "have undertaken psychoanalysis and spent countless hours agonizing" over this presumed inadequacy (1994:250). It is no wonder so many critics have believed that Freud's theory was a self-interested attempt to validate the male role in heterosexual lovemaking.

But Masters and Johnson established that there were fairly predictable physiologic patterns in the sexual response cycles of both males and females (see Brecher and Brecher 1966:18–32; Hyde 1994:242–48).[1] Whether these physiologic responses are possible for severely circumcised women should be an important consideration in the debate over sexual response, so I will outline them briefly.

In response to some sexually arousing stimulus, the excitement phase begins. The vasocongestion (increased blood flow to the genitals) characteristic of this phase produces erection of the penis in the male and vaginal lubrication in females. A secondary reaction at this phase is muscle contractions (myotonia), such as those that cause nipple erection. The research found that the female response was equally prompt (about ten to thirty seconds after stimulation begins) regardless of the source of stimulation, whether direct stimulation of the genitals, stimulation of the breasts, or even erotic thoughts.

The excitement phase also includes changes in the clitoris, where the clusters of very sensitive nerve endings are found. In most women studied, the clitoris (consisting of a shaft and bulb or glans, which vary in size) becomes engorged and enlarges somewhat in response to stimulation, especially direct stimulation but also the stimulation of areas near it. Because the prepuce (hood) of the clitoris is attached to the labia, general movement around the labia can stimulate the clitoris by causing the prepuce to rub against it. For other women, direct stimulation is possible as the enlarged clitoris emerges from the prepuce. The inner and outer labia also generally enlarge, opening and flattening against the surrounding tissues or becoming distended. The vagina also responds as excitement progresses. Its unexcited collapsed state gives way to what is described as "ballooning" of the inner two-thirds of the vagina barrel as the cervix and uterus are pulled up and back and the vaginal walls become smooth and change color as surrounding tissues engorge. The entire body is responding, as the heart rate and blood pressure rise.

Although there is no precise shift between phases, the research identified what Masters and Johnson labeled a plateau phase, as the rate of breathing, pulse, and blood pressure rise, the tension of voluntary and involuntary muscles increases, and effects such as the "sex flush" may be

---

[1] Masters and Johnson focused primarily on heterosexual sex and self-stimulation, but the stages of response are applicable to oral stimulation by a same-sex partner.

noticed. People may intentionally tighten muscles in the buttocks and rectal areas to heighten the sensations.

For women at this plateau phase, the inner two-thirds of the vagina continues to expand while the outer third becomes constricted because of the engorgement of the surrounding tissues. As a result, in intercourse the sensation may be that the vagina "actually grips the penis, and the erotic stimulus experienced by the man is notably increased" (Brecher and Brecher 1966:28). This phase is termed the "orgasmic platform," but it does not necessarily mean the woman is close to orgasm. The clitoris, meanwhile, is generally retracted upward, farther from the vaginal orifice and may be difficult to find. But it can continue to respond to either direct or indirect stimulation.

Then if successful sexual stimulation continues, the plateau phase leads to the orgasm, the intense climax of sexual arousal when muscles contract throughout the body. For males a spasm followed by rhythmic muscular contractions occurs in the penis and urethra. In females the spasm and rhythmic contractions occur in the vagina and in the orgasmic platform, that is, around the vagina and from the top of the uterus toward the cervix. Orgasm in both males and females may be described as mild or intense, with a number of contractions varying from three or four to a dozen, with one laboratory-recorded orgasm going on for twenty-five rhythmic contractions. The first few are rhythmic with intervals less than one second, slowing down as the intensity of the contractions wanes. Some people also experience rhythmic contractions of the anal sphincter or other muscles.

Following orgasm is the resolution phase, when congestion of the tissues reduces and the organs return to normal. For males, a refractory period ensues during which they cannot be sexually aroused. For women, however, Masters and Johnson noted an ability to return to aroused states and achieve orgasm again, even several times. If no orgasm is achieved but sexual stimulation is discontinued, it can take a fairly long time (up to an hour) for the resolution phase to occur.

Although Masters and Johnson found there was a range of variation in the intensity, length, and repeatability of the female orgasm, the location of stimulation did not produce fundamentally different types of orgasms — the muscles around the vagina contract, the uterus contracts, and the other physiological reactions are the same.

Masters and Johnson found that clitoral stimulation (whether direct or indirect) is almost always involved in a woman achieving orgasm. For some women, the movement of a male in intercourse rubs or presses directly on the clitoris to produce the necessary stimulation, while for many it is indirect, with the movement against the labia causing the clitoral hood (prepuce) to move against the clitoral erectile tissue. The research demonstrated that regardless of the source of the clitoral stimulation, it seemed to be a regular part of bringing about an orgasm. Because of the movement of the labia and attached clitoral prepuce in vaginal intercourse, the clitoris is being stimulated even if neither partner is intentionally stimulating it. Masters and Johnson did not, apparently, attempt to test the notion that a female orgasm could be brought about while depriving the clitoris of stimulation, that is, with vaginal or other stimulation alone, which would have been a significant piece of information in the discussion of the effects of clitoridectomy in circumcised women.

Although there are reports of female orgasms achieved by other means such as breast stimulation and fantasy, it is assumed that the physiological responses would be the same. However, because none of the 382 women in Masters and Johnson's study was able to achieve orgasm through fantasy alone (all required some physical stimulation), physiological responses in such a case could not be studied in the research laboratory.

The discovery of the important role of the clitoris in female sexual response contributed to more attention. An entire book entitled *The Clitoris* appeared in 1976 (Lowry and Lowry); one contributor considered the attention overblown: "The gynecological aspects of the clitoris, when compared to the mythological or psycho-physiologic features, are very modest indeed. This small organ, almost vestigial in the female . . . has achieved recently almost unjustifiable importance" (Wolkoff 1976: 104). But the emergence of the clitoris was celebrated by the feminist movement in a variety of ways, in literature, art, and the health movement. The venerable volume *Our Bodies, Our Selves,* inspired by the feminist self-help movement, gave attention to female sexual response, and *The New Our Bodies, Our Selves* described the clitoris's "central role in elevating feelings of sexual tension" (Boston Women's Health Book Collective 1984:169).

The validation of the role of the clitoris made possible strong advocacy of changes in lovemaking. As counter to the previous advice about "the power of sexual surrender" and the assumption that proper women should be passive or simply move with the moves of the male partner, the glorification of the clitoris allowed women to wish for, and ask for, stimulation of it. Whether through manual stimulation during intercourse (by one's partner or oneself) or oral stimulation or self-stimulation in the absence of intercourse, the clitoris became central to female sexuality in Western feminist thinking. The male's penis and its penetration of the vagina could be dispensed with entirely, or at least put in proper perspective as an optional part of sexual activity, not its sine qua non. And among those most aware of the negative effects of sexism, women's oppression by men, and violence against women, this seemed an added reason to value the alternative lifestyle of lesbians.

From the perspective that the clitoris is central to female sexuality, it is quite understandable that the idea of clitoridectomy should be equated with destruction of female sexuality, as terms such as "sexual castration" (Hosken 1982), "sexual blinding" (Walker and Parmar 1993), and "mutilation" suggest. The additional tissue damage from infibulation would presumably be even more destructive to responsivity.

Yet I was reluctant to conclude that the only sexual activity that could be considered satisfying was that leading to orgasm. Further, the "no clitoris, no orgasm" assumption was not fully convincing. First, cross-cultural perspectives on sexuality, such as those offered by the early study by Ford and Beach (1951) and the recent edited collection by Suggs and Miracle (1993), strongly suggest that culture structures sexual response in fundamental ways. When and where sex is performed, with whom, with what meanings, how often — all these are influenced by how one's culture shapes the individual's learning about sex. The response cycle, though based in human physiology, clearly involves the mind, and it is really no surprise — once ethnocentric perspectives are questioned — to realize that cultural patterns structure the sexual experience. Suggs and Miracle refer to that perspective in anthropological studies of sex as particularistic, focused on "the elucidation of the diversity in the 'culture of sex'" (1993:484). Given the variation in practices, symbolism, morality, and beliefs, could we not consider the possibility that there are other routes to pleasure and even orgasm? It is possible that for circumcised women, the loss of some tissue that is involved in sexual response is not as debilitating as one might imagine?

During my research in Sudan in 1989 and 1992, I focused on this issue, but it was an awkward topic. It is not the sort of thing to bring up in your first conversation with someone: "None of your business" would be a very legitimate response. Even the Sudanese women interviewers in El Dareer's research project initially found women reluctant to discuss so private a matter (El Dareer 1982:40–41).

Fortunately, my Sudanese women friends and acquaintances in the villages where I conducted research really wanted me to understand their lives and seemed amused rather than offended by my curiosity on the topic of sex.

Since Arabic vocabulary I had not yet learned often appeared in these conversations, I took to making drawings in my notebook and eliciting the various terms for anatomical parts. This became a further source of amusement for the women. More than once, when another woman dropped by following one of these vocabulary lessons, my teachers would urge me to recite my new words. It reminded me of the old trick of older siblings teaching the toddler to say a naughty word to shock the adults: my recitations were always met with peals of laughter. Once, when a man approached to ask what we were laughing about, one of the women grabbed my notebook and stuffed it under a cushion. "Shh!" she said. We all became suddenly sober and sensible, switching to idle conversation about an upcoming wedding. When he left, one of my teachers reminded me not to talk about these things in front of the men.

But the vocabulary lessons taught me more than words. They helped me understand more about the physical self-image of some circumcised women and how they view uncircumcised women. In the Gezira village one day, Sadiya (a pseudonym) helped me with words for male parts. After the usual laughter, she grew more serious and asked me to tell her how we uncircumcised women have intercourse. She asked me if we put "the whole thing" inside. Pointing to the drawing of penis and testicles in my notebook, she said, "Do you put the 'balls' in, too?"

I was taken aback by what must have been her image of the uncircumcised woman: a large, gaping hole capable of accommodating both penis and testicles. She was relieved when I corrected that impression. For Sadiya, the small opening of the infibulated vulva is what is normal, while the uncircumcised vulva is imagined as rather repulsive.

Sadiya was the happily married mother of more than ten children. She had married her cousin at a fairly young age and described sex with evident delight. Following the birth of each of her children, she was tightly reinfibulated, leaving the opening very small. She told me that when she and her husband are ready to resume intercourse (following the customary forty-day postpartum period without sex), they cannot achieve intercourse for a long time. They try and try, she reported, and it is very frustrating — and enjoyable — for both of them. Some women have described this period of resuming sex after the postpartum hiatus as rather like being a new bride. Husbands, I was told, can be very generous with gifts of gold or other precious things when they find the tightness of the opening to their liking. Eventually they succeed at stretching the opening enough for intercourse.

It was obvious to me in Sadiya's description that although there may be pain, frustration, and discomfort involved with sex, there is also a great deal of excitement, a common goal, and pleasure that she and her husband share.

But what effect does the reinfibulation have on the woman's potential for orgasmic response? I discussed this matter with several groups of women in the Gezira village, telling them that this was something my American students wonder about and I didn't know what to tell them. I knew that men have orgasms ("finish") in sex, but do women also?

Yes, I was told, women "finish."

I wanted to ascertain that what they were talking about was a true orgasm and not some vague conceptualization by women who had never personally experienced them. I pressed for a clearer description. Somewhat exasperated that I didn't seem to understand plain Arabic, a visiting midwife named Miriam grabbed my hand, squeezed my fingers, and said, "Look, Ellen, some of us do 'finish.' It feels like electricity, like this . . . " and she flicked her finger sharply and rhythmically against my constricted fingers. I was convinced we were talking about the same thing.

There is little systematic data on the effects of female genital surgeries on sexual response in any of the countries affected. Dr. B. C. A. Johnson, working in a psychiatric hospital in Yaba, Nigeria, notes that it is "tempting to postulate that female circumcision could lead to disturbed sexual functioning in the woman — frigidity, vaginismus, etc.," but states: "as far as I know there is no reported case of a patient complaining of frigidity, because of circumcision. Furthermore, many women who have not been circumcised are frigid" (1979:4). In some cases, however, circumcised women have offered testimony on the damage done to their sexual functioning as part of their efforts to convince others of the urgency of reform. Although it is not possible to know if they represent a common experience of the other women of their societies, there is a tendency to overgeneralize from their experiences and conclude that circumcised women are sexually impaired, regardless of the type of surgery they have had.

Based on my interviews and the limited data available, I believe such conclusions are unwarranted. Sexuality research is inherently difficult to carry out. For countries affected by the female circumcision debates, sexuality research would be, at this point, thoroughly embedded in the politics of reform. That is, as a rationale for ending the practices, there is a tendency to investigate and report the complications and problems rather than the cases where no problems have resulted. Complications and problems are, after all, more important from a medical perspective and more compelling from an activist perspective. Among reformers in Sudan, there is also a recognition of the harm the practices can cause for female sexuality.

Many of those educated people who opposed circumcision in a preliminary study done by Asma El Dareer opposed it because they believed "it denied sexual fulfilment to women and for general humanitarian reasons" (1982:iv). According to the larger research project on female circumcision conducted by the University of Khartoum's Faculty of Medicine (under physician El Dareer's supervision) in northern Sudan, 50 percent of the women interviewed said they had not experienced sexual pleasure, while 23 percent expressed indifference. El Dareer also reported cases of very painful sex, as in the following quotation from a forty-five-year-old infibulated woman in the city of El Obeid in Kordofan (west central Sudan) who had married at the age of fifteen:

My first sexual experience was very painful because I was so tight, and the following experience was equally painful. On one occasion my husband tried to force penetration and the flesh tore. This wound became infected, so sexual intercourse became even more painful for me. . . . I hated to have sexual relations, and my husband complained about this. I was so pleased when I became pregnant, because the tradition in our tribe is that a husband may not have sexual intercourse when his wife is pregnant. When I was delivered the opening became wider and I could have normal sexual relations. But my sex life is still of no enjoyment or interest to me, I perform it merely as a duty. (El Dareer 1982:36)

The investigation of sexual responsiveness should not be construed as an effort to minimize such experiences as that just described; female circumcision presents a very real threat to healthy sexual responsiveness. But there is reason to question the assumption that all circumcised women, regardless of the type of surgery or social meaning given to it, experience the same harm to their sexuality. The minimal data that do exist suggest that female genital surgeries are not uniformly destructive to female sexuality, even in countries where infibulation is the norm.

In Egypt, for example, where the less severe forms are practiced, a study by Marie Assaad (1980) found that a large majority of women reportedly enjoyed sex. Yet even in Sudan, where infibulation is most common, Janice Boddy found that some of the women of Hofriyat, a Nile Valley village in rural northern Sudan, said they enjoyed sex, while others considered it a marital obligation and did not enjoy it. And in the sample of 3,210 northern Sudanese women surveyed in the University of Khartoum study, 27 percent of the circumcised women found sex "pleasurable altogether or only sometimes" (El Dareer 1982:48).

Sex researcher Hanny Lightfoot-Klein carried out an unusual study focusing on sexuality and marital adjustment in Sudan. Spending several months in the capital Khartoum and neighboring Omdurman and traveling to many other parts of Sudan between 1979 and 1983, she used connections at hospitals to obtain opportunities for interviews and the services of translators. Lightfoot-Klein's observations lack methodological rigor and the sound ethnographic contextualization that would enable me to report her findings with confidence. Still, although I disagree with her interpretation that Sudanese are "prisoners of ritual," some of her interview findings are extremely interesting. She estimates that she interviewed around four hundred people, one hundred of them in one hospital in Omdurman where two nurses who had trained in London and spoke excellent English translated for her. The women interviewed there were employees of the hospital, mothers of pediatric patients, or pregnant women waiting to deliver. She also interviewed university students and interviewed some men. She estimated that one-third of the interviews were conducted without a translator in English. Clearly, as she recognizes in her book, her sample was biased in favor of those who might already be opposed to the practice by virtue of their roles in medical services or their educational status.

In these interviews Lightfoot-Klein found many women expressing passionate feelings, many deeply in love with their husbands and well-adjusted to their marriages and life in general, including sex. She found many women who convinced her of their ability to have orgasms. Although she herself recognizes that because of sampling bias her estimate is "unduly high, and no doubt out of proportion to the true state of affairs," she reports that "close to 90% of Sudanese women interviewed claimed to regularly achieve *or had at some time in their lives* achieved orgasm" (Lightfoot-Klein 1989:80, italics in original).

It should be noted that many women were initially reluctant to discuss such matters until Lightfoot-Klein learned to begin with the subject of the "smoke ceremony," the sandalwood incensing reserved for married women that signals sexual interest. After that icebreaker, frank discussions often took place. Some told her they thought that showing sexual interest or responsiveness was shameful, so they tried to remain totally passive and motionless during intercourse. Lightfoot-Klein is guilty, however, of unwarranted overgeneralization when she states: "Custom decrees that a Sudanese woman remain totally passive during the sex act. She must lie like a 'block of wood' and participate in no way whatsoever" (1989:89). But Lightfoot-Klein's impressions could have been formed by a context such as I experienced: the giggling and secrecy of women when discussing such topics. Showing open interest in sex in general, and especially when in the company of men, would be seen as shameful for respectable women.

To understand how orgasmic response could be possible for circumcised women, it is necessary to consider three distinct issues: variation in the tissue removed, variation in erogenous stimulation, and the possibility of a role for the "G-spot."

Variations in Tissue Removal

The many different forms of female circumcision in the various countries where it is practiced, which are discussed in the Introduction, can be expected to affect sexual response differently. If erectile tissue or other sensitive tissue that would become engorged during sexual stimulation is removed in the cutting, it is reasonable to suppose that sexual responsiveness will be affected. But if only the clitoral hood is cut, there may be increased exposure to stimulation of the clitoris. If only part of the clitoris is cut, does the remaining portion still function effectively to provide sexual stimulation?

Although the answers to these questions are still not fully available in the research, the variation in what is removed should be considered as we hypothesize about the effects. Although the patterns of differences in the operations geographically can be seen in general terms from Map 1, the variation among the population even within one geographic area can be quite great, as my experiences in the Gezira Province of Sudan demonstrate.

My initial observations of the surgeries of the midwife Besaina in Abdal Galil village were of the very severe pharaonic form, and she did very tight reinfibulations after childbirth. But it would have been a mistake to generalize to the entire region from those observations, as my later experiences in Wad Medani, the provincial capital, attest. (See Map 2.)

Delivery Room in Wad Medani

I spent a most memorable day in the delivery room of the Wad Medani hospital in the summer of 1989, a day that afforded me an opportunity to see and discuss the variation in circumcisions. I was invited to visit by Miriam, mentioned above, a member of the hospital's midwifery staff who has family ties in Abdal Galil village. While visiting there during my stay, and upon learning of my research interests, she urged me to come to the hospital the next time I was in Wad Medani.

As mentioned before, Jay and I had lived in Wad Medani for a year (in 1978–79), when he was teaching at the University of Gezira during its opening year. It is a beautiful city located on the banks of the Blue Nile, with many large old trees and a few stately colonial buildings and older neighborhoods where the British administrators lived during the colonial period. There are some sprawling neighborhoods laid out in grids and others with narrow winding streets and high walls. Served by the main rail line and located just a few miles from the administrative center of the massive Gezira Irrigated Scheme, Wad Medani is a vibrant commercial city with a large market area of two-story buildings of shops selling imported commodities and numerous streets of businesses, including bedmakers, fruit wholesalers, small manufacturing, tailors, auto repair, jewelers, and many small shops. A large, more open bazaar area hosts hundreds of merchants selling fabrics and ready-made clothes, spices, and all manner of foods. Farmers sell produce spread on mats on the ground, and rows of young girls line the walkways, sitting with their bowls of homemade peanut butter or toasted nuts and seeds for sale. One area designated as the "women's market" provides a place for

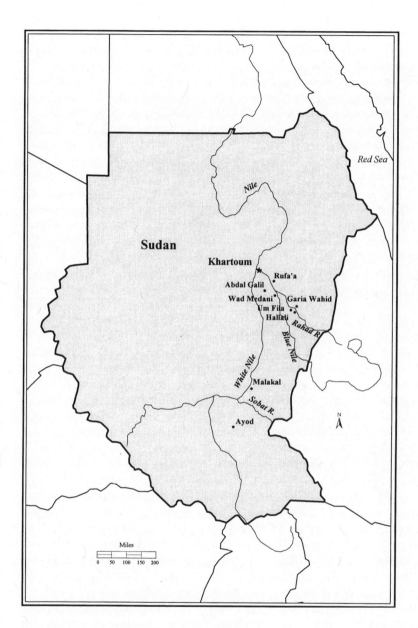

Map 2. Sudan: Locations of author's research.

craftswomen and merchants to sell products that are bought mostly by women — baskets and decorated straw food-covers, round mats with central holes used for incensing, carved stirring implements, charcoal braziers and cooking equipment fashioned from scrap metal, decorated round clay coffee pots and beaded soft rings to stand them on, and homemade cosmetic products. Some of these merchants travel to villages where they buy crafts from local women to sell in this market or come from villages for a few days at a time to sell their goods before returning home. One area is quite makeshift, with burlap shelters and rope beds where market women can sleep with their merchandise, at least during the heat of the day. In another area, women merchants rented space in a shaded, open, well-built pavilion with a wooden floor. The grandmother of my university-educated frient Shadia had a stall there, and she invited us to drink tea whenever we stopped by. She had a comfortable spot for her low stool and trunk of goods, and she sold various scents, cosmetics, and home remedies. In the evening she returned to her house in one of the "second class" neighborhoods of the city, leaving her goods in the safe care of the facility's guard. It was considered an occupation quite acceptable for an older woman of a working-class family, and her educated descendants were proud of her.

The government-supervised transport areas allow drivers to organize vans full of passengers to various destinations. Small restaurants, shops with electric blenders that specialize in lime and lemonade and mango and guava drinks, tea sellers, and sandwich vendors serve the needs of travelers, shoppers, and workers. There are many mosques throughout the city, but in addition, the area is also rich in religious shrines and the homes of shaykhs, or religious leaders, and their places of worship (known as a *mesjid*), where disciples gather for worship and teaching.

As a provincial capital, the city has much better health care facilities than most of the country, including a large hospital with several specialty clinics. Both in-patient and out-patient services are provided, but like clinics wherever they are found, long waits and inadequate supplies and drugs are the norm.

The Wad Medani Hospital had some fine facilities, such as the surgical facility in the obstetrics department built with German aid. But in general, the hospital's well-trained physicians tended to be somewhat frustrated with their working conditions, bemoaning the inadequacies of some of the facilities, lack of the modern equipment they had been trained on in medical school, and the unpredictability of electrical services, drugs, supplies, and even their salary payments. It was not surprising that so many of them opened private clinics outside, where they could benefit from their own investment in equipment, laboratory facilities, and comfortable furniture. And the patients they served in these private clinics were usually more affluent. Commercial pharmacies catered to the needs of the private clinic patients and those who could not find the medication they needed at the government clinics.

All manner of patients used the delivery room services. Although many urban women continued to give birth at home, many, such as my educated friend Shadia, chose the hospital as the modern alternative that was equipped and staffed to be safer in the event of complications. Poor women who could not pay a midwife could at that time deliver their babies in the hospital gratis, and neighborhood midwives referred any difficult cases there because physician backup was available.

The labor and delivery area was in an older building that probably dated back to the colonial period. The labor room was directly off the main corridor of the ground floor. It adjoined the delivery room and was fully visible from it. The delivery room was lit by large, high windows and electric light. It had two delivery tables and an alcove where the nurse midwives sat. Because this alcove was marked off by a low wall that one could see over from a seated position, both delivery tables and the labor room were easily visible, so the midwives could easily respond when needed.

I joined the nurse midwives in their alcove and spent several hours observing their work. The labor room was overcrowded, usually with two women to each of the five beds, often with a bag of belongings. Down the hall was another area where patients could wait for a spot to become available and where family members were supposed to wait. But female family members filtered into the labor room to look after the women in labor. Periodically, when the room became too crowded, the nurses ushered the visitors out, only to have them return again a few minutes later.

The midwives' alcove also served as their lounge. In fact, when the midmorning breakfast time approached, I was rather surprised when they pulled out their breakfasts. A sandwich from the market was delivered for one of the women by a messenger she had dispatched. And a peanut vendor came into the delivery room to sell peanuts to the nurses. I joined them in buying a newspaper cone of the toasted shelled peanuts in their papery red skins. Usually people drop the papery skins on the ground as they pop each peanut into their mouth, and even here in the delivery room that is what they did.

Clearly there was no expectation that an aseptic environment would be maintained. But it was considerably better than village birthing conditions, where most births take place on rope beds in rooms with dirt floors and flies. Still, I was dismayed when a prepared hypodermic needle rolled off the table in the center of the labor room onto the dusty floor. A nurse picked it up. Apparently she thought it looked clean enough, and she went ahead and used it on her patient.

In the delivery area, however, the midwives were careful to ensure far greater hygiene than was likely in home births. The antiseptic Dettol was used liberally to wash the delivery surface and the instruments, and the midwives washed their hands before touching the patients on the delivery tables. There was also physician backup available. A group of medical students (in this case all male) was ushered in to observe one of the deliveries, standing to one side of the laboring woman but not touching anything.

The midwives described for me the many different types of circumcision conditions they must handle in these deliveries. Some women have very tight scar tissue, which they must cut open at the appropriate moment and reinfibulate afterward. Other women have had much less removed, and the midwives must evaluate the degree of cutting and restitching necessary when the time comes. The first woman to deliver while I was there that morning was a woman of rather small stature who delivered relatively quickly. I noted no particular difficulties as a midwife delivered her small baby, and no cutting was needed. Since I had assumed all women here would be circumcised, I asked the midwife what sort of circumcision I had just seen because it was not obvious. The midwife replied, with what seemed to me to be mild disapproval, "She isn't circumcised at all. She's a southerner." A long-term migrant from the south, I assumed. She wore a simple dress, tobe, and sandals (the tobes were removed during delivery, but the dresses only lifted). She was a fellow countrywoman, but seen as "other" because she lacked circumcision.

The next woman, however, was an Arab-Sudanese. She appeared to be better off than the first, healthy and well-nourished, dressed in better clothing that was carefully adjusted to avoid soiling. Her circumcision was an intermediate type, where the inner labia rather than the outer labia were joined, the type called *al juwaniya* (roughly, "the inside type"). I was struck by the looseness and motility of the tissues, in comparison with the more rigid scar tissue of women with pharaonic circumcision. The joining was not continuous either—fluid emerged from two or three openings above the vaginal opening as the pressure of the baby and the contractions brought her closer to delivery. When the moment was right, the midwife incised upward through the scar tissues of the joined labia minora to deliver the baby. While one of the staff took over the care of the baby, another took charge of delivering the placenta and then sutured the area that had been cut.

If one has seldom seen stitching of tissue, it can be something of a surprise to see the apparent imprecision and randomness of where the suture needle goes. But I understood it better after witnessing an expert obstetrician at Loma Linda Hospital perform a tear repair after an American friend of mine had delivered. The texture of tissue from a lay perspective is not easy to make sense of, with mottled color and what looked like moist, granular bumps on the uneven, spongy, three-dimensional surface. The surgeon in California patiently and gently manipulated the surface, matching the two sides to each other as well as she could and suturing in such a way that the surfaces would stay in contact for healing. It was not, as one might imagine, a matter of sewing together the edges of two flat surfaces of skin. It did not at all look like precision work, but the human body's healing responses made it work, and my friend was fine in a few days.

The Sudanese woman in Wad Medani also had relatively few stitches done, drawing the labia minora together again over the urethra and the area where the clitoris had been removed or reduced at the time of her original circumcision. Whether she would again have small openings for leakage or whether the scar tissue would form a complete seal above the vaginal opening would probably depend both on the skill of the midwife's sutures and the subsequent care of the wound during healing.

Although I did not stay for the delivery of one of the pharaonically circumcised women, I had seen the delivery of such a woman in Abdal Galil. The relatively hard scar tissue of a pharaonically circumcised woman cannot stretch very much as the baby presses down, so when the head begins to crown, the midwife must be prepared to do the long upward cut. It is hard to imagine that after a few such births, the thick scar formed after several repetitions of the opening and reinfibulation of such vulvas would allow any sexual sensitivity, at least in those outer areas.

The observations that day in Wad Medani strengthened my impression that the condition of women's bodies in this single geographical region, the Gezira, is highly variable. When the whole of Sudan is considered and when the many countries and cultures of the several regions of Africa where circumcisions are common are included, it is clearly a mistake to generalize about the effects of these operations on women's genitals. It is similarly inappropriate to conclude that there is a uniform effect on sexuality, not only because of the variation in what is altered, but also because of the complexity of erotic response.

Erogenous Zones

As is well known, many parts of the body are sexually sensitive. In addition to the genitals, stimulation of a woman's lips, nipples, and thighs, for instance, can contribute to sexual arousal. Many people find other areas to be particularly stimulating — the back of the neck, ears, buttocks, or stomach. These areas are generally termed erogenous zones, and tremendous individual variation exists in the location and subjective experience of such stimulation.

In fact, some people achieve orgasms without direct (only indirect) stimulation of the genitalia. Some breast-feeding literature in the late 1970s reported that the nipple stimulation of breast-feeding occasionally resulted in orgasmic response for some women. Although perhaps rare because the emotional context tends to be nurturance rather than eroticism, this is consistent with reports of orgasms from nipple stimulation in sexual relationships.

Given that the clitoris and labia are not the only sexually sensitive areas for women, then, it seems reasonable to suppose that circumcised women, even with the most severe forms, need not be considered totally sexually impaired because other erogenous areas survive the genital surgeries.

If sensitive nerve endings are damaged in these female genital surgeries and some impairment of sensitivity and sexual responsiveness results, the nerves themselves presumably continue to transmit sensations, much as the nerves of amputees continue to function to transmit sensations (including the phantom limb sensations) and impulses.

A comparison to the experiences of people with quadriplegia and paraplegia suggests that there is still much to learn about sexual responsiveness of damaged bodies. For example, according to Hyde, women with spinal cord injuries in whom nerves cannot transmit sensations to the brain are reported to experience many of the same sexual responses as other women (i.e., engorgement of the clitoris and labia when stimulated, erection of nipples, changes in heart rate). But of course such women would not be able to feel sensations in the areas of paralysis, and orgasm apparently results only in rare cases. Hyde notes, however, that "some spinal-cord-injured women develop a capacity for orgasm from stimulation of the breasts or lips" (1994:263). And other people with spinal cord injuries report that they have learned to achieve a "psychological orgasm" that is reportedly "as satisfying as the physical one" (Hyde 1994:263).

The sexual experiences and sexual potentials of disabled women have not been studied extensively, just as the sexual experiences of circumcised women have not. But it seems to me that at the very least we should consider the possibility that the ability of other areas of the body to respond sexually allows circumcised women — even pharaonically circumcised women — to maintain the capacity for sexual pleasure, including orgasm.

Perhaps the most valuable piece of wisdom offered in the human sexuality course I took as an undergraduate was the idea that the mind is the

most important erogenous zone. Indeed, without the confidence, emotional arousal, and sense of safety and propriety that comes from pleasant, socially acceptable, and loving contexts, sex can be a nonstarter for
many people.

Egyptian physician and novelist Nawal El Saadawi cautions outsiders to
beware of the paternalistic " 'them' helping 'us' " approach to solidarity
over female circumcision that sometimes takes the form of pitying circumcised women for the damage to their sexuality. She notes that many
Western women experience psychological impairment of their sexuality
that may be equally damaging. The puritanical values and suppressed
sexuality of some Western cultures have, she argues, contributed to frequent psychological impediments to sexual fulfillment, that is, "frigidity"
(El Saadawi 1980).

The G-Spot

A current research controversy surrounds a feature termed the Gräfen-
berg spot, or G-spot. Sometimes called the "female prostate," it is a small,
spongy gland located on the front wall of the vagina, lying near the
urethra (Hyde 1994:257). According to some research, the gland is responsible for a female ejaculation in which a fluid is released into the
urethra at the time of orgasm. In some studies the fluid seems to be
chemically like semen without sperm, but another study claims it is chemically like urine, which would suggest that it was not an ejaculation but
perhaps leakage from the bladder.

But what is significant about the current speculations about the G-spot
is its potential role in female sexual enjoyment. It is not clear that all
women have such an organ, though Ladas, Whipple, and Perry (1982)
claim that of over four hundred women examined, each had one. A
smaller study by gynecologists found G-spots in only four of eleven women
(and presence of a G-spot did not correlate with whether they were ejaculators or not) (Goldberg et al., 1983, reported in Hyde 1994: 258). Those
researchers who are convinced of its existence in virtually all women
(Perry and Whipple 1981) also have identified it as a powerful erogenous
zone. As described in Hyde, "stroking it produces an urge to urinate, but
if the stroking continues for a few seconds more, it begins to produce
sexual pleasure" (1994:257). This idea of the G-spot as an important
region for female sexual enjoyment has entered the popular culture in
the United States to such an extent that its reality is almost taken as a given
and its role in sex is widely alluded to in U.S. popular culture.

Perry and Whipple go so far as to suggest that stimulation of the G-spot
produces a "uterine orgasm" with deeper sensations than "vulvar" or-

gasms that result from clitoral stimulation, a differentiation reminiscent of Freud. But the location of the erogenous stimulation is not the same as the location of the muscles involved in orgasmic contractions. Thus is seems to me quite reasonable to assume that female orgasms can differ in intensity and involve different parts of the anatomy in contractions regardless of where the stimulation that leads to the arousal, plateau, and contractions of orgasm occurs. Thus even assuming there is an erogenous G-spot, we need not conclude on the present evidence that there are two kinds of orgasms.

The potential role of a G-spot in female arousal is an idea that may go a long way toward explaining the orgasmic experiences of circumcised women. Embedded as it is deeper in the vagina, the G-spot would be protected from the direct effects of cutting of the external genital tissues. Even a severely infibulated woman would still have her G-spot from which to derive erogenous sensation.

Male Sexuality and Female Circumcision

"It is the men who want it to continue," claimed a midwife I interviewed.

I knew, of course, that some men did not. But in searching for the answer about why so many seem to promote or tolerate the continuation of female circumcision, I found that their attitudes were not related only to ideas about what it does to women's sexuality. Female circumcision plays an important role in male sexuality as well.

It must be remembered that male sexual interest is sometimes of vital importance in maintaining the reputation of a bride and the endurance of a marriage. One elderly father I knew in one of the Rahad Valley villages told me, with some disgust, about his son's rather controversial behavior following his marriage. Within a day or so of the celebration, the son exercised his right to divorce his wife unilaterally, against her wishes. The father had no enthusiasm for discussing the matter, particularly because the young woman was a close relative and the incident had caused a stir in the family.

Some hours later when I had the opportunity to talk with his son, I asked why he had divorced so soon after marriage. "I didn't like her body," was his reply. He declined to elaborate. I did not think he was referring to female circumcision per se because he does not belong to an infibulating ethnic group. But my point is that a husband can and sometimes does divorce rather abruptly following a marriage. If that happens, it can be a shameful situation, especially for the rejected bride. A fear that one of my educated Sudanese women friends expressed was that people might assume that the husband had discovered she was not a virgin. For parents, the moral of a story like this is that it is best to endeavor to make their daughters as acceptable as possible for their future husbands, lest they risk such rejection. And if tight infibulation is valued, then tight infibulation may be part of preventing such potential disasters as unilateral divorce immediately following the wedding night.

Male sexual desire in circumcising cultures as anywhere else is influenced by both biology and culture in a complex interrelationship. If men in an infibulating culture prefer that their wives have tight vaginal openings, their attitude is probably based on what is considered appealing in their cultural circumstances and what they have been socialized to expect, as well as what is found to be stimulating. But there is also the strong possibility that tight openings have an effect that is desirable for physical reasons, regardless of cultural expectations.

For sexual intercourse, men of many cultures seem to prefer tightness of their partner's opening. Presumably, as men have reported, this is because it produces increased friction, which is experienced as more sexually stimulating than less friction. Sex with a virgin is also supposed to be pleasurable for that reason — a tight opening.

Although tightness and pressure around the circumference can also result from voluntary and involuntary contractions of a woman's vaginal muscles during intercourse, some men have reported that a more continuous and firm pressure around the penis as it is repeatedly thrust into the opening and along more of the shaft is more pleasurable. This added pressure can be produced by using different sexual positions, such as having the woman cross her legs. An alternative means to produce added pressure on the penis, both at the opening and along the shaft, is anal intercourse, a practice that varies widely from one culture to another worldwide. In the regions of Northeast Africa where infibulation is practiced, anal intercourse is apparently highly stigmatized and rarely practiced, though not entirely unknown. Because it is associated with male homosexuality, a man would presumably not want to risk his wife thinking he was a homosexual. I am told, furthermore, that "sodomy" is illegal in Sudan. In any case, for men whose female sexual partners are infibulated, the tightness of the infibulation itself can be expected to produce a very high level of such stimulation.

The preference for tightness during intercourse is so well known in Western culture that U.S. obstetricians even have a term for the extra stitch they often perform when doing episiotomy repairs following childbirth: the "husband's stitch." The husband's stitch is intended to produce a smaller vaginal opening, to counteract the natural stretching of the tissues from sexual activity and childbirth and even to make the opening more constricted than it might have been before. As its name suggests, the husband's stitch is for the purpose of greater stimulation of the penis during the thrusting of intercourse.[2]

Sudanese women told me that tight openings are desired by males, a belief for which there is ample supporting evidence. Both urban middle-class and rural poor women told me that a husband is more generous in his gifts to his wife when she has a baby if he finds her to be as "tight as a new bride" when they resume sex after the forty-day postpartum hiatus. A well-known midwife in Wad Medani, Sister Battool, whose work is discussed further in Chapter 7, considers men's desire for a tight opening for sex to be the main reason the practice of infibulation continues. And as Sadiya's experience (discussed earlier in this chapter) indicates, her husband reportedly found great pleasure in the challenge of achieving entry and in the tight sensation of her reinfibulated vulva after childbirth.

Although the sexual desires and pleasure of *all* men may not require tightness, the cultural expectation that men are likely to have such preferences surely influences parents to continue to infibulate their daughters rather than risk change that might make her unappealing as a wife.

Another means of producing additional stimulation for males during intercourse is what has come to be known as "dry sex." Applying an astringent substance or absorbent material to the vagina prior to intercourse results in greater friction, which is preferred by some males but is often painful to the woman and damaging to vaginal tissues. Dry sex has received much attention in Africa for its role in HIV transmission in the AIDS epidemic. To my knowledge, dry sex does not seem to have become popular in the areas where women are infibulated. When infibulation declines, public health education efforts might be needed to prevent the spread of dry sex as an alternative means of stimulation.

A second aspect of male sexual pleasure that should be noted is, it seems to me, more of an aesthetic consideration, but one that clearly could be linked to culturally defined male sexual preferences. That aspect is the male preference for smoothness of the vulva in cultures practicing female circumcision. Women in these cultures, of course, share this aesthetic preference, as Janice Boddy's writings argue persuasively (1982, 1989). But there is an added fear that a husband may find one's body distasteful if the vulva is not smooth.

Considerations of male sexual pleasure arose in my interview with

---

[2] One interesting case reported in the U.S. press concerned a woman who sued her anesthesiologist husband, present during her surgery, for directing the surgeon to "circumcise" her while she was under general anesthesia. (The journalist did not report the details of what was done surgically.) Could this have been motivated by the husband's desire for a tighter opening?

Sister Battool. A woman who was visiting her joined in our discussion of the changes in what people ask for when they bring their daughters in for circumcision. Sister Battool described some of the variations people were asking for which were less severe than the traditional pharaonic form, such as the *nuss* (half) or *juwaniya* (inside type). When she said the men really wanted the closure, I raised the issue of sexual pleasure:

"Isn't it important that both the husband and the wife be happy in sex? If you leave the clitoris inside but sew the labia shut, then couldn't both the husband and the wife enjoy sex more?"

"Some of my clients insist I take off the clitoris. I don't know why," said Sister Battool. The two Sudanese women laughed.

"Yes," replied the other woman. "Both should be happy in sex. But it won't happen if something is there that shouldn't be."

"What do you mean?"

"Hair, for instance," she replied. "You have to remove it with *halawa*" (a depilatory made from sugar syrup and lemon juice that is used for removing body hair from the arms, legs, and vulva). "Hair is *eyb* (bad). If she hasn't removed her hair, a woman can tell her husband [when he desires intercourse], 'Not today—I'm not ready.'"

Sister Battool explained further, "If men say they don't want the external genitalia, then women won't want to have it. Many people view those parts as abnormal for a woman." She put my question to the other woman—wouldn't it be better to keep the clitoral tissue inside (a technique Sister Battool used when possible) so that both the man and the wife could be happy in sex? The woman's reply was one I often heard, "Of course the wife will be happy if her man is happy." Sister Battool glanced in my direction and said no more for the time being.

The visitor left a few minutes later, after making an appointment for 4 P.M. for Sister Battool to do a small surgery for a neighbor from a family without much money. Sister Battool, in the charitable tradition of most of the Sudanese midwives, assured her that whatever the family could pay would be enough. The woman turned back from the doorway, still uncertain, and named a figure (equivalent to about eight dollars). "Will that be enough?"

"Go!" Sister Battool replied, implying acceptance of the amount while rejecting any notion that money was a consideration for her.

Once the woman was safely out of earshot, Sister Battool confided that she was probably not the right person to ask about clitoral stimulation, orgasms, or mutual sexual pleasure for husband and wife. "She's probably never experienced what I'm talking about."

As one final example of the effect of male sexual pleasure, let me return to the case of one of the families I worked with in Garia Wahid village in the Rahad Irrigation Scheme. The devout Zabarma husband of two wives had for many years been satisfied with their condition as women with no infibulation (only minimal sunna, according to their descriptions, which was described as "none at all" by their neighbors, the Kenana Arabs). After the husband married a third wife from another village, one who was infibulated, he was pleased, and he persuaded the younger of his other wives to be pharaonically circumcised. She was very unhappy with the result, which made sexual relations painful for her. The senior wife, who rejected the idea, thought she had been right to do so.

Sex and Female Circumcision

The effect of female circumcision on sexuality is not uniform or sufficiently well understood. It does seem clear that the various forms of female circumcisions are not equally devastating to female sexuality. Writers who claim that the purpose of female circumcision is to destroy female sexual pleasure have in my opinion gone too far. As I will discuss in a later chapter, there are even those who would argue that female circumcision done in a "proper" way will enhance sexual pleasure for both women and men. There is evidence from studies in Egypt that female circumcision is sometimes viewed as a precursor to and celebration of womanhood and sexual activity and that women are conscious of the need to limit the amount of tissue taken so as to preserve sexual sensitivity.

Yet there can be no doubt that many of the circumcision practices do affect girls' and women's physical well-being, including their sexual responsiveness. Psychological aspects of sexuality are surely also affected for some or most of the women who underwent surgeries as girls, as several writers have suggested (for example, see El Baashar 1979 and El Dareer 1982). In a radio interview on *Fresh Air* (1996), Nahid Toubia described her own mother's comment that the trauma of circumcision was always with her and influenced her sex life. Nawal El Saadawi's vivid description of the memories of her traumatic childhood experience of circumcision has led many readers in the United States to conclude that sexuality is always damaged (1980b).

In summary, it is clear that female sexuality is neither destroyed nor unaffected by female genital cutting. U. Megafu (1983, cited in Kassamali 1998) reported in a study of Ibo people in Nigeria that clitoridectomy did not diminish a woman's libido, contrary to the widespread belief that excision would affect sexual desire. Still, if sex becomes painful or is associated with psychological trauma, that is likely to decrease orgasmic ability. But if female circumcision does not reduce desire, then one of its presumed explanations—control of female sexuality—can be seen as erroneous. Female circumcision does not totally eliminate sexual satisfaction in all women, even in severe forms such as Sudanese infibulation (Lightfoot-Klein 1989, Gruenbaum 1996, Obermeyer 1999). The variability of experience — not to mention the variability of importance of sexuality in people's lives — means that improving female sexuality, as important as it may seem from a North American or European perspective, should not be assumed to be a universally persuasive reason for people to give up any of the forms of female genital cutting.

Chapter 6
Economic Development

Economic development and the provision of better health and education services to rural areas have the potential to boost efforts to change female circumcision in Africa. Bringing in staff for a health clinic increases the chance for people to learn about the health risks involved. Education and increases in general literacy improve the likelihood that people will be aware of programs and new approaches to change, including challenges to erroneous information they may hold. Economic development and the opportunity for increased commerce, migration, and employment has the potential to expose people to challenges to current practice and alternative views in urban areas or other countries.

The Impact of Development Projects on Women

Economic development, though, is not a magic bullet, particularly when programs do not provide a structure that benefits women, children, and families. It took many years for the critique of male-oriented development planning to gain the widespread recognition among scholars, activists, and officials that it has today (see, for example, Boserup 1971, Women in International Development series, and numerous UN documents addressing women's issues). The failure of development projects and policies to address the needs of women and children is essentially based on the failure to investigate seriously the social and cultural context of innovations. Production systems that are right for Iowa may encounter unforeseen obstacles when introduced elsewhere, obstacles that undermine productivity and also disrupt the social fabric in some unforeseen way. There is ample new attention being given to these matters in international organizations doing aid and development work in poor countries as was evident from many presentations at Forum '95, the NGO sessions of the Beijing Fourth World Conference on Women. It is now routine to employ sociologists or cultural anthropologists to advise on the planning of projects and to include social impact assessments in follow-up evaluations.

But many of the patterns of development projects were established prior to these insights and did not consider the social and familial impacts. In other cases, development planners, focusing on some other goal like increasing the output of a raw material needed elsewhere or trying to produce for export to improve the flow of hard currency to a government, may have sought to enhance public acceptance of the project by incorporating some elements of traditional social arrangements, whether or not they fully understood how those social arrangements worked.

As a result, many of the tenancy arrangements established for irrigation projects in Sudan, for example, were set up with male heads of household who could command family labor. The resulting male control of the cash revenues from cotton production has altered the complementarity of gender roles in work.

Female circumcision practices have been impacted by economic development projects in contradictory ways, largely depending on the degree to which the projects include development of social services, especially schools and clinics, and the type of effect on women's economic and social roles. Where girls are sent to school, where women are increasingly literate and have access to biomedical and public health services, and where employment opportunities for women exist, the incidence or severity of female circumcision may be reduced. Schools, clinics, and employment opportunities offer access to more critical knowledge and alternative practitioners as well as the confidence that a daughter's life might actually be better, not worse, if she is not altered so severely.

But economic development can also have a negative impact on female circumcision. If development projects have minimal or negative effects on women's work, family, and social roles and on their long-term economic security, an obstacle to circumcision reform may result. Planned development efforts that have focused on the male head of the household as owner / tenant (as has been the case for both the Gezira and the Rahad irrigated schemes in Sudan) can affect female circumcision in two ways. First, because the development pattern reinforces patriarchal relations and women's economic dependency, it undercuts the potential for women to cultivate alternatives to marriage or to gain economic leverage in families. The formalization of the male tenant role in the Rahad Irrigated Scheme actually weakened women's ability to gain direct access to resources that are produced in part by their own labor, while offering a new, more modern, image to patriarchy. Reducing women's economic autonomy erodes the basic condition for challenges to any aspect of their situation. In the case of female circumcision, this reduction in women's economic autonomy can be expected to strengthen, rather than weaken, a family's resolve not to take risks with a daughter's marriageability.

The Gezira Irrigated Scheme, though, offered more educational opportunities for women and girls because of the circumstances of its origin (large landowners were allowed multiple tenancies that women heirs could acquire in the next generation and scheme managers prevented these tenancies from being fragmented completely) and because of the political activities of the Tenants' Union, whose members demanded schools and clinics for their region during the colonial years. Although girls' education came later and is still less well developed than opportunities for boys, there is nevertheless a small but significant percentage of adult women who are educated and involved in discussion of community affairs, proper Islam, social policies, and national politics. Some have had opportunities for employment, periods of residence in towns, and opportunities for marriage with educated men. As a result of these women's engagement with the issue, prospects for early female circumcision change in that region are better than in other places.

A second effect on female circumcision derives from the situations in which women's economic dependency is increasing and male control of resources has led to increasing rates of polygyny. While this is by no means a general trend for all irrigation projects, the tenancy form of development in Rahad has led to increasing rates of both child-bearing and polygyny, and such trends deserve observation. How increasing rates of childbearing and polygyny contribute to continuing female circumcision requires further explanation.

Polygyny

Polygyny (or polygamy) is the marriage rule that allows a man to be married to more than one wife simultaneously. It is a very common marriage rule found in many of the world's cultures, and it is widely accepted in African and Middle Eastern societies among both Muslims and the followers of traditional African religious beliefs. The number of men who are actually able to practice polygyny, however, is usually limited to a small minority of individuals in any given society. Nevertheless, the existence of the institution of polygyny, its popularity among men, and women's concern that it might become a reality in their own family can all be significant factors in women's decisions about their own and their daughters' lives. Concern about polygyny can create a dampening effect on female circumcision change efforts.

One study that investigated whether polygyny was related to infibulation or female circumcision generally was Esther Hicks's comprehensive cross-cultural review of the ethnographic literature. She found several correlates of infibulation that, she stresses, are not to be inferred as causal. The primary variables that were correlated were wives retaining full membership in their natal groups, male absenteeism, unstable marriages, low position of women, sheep and goats cared for by wives, high "brideprice," and the practice of Islam (1993:162).

Although the variable of polygyny did not emerge as an independent correlate of infibulation, Hicks found that it was related to other variables for which she discovered strong independent correlations. For example, among northeast African pastoralists the frequency of polygynous marriages is higher for older, wealthier males. Mixed herding that necessitates seasonal nomadism to provide for some of the types of animals herded can result in male absenteeism, a variable Hicks found to be strongly correlated with the existence of infibulation practices (1993: 165). The difficulties of managing a large herd encourage wealthy men to seek additional wives to provide more help and to produce more children to manage the animals. Polygyny, particularly where wives live in different settlements from one another (which may be necessitated by their arrangements to be near other family members during periods of husbands' absence), contributes to the tendency for male absenteeism because the husband (even when he is not away with his herds) splits his time between different households.

How could this pattern — mixed herding, nomadic or seminomadic movements, and polygyny, an ancient pattern that predates the arrival of Islam in northeast Africa — have contributed to the practice of infibulation? The answer is not clear from Hicks's exhaustive testing of variables based on data drawn from ethnographic sources. But she points us in the direction of composites, clusters of related variables rather than single determining factors. Polygyny, as one such variable, should not be given great importance in and of itself because there are plenty of noncircumcising societies that do practice polygyny. But it may play a role in a set of conditions conducive to the practice of female circumcision.

Positives and Negatives of Polygyny

Polygyny has been very common in the southern part of Sudan among the non-Muslim, noncircumcising peoples such as the Nuer, who are well known to anthropologists from E. E. Evans-Pritchard's detailed ethnographic work carried out in the early 1930s. In my own research in that area (in Upper Nile Province in the mid-1970s with the Jonglei research team from the Sudanese National Council for Research), we found that some of the rural families among the Nuer, Dinka, and Shilluk peoples included several wives of the same man, even ten or more for a particularly wealthy or powerful man. This was certainly true in the village of Ayod, where I was based.

A Nuer lineage leader with a large herd of cattle might have acquired some of his wives through marriage contracts and the payment of cattle and others through "inheritance," a custom whereby the brother or son of a man who has died takes over the duties and rights of husband to his widows (anthropologists call this custom the "levirate").[1] The widow can object to a particular kinsman, but particularly if she is a young woman still able to bear children, the bridewealth cattle transaction that contracted her marriage is still considered to be in effect and the family of the deceased man has the right to continue to father children in his name unless the bridewealth cattle are returned. For older women, though, who have already borne several children or are past menopause and generally grow their own food and can affiliate with another kinsman's household if they wish, their lives are in practice fairly independent if they want them to be. Such old women can decline to be inherited and go their own way, though it is more usual to be counted among the wives of someone, even if the man is much younger, far away, or uninvolved on a daily basis. There is no expectation that such wives live in a particular place, although no one wants to live in an isolated place without the security of other people as some measure of protection against wild animals, thieves, fear, and now the ravages of civil war. And one must live where clan membership offers rights to cultivate and be protected.

In Nuer society if a man has several wives, they may live in widely separated homesteads, having relatively little contact with one another unless they happen to be friends, or they may share a homestead. Adult Nuer women have more autonomy and may well have independent economic activities like brewing and distilling that provide personal income. On my last night at the end of two months in the village of Ayod, for example, as I went to say my good-byes to one of the women, I found her and a couple of her co-wives operating an elaborate still constructed of tins and pottery and glass.

The women offered me a glass of the hot clear liquid that dripped from the pipe. I had not realized it, but these women must have been the source of the illegal, strongly intoxicating alcohol called *aragi* that some of the members of our research team had obtained. Co-wives with access to resources had prospered in their own right through a cooperative venture, under the aegis of their powerful husband's shelter from the law.

Polygyny was widespread in these southern Sudanese ethnic groups,

---

[1] If a son is involved, he would become husband only to wives who are not his mother, of course.

but they generally eschewed female circumcision. No group had adopted it, despite individual cases of experimentation.

Polygyny can contribute to perpetuation and spread of the practice of female circumcision when husbands of circumcising groups intermarry and make comparisons of wives, as in the case of the disillusioned Dinka woman married to a northern Arab trader who was mentioned in Chapter 4. Given a woman's sexual rivalry and desire for children, it is not difficult to understand why an uncircumcised co-wife might consider undergoing circumcision if a husband wanted her to. In the case of the two co-wives of the Zabarma man discussed earlier, even though the husband was from a noninfibulating group, his sexual experience with a new third wife, who was infibulated, led to the second wife undergoing the procedure.

Of course, it is not primarily the circumcision issues that influence women's views on polygyny. Women from ethnic groups where polygyny has been common are more likely to find ways to cope with polygyny and even to see positive aspects of it. Yet even where the practice is well accepted, certain fears remain. Sometimes men are concerned about the potential for conflict among their wives, based on sexual jealousy and rivalry, anger about favoritism, or other issues.

From many women's point of view, polygyny confers a number of economic disadvantages. If women are fairly independent in production, as is the case of Nuer women who plant their own fields and have separate residences and contribute to a husband's support, having more wives to take care of him might reduce the obligations of each wife. But whatever his responsibilities are, such as the provision of cows for milking, his contribution will still be divided.

Based on my observations in the rural contexts where I did research, a woman whose husband is polygynous must expect to share with another wife whatever their husband provides. Unless the man is wealthy, she will have less of all the good things in life: less sugar, less coffee, and smaller quantities of spices, incense, and perfumes. New sets of clothing and sandals will be offered less frequently, and basic supplies will have to be shared more widely. Unless he is scrupulously fair, jealousy and conflict can arise over who got more supplies or better cloth or special treats. These resources must be shared not only between wives but also among more children. A woman's own children, on whom she expects to rely for support in her old age, will have to share the inheritance with another woman's children. Although the family's prosperity may be enhanced by more hands to work, there are also more mouths to feed. Insofar as the hands of many children make for a man's ability to cultivate larger fields, care for larger herds, and engage in more diversity of enterprises, however, the family may enhance its prosperity and prestige to the extent that both wives think they are better off. And most Zabarma co-wives seem genuinely to appreciate the cooperative work and communal living they share — so long as their husband is fair.

Some of the women I spoke with truly appreciate these potential advantages, yet even the Zabarma, and to a greater extent the Kenana, are concerned with the potential diminution of their own and their children's economic resources in the long run. For the polygynous father, though, the larger family enhances his personal reputation and if he plays his opportunities for alliances cleverly, he may eventually be able to provide his children with other sorts of opportunities based on his prestige and political clout.

Economic Dependency of Women

The Gezira and Rahad development projects have had strong impacts on women's work, reproduction, and health that in turn place pressure on their circumcision practices. As discussed earlier, Garia Wahid in the Rahad irrigation project is inhabited by former residents of several old villages, including Zabarma and Kenana families from the two Rahad River village sites I studied in the 1970s, who are now neighbors.

The division of labor and the family systems of the two groups were somewhat different before the move. For the Zabarma, large patrilineal extended families had been the common production and consumption units in the 1970s (see O'Brien 1980). Men and boys of an extended family worked together in the agricultural fields under the control of the senior male, while women avoided agricultural work in the fields.

In the irrigation project, the most basic factor in women's increasing economic dependency was the fact that the tenancies — the standard-sized plots of land that were to be farmed in accordance with centralized management decisions and water regimens, but with economic risk carried by the tenant — were given out almost exclusively to males as heads of households. Only a few widows with children received tenancies in the original allocation, and officials of the Rahad Corporation whom I interviewed in 1992 estimated that less than one percent of tenants were women at that time. The mostly male tenants have been able to treat the income from the tenancies — most of which is paid out in one annual lump sum share of the project's cotton profits — as personal property, even though family labor contributes to the productivity. Many women complained that their husbands seldom paid them for their work, although men did provide for their families' basic needs (food, clothing, and shelter, an expectation reinforced by Islam) out of these incomes. Nevertheless, this structure that transforms the family's work into the man's property reduces women's economic autonomy in comparison with the previous situation; in the past, when they picked cotton for others, each woman could keep her own wages.

It is this masculinization of cash income that has served as the impetus for increasing polygyny: it has become more of an option than it used to be. Husbands' control over discretionary funds has enabled some to pay the costs of second and even third marriages. Although prior to the irrigation project the Zabarma were accustomed to polygyny (see demographic information in O'Brien 1980), for the Kenana community, polygyny was extremely rare before the project.

Polygyny, Work, and Reproduction in the Rahad Irrigation Scheme

The structure of economic relations in the Rahad Irrigated Scheme increased the possibility and economic desirability for men to marry second and third wives. Not only did they find the labor of the additional wife useful, but having more children over a longer period of time guaranteed a core labor force, some of whom could also be sent to school to generate longer term economic opportunities for the family. And because the cotton profits were under male control, the opportunity was there for men to take second and third wives, taking on the cost of bridewealth, wedding, and building a new house.

The women I interviewed in Garia Wahid had two sorts of reactions. The Zabarma group had already experienced numerous polygynous marriages prior to the move to the Rahad irrigation project, and for them it was more acceptable. Their saying, "a man is not a man without two wives," could only be realized by a minority of men, but it was frequent enough that they had learned how to make it work. Zabarma husbands had strong traditions of rotation among wives and fairness in dividing resources, and co-wives commonly managed to coexist harmoniously in the same compound, although there were exceptions.

For the Kenana it was an entirely different story because for them polygyny was previously quite rare and not well accepted. The Kenana women I interviewed had negative feelings about polygyny and the new trend toward it, even though they acknowledged it was men's right. Kenana women were well aware of the many pitfalls of emotional attachments, stretched and potentially unfairly distributed resources, and the risks to the inheritance of one's children. On formal questioning, women often gave the dutiful answer that they would not object if their husband wished to take a second wife, but their banter among themselves and their ridicule of old men who wanted second and third wives belied their sanguine attitude.

The new possibility that a husband might want another wife offered an incentive to conformity with infibulation, if one was needed. Insofar as husbands' preferences are for infibulated brides and tightly reinfibulated wives after childbirth, it would be the rare Kenana mother indeed who would risk not infibulating her daughters. Especially now that polygyny was a real possibility for the Kenana, there was all the more reason to conform and a strong disincentive to risking modern innovations like sunna, lest the husband become more interested in additional wives.

The Kenana and Polygyny

Nur was a man whose energetic wife, Miriam, had not become pregnant in the last three years. As part of the extended family I lived with, he frequently joined my conversations with the women. Some of the women hinted, when he was out of earshot, that he might be interested in my research assistant, an unmarried young woman who had a high school education. More than once there had been considerable banter among the kinswomen, teasing his wife about the idea. Her wiry mother-in-law said Miriam would be upset if Nur took another wife, but Miriam laughed and denied being jealous or angry. The other women persisted, as if to give her practice at denial.

Later, when his wife was not present, I had the chance to ask Nur if he was really interested in taking a second wife. He said yes, of course. Why not? After all, his wife would soon reach menopause, and although he had a number of children already, the more the better from his point of view; he would need more children to help with the work when these ones were grown.

I asked if he didn't think it was unfair to her to want another wife.

Not at all, he said. He then pursued a line of questioning to demonstrate the fundamental good sense of it all.

"Ellen, what happens in your culture if a man and his wife get a little older? Does it ever happen that a man becomes interested in a younger woman?"

"Well, yes, sometimes," I had to admit. "In fact it is not at all uncommon."

"Okay," said Nur. "Then what happens, what does he do about it if he loves a younger woman?"

"He might have an affair, although that is frowned upon, or he gets a divorce so he can marry the younger woman."

"There, you see what the problem is?" he retorted. "We Muslims would never reject our wives for that. I would always keep my first wife in her respected place as the mother of my children. She would be the senior wife, and I would just add another wife to the family. Isn't that kinder and more respectful of her than to divorce her and send her away?"

He had a point, though I disagreed with his premise that it was almost inevitable that a man would want a younger woman as his wife got older. He pursued it: "Isn't your husband attracted to younger women?"

This was territory I did not want to get into, so I turned to the law: "In the United States, it would be illegal to marry more than one woman at a time."

"Illegal? But it's natural to want a second wife!" He shook his head at American law.

Turning it around with my innocent feminist logic, I said, "Well, what if women want to have two husbands?"

He could not control his laughter. "How could a woman have two husbands at the same time?" I think I had just offered the most absurd idea he had ever heard on the subject of marriage. That ended the conversation as he went off to share the hilarity with another of the men.

Nur did not in fact marry my research assistant, who married someone from her home village the following year, I learned, but such discussions may have helped prepare his wife psychologically for a future more serious proposal. I don't know whether Nur ever did marry a second wife, but there were others who had. That same week I attended wedding festivities for a fourteen-year-old girl who had been taken out of school (sixth grade) to be married as a second wife. Another man invited me to dinner with his young third wife, who was about sixteen.

Demographic and Health Implications

Because one of the goals of husbands in taking a second wife is to have more children to participate in the economic enterprises, the main tool available to a woman to forestall her husband's taking another wife is to maximize her reproduction. Some of the women I interviewed were actively seeking to have as many children as they could to prevent their husbands' opting for polygyny to get an additional childbearer. Indeed, many people commented that since they moved to the irrigation scheme, the usual three-year intervals between babies had shortened. Two years had become the norm.

While the reduction in birth intervals probably has not been as dramatic as that commonplace observation made it sound, data from my twenty-nine reproductive history interviews (ten Zabarma and nineteen Kenana women) conducted in Garia Wahid in 1992 support the widely held contention that the birth rate was increasing through the shortening of birth intervals (Gruenbaum 1996).

Women's desire to prevent their husbands from resorting to polygyny

The Rahad Irrigated Scheme led to an improved standard of living for the Kenana women of Garia Wahid.

was not usually explicitly acknowledged as a reason for high birth rates. Both women and men would agree on their main conscious reasons for wanting more children: (1) they had always preferred lots of children and now the sense of family economic security based on irrigation project income made that possible, (2) they now had the opportunity to send children to school, which offered future economic security, as employed offspring could be expected to send remittances to their parents, and (3) the additional labor could be put to work on animal care or on the tenancies to increase productivity and reduce the cost of hired labor.

Since the move to the Rahad project, not only have the intervals between births become shorter, but the survival rate of infants and children has improved significantly, especially for the Zabarma. In fact, of those births to the Zabarma interviewees that occurred prior to the move, only 65 percent survived to age five and only 52 percent until age twelve. Since the move, which resulted in access to a local clinic, 80 percent of Zabarma live births (occurring at least five years before the interviews) survived to age five. For the Kenana (who had more often traveled for health care even before the move), the pre-move five-year survival rate of 87 percent was virtually unchanged (86 percent) for births after the move. The combination of increased survival and accelerated births could be leading to significant population growth for the area.

Health conditions have shown improvement since the move to the irrigation project. Most of the women I interviewed noted the health benefits of improved housing, but some complained that their diet was not as good in the project scheme as in the old villages. This was primarily because of an inadequate milk supply resulting from the lack of year-round grazing on the project, which meant that the herds must be taken far away. The biggest health problems were sanitation and the water supply. The water supply, initially improved by a pump system that filtered and piped canal water into the housing area, had become woefully undependable by the early 1990s because of pump breakdowns and the lack of spare parts. On the positive side, pregnant women and children have been receiving immunizations at the local clinic and during periodic public health immunization campaigns. Many of the Kenana children and a few of the Zabarma children are also now going to school.

It was still extremely rare to see a family build a latrine in the family compound or extend water pipes into the courtyard for convenience, both of which actions might improve health conditions. Water was generally carried by women in unsanitary plastic cans and stored in clay pots in the houses. People owned many more dishes and better furniture than before, however, and the housing was somewhat better than at the river. Nearly all the dwellings were round, mud-plastered houses with thatched roofs and dirt floors, whereas some before did not have the mud plaster.

But it was rare indeed to see window screens installed against malarious mosquitoes. The cotton profits that might have been used to fund such improvements were in the hands of husbands who might decide polygyny was a higher priority.

The Zabarma and Polygyny

A couple of specific cases may help to illustrate the variety of women's experience with marriage and polygyny, reproduction, work, and health. Hawa and Kalthoum, two co-wives mentioned above, serve as good examples of a family successfully adapted to polygyny; their work has changed considerably over the years.

Hawa, the senior wife in a household of three wives, was a heavy-set, mature, and confident woman in her late forties at the time I last interviewed her. Friendly, likable, and enthusiastic, Hawa enjoyed visiting her neighbors, including those of a different ethnic background. Normally, she visited with her closest co-wife, the second wife, Kalthoum, whom she jokingly described as her "twin." I found the term particularly apt because not only were they seemingly inseparable away from home (which serves as a form of chaperoning), they sometimes wore dresses of matching cloth, the result of their husband's desire to treat them equally in the provision of clothing.

Hawa was very proud of her own religious practices and cultural values, particularly her observance of female propriety. Before moving to the irrigation project, Hawa did not do any labor in the agricultural field, which was the Zabarma preference, although she did gather wild okra in season. In the old village of Um Fila, she had done some embroidering of sheets and weaving of mats, a few of which she sold from her home for personal cash income. She had plenty of work to do at home pounding and grinding grain to feed the family, hauling water from the well or river, cooking, cleaning, and caring for children. There was an important shift in her activities after the move to the new irrigation project, however, because she took up field labor, particularly in harvesting cotton and peanuts; crops not grown in the old riverbank village. (She does not use the large hoe used by Zabarma men, though.) Some years she and her co-wife took turns going to the field and caring for the young children, each of them harvesting and selling her own sacks of peanuts, an arrangement that could only work well if the children were not too small. The older children helped in the field, though a daughter would do so only until the age when someone had asked to marry her. Selling the peanuts was done from home, to maintain propriety, with Hawa's grown son making inquiries and bringing any prospective buyer to bargain directly with her.

Married when she was eleven, Hawa had her first child at about the age

A mother who is a co-wife of a Zabarma family, Garia Wahid.

of eighteen. She has had no pregnancies in five years, and it is likely that she has completed her reproduction, having given birth to nineteen children in all (full-term pregnancies). Twins figure prominently: she had four sets, but two of the sets were stillborn. Only one of the first pair survived and another set died when three years old. The other eleven pregnancies were single babies. The reproductive history was full of grief. Of the fifteen live births, only seven children were still living at the time of my interview. The youngest was five. The ones who had died were lost at ages between fifteen months and three years.

Hawa's co-wife, Kalthoum, was a soft-spoken woman with a fairly light complexion who wore a nose ring. She had given birth to nine children, seven of whom were still alive (the oldest fourteen and two still under age two). She, too, had not done field labor before the move to the irrigation project but had collected firewood and wild okra for subsistence use and to sell from home (buyers came by vehicle to the village). Kalthoum appreciated the lightening of some of the drudgery that the move to the irrigation project afforded because their husband had extended a pipe to their yard, water was more convenient (at least on days when water pressure was adequate), firewood was delivered for purchase, and the flour mill reduced the pounding and grinding efforts necessary.

For Kalthoum, her work role changed as the women's concept of propriety shifted. Earlier, in the 1970s, Zabarma women (including Hawa and Kaltoum) had told me it was "haram" (forbidden or sinful) for women to work in the fields. But in the 1980s and 1990s, since they had begun doing field labor, Kalthoum was very clear that field labor was not haram, it was just "not our custom" before. Meeting men, which had been so rare before, had now of necessity become more common, and Kenana neighbors and buyers came to the house and entered the courtyard. Before, that would have been "haram." The Zabarma women didn't like the change but were adapting.

"Lots of things are haram," Kalthoum said. "Women are supposed to shake hands through the tobe." She demonstrated by extending her right hand covered by the final drape of her veil as it rose toward the left shoulder, so that her hand would not touch a man's hand directly. "But we've had to change in the new situation."

Saida, the schoolteacher who was with me for this series of interviews, joined in the discussion authoritatively: "The religion is one. All the things that are haram are haram, regardless of customary differences."

"Well," said one of the Kenana women who sat with us, "some of us just go [*mashi sai*]. We don't know any better." Although this young schoolteacher was thought to be ignorant of many issues that she, as an unmarried woman, could not yet understand, when it came to religion, Saida's literacy and education commanded the respect of the village women.

Kalthoum was certainly pious and came from a family in which her own mother had gone on the pilgrimage to Mecca three times. But she and these other illiterate women could not study Islam for themselves. "The men tell us about religion," Kalthoum explained.

Hawa and Kalthoum's husband had married a third wife as Kalthoum neared the end of her reproductive years. The three all shared one courtyard and cooperated smoothly. The fourth house in the courtyard was that of their mother-in-law, the elflike old woman who had befriended me on my first visit to Um Fila, before the move.

Khadija, by then in her seventies, was the eldest wife of her husband, who also had three wives. She had only two surviving children, and a third had died. She recalled nursing each of them for three years, which resulted in longer intervals of child-spacing than in more recent years. She often commented, with the amazed and long-term view of the philosophical elderly, that their customs have changed a lot, with girls and women now going to the fields to pick cotton and other changes in work. As for female circumcision, from her point of view the main change had been that now they went out of their way to find a midwife with local anesthetic for the girls.

Nursing periods are significant for child-spacing, of course. Another of the women I interviewed, Zeinab, age forty-five, explained that in the past she had always nursed her babies for two years, whether they were boys or girls. In doing so, she ignored the advice of other women who told her that you should nurse boys for only eighteen months, to make them smarter. She didn't believe that, so she went ahead and nursed for two years, at least in most cases. Her ten children from two marriages thus had been in most cases a little more than two years apart, but there was an exception because of divorce. When her first husband, whom she had married when she was fifteen, had divorced her, she still had a small son who was nursing. The husband took custody of the older children, as was his right under Islam, leaving the young child with her until he was five. Usually after divorce, girls can remain with their mother until age nine and boys until age seven, but local custom varies. A woman cannot, however, take the children of one father into a marriage to a new man. This forces a young divorced woman to make a difficult choice: she must give up custody in order to take advantage of an opportunity for a remarriage and the chance to have more children to give her long-term security. In Zeinab's case, she returned to her father's home during the two years of being divorced, and when she remarried, her son's father took him. She did not see the boy again until he was an adult and chose to come and find her on his own.

This kind but slightly melancholy woman Zeinab found polygyny unhappy because her husband's first wife did not welcome her. Nevertheless, she did not complain but gave the standard opinion of polygyny: "It should be no problem if he always divides in half." She was an outsider, with no relatives in the village, and she came from a different West African ethnic group, so it had been especially hard for her to adapt and be accepted.

Hawa, Kalthoum, Khadija, and Zeinab are ordinary women whose lives are marked by hardship and hard work at changing tasks. Their lives have been significantly changed by the social and economic developments around them. In this context young women are committed to rearing as many children as they can, as the route to a woman's security. Each recognizes her own husband's desire to do the same, although the male strategy encourages polygyny. The longer women can continue childbearing, the later polygyny may be delayed, but each of these women has clearly found satisfying ways to accept polygyny.

Summary

Economic development is no panacea for ending female circumcision. The problems faced by these rural families are monumental. While conditions are fairly good in the older, well-established areas like Gezira, as examples in the next chapter illustrate, newer irrigation projects like Rahad still have many problems. Obtaining clean water is a challenge, and women in Garia Wahid have to carry heavy tins from distant canals, store the water in clay pots, and hope that water-borne diseases will not afflict them and their families. Latrines are not available to the majority of families. Sick children still die at high rates, and the clinic is undersupplied with medicines. The school does not accommodate enough children. People in Garia Wahid want more tenancies, more educational and employment opportunities, better health services, clean water, and reliable services of flour mills and bakeries. They have been awaiting electricity and a paved road, and hoping for better and more varied food supplies, and they are interested in better religious instruction.

Under such circumstances, reform of female circumcision has not been at the top of the list. But the exposure to other ethnic groups and to more national influences through the market, the school, and other services offers paradoxical possibilities for change. As we have seen, there are new opportunities and pressures for those who did not previously practice infibulation to do so now, and it can be hard to resist these pressures. On the other hand, as education takes hold with the children, the idea of changing the kind of female circumcision practiced to one of a lesser severity may be expected. The ideas of the anticircumcision movement have remained somewhat alien, however, in areas far from cities like Khartoum and Wad Medani. "That hasn't come to us yet," they said.

But even for those who might consider reform, the fact that development has enabled more men to marry second and third wives has made it harder to imagine fundamental challenges in female circumcision. Keeping a husband as happy as possible with frequent reproduction and (for the Kenana) tight reinfibulation can help to prevent or delay the husband's becoming polygynous.

Yet it is obvious that these rural Sudanese communities, as elsewhere in Africa, are not culturally static. Expectations are rising, and change is occurring. The next two chapters look at the process of change in the practices of female circumcision, first at the grassroots level and then from a global perspective.

Chapter 7
Change

The followers of mutilation are good people who love their children; any campaign that insinuates otherwise is doomed to provoke defensive reaction.

— Gerry Mackie (1996:1015)

More than two decades have passed since the watershed 1979 United Nations Conference on Traditional Practices Affecting the Health of Women and Children drew medical, public health, and other experts to Khartoum from dozens of countries. The research presented at the Khartoum conference had a particularly strong influence on the discussions about this harmful traditional practice in Sudan because so many Sudanese were able to attend, presented research, or heard about the discussions that week. The result was an intensified commitment of many Sudanese health workers to end the harmful genital cutting of young girls.

Prior to that time, female circumcision was accommodated by the government health care system, despite the fact that a law against it had been enacted in 1946. The government had realized that many other traditional practices such as treatments by spirit-possessed zar healers and Islamic *fakis,* would continue to be relied on, even as people increasingly accepted the biomedical services that were gradually being made available to them in more parts of the country. In knowing defiance of the legal prohibition, many doctors performed circumcisions in their offices, justifying the practice by the greater safety afforded by superior medical techniques and more hygienic office conditions than could be offered by a lay midwife working in people's homes. Through their tolerance and participation, health practitioners had reinforced the practices, medicalizing them.

In the colonial period in Africa, as discussed earlier, anticircumcision efforts by British imperial governments and missionaries had not been handled well. In response, Jomo Kenyatta made the right to circumcision as part of the national heritage a rallying cry in the Kenyan independence movement (1965, originally 1938). In Sudan, too, there was opposition to outlawing it.[1]

After independence, medical tolerance and acceptance prior to 1979 did little to discourage female circumcision. But already at midcentury, activists from the Sudan Women's Union, which was affiliated with the Sudanese Communist party, had developed a political position opposing the practices. As Sondra Hale has noted in her research on gender politics in Sudan, however, the call for eradication of female circumcision never became a major Women's Union or Sudan Communist party agenda item because some of the leaders "saw the eradication campaign as a Western importation," and the leadership of Sudanese efforts against female circumcision was then left to "the liberal women of the Babiker Bedri Scientific Association for Women Studies" and others (Hale 1996:230–31).

Public health education campaigns since 1979 have made some progress toward expanded awareness of the need for change. Various techniques have been used to mobilize against female circumcision, such as training health workers, resolutions by the doctors' union, radio talk shows, and public forums. Although elaborate celebrations of circumcisions, featuring hired musicians, were continuing in Khartoum in the late 1980s among urban educated people, change no longer seemed as remote as it had in the 1970s. Many of the urban educated families I knew either had stopped circumcising or were considering it.

How do such changes occur when the practices have been so important? Although education about health risks is a contributing factor to change, social change seldom happens in a straightforward manner in response to information alone. In my earlier writings, I argued that women's insecure position in society needs to change before fundamental rejection of circumcision can be achieved. In my discussions with exiled Sudanese Women's Union leader Fatima Ahmed Ibrahim in 1995 at the NGO Forum of the Fourth World Conference on Women in China and in 1997 in California, she expressed the same belief that the practices will change when other aspects of women's oppression changes.[2] Ignorance, Fatima Ahmed Ibrahim said, is far more serious of a problem than female circumcision. She is quoted in Sondra Hale's book as saying, "The Women's Union is trying to tell women that circumcision is not the cause of a

[1] The Rufa'a incident of 1946 is discussed in Chapter 8.

[2] Fatima Ahmed Ibrahim was a visiting scholar in the Women's Studies program at UCLA for several months, and I invited her to lecture at California State University, San Bernardino, during that time.

problem, but is the result of a situation. . . . The cure is not to spend lots of money to convince women to stop. . . . The solution is to educate women, raise their consciousness . . . so they will not feel in need to circumcise to keep respect" (1996:238).

An outspoken critic of the current Islamist government of Sudan and a long-time supporter of the leftist movement there, Fatima Ibrahim's current efforts to challenge the government's interpretation of Islam and to investigate ways that the Islamic religion can be used to support women's rights and social justice are examples of precisely the type of creative role individuals can play in social change. The process of change for female circumcision, while owing much to the educational, social, and economic transformations of the twentieth century, benefits from the individuals and organizations that fit the category of change agents. Those working at the "grassroots" level are not likely to achieve international fame as anticircumcision leaders, but their impact is significant.

The Context for Change

To understand the significance of the efforts of Sudanese change agents described below, it is helpful to understand the obstacles they faced in the recent social and political situation. When I first left Sudan in 1979, the economic situation was fairly dismal, worse than in previous years. But at that time it appeared the civil war had been settled (only temporarily, unfortunately), food production was increasing, and poverty, though rampant, was mitigated by kin and community supports. When I returned to Sudan in 1989 after a ten-year absence, it seemed as if the scale of human suffering had reached an unprecedented order of magnitude. Famines and massive population displacements had taken place in the previous few years, primarily because of the renewed civil war, which resulted in an estimated one million deaths during the period of 1988 and 1989. And yet during the 1980s the huge Rahad development project, where Garia Wahid is located, had been brought into full production and numerous other development projects had been undertaken. There had been an influx of hard currency from Sudanese working in the oil-rich Middle Eastern countries. New financial influences, such as the Islamic banks founded with infusions of Saudi Arabian capital, resulted in significant restructuring of the Sudanese political economy.

Such changes were harbingers of the widening gap between rich and poor in the country, exemplified by the all too frequent sights of stark contrast between the shanty dwellings on construction lots and the modern villas next door, between the huge numbers of homeless, begging children and the unprecedented wealth of the upper class. The presence of so many Mercedes Benzes and the construction of new high-rise build-ings have altered the urban landscape, changing the look and feel of Khartoum from its earlier languid "colonial outpost" feel to a Third World city. Further, the Islamist movement had made surprisingly deep tracks in the Sudanese social landscape. Gone were the liquor stores and the cold bottles of locally made Abu Jamal (Father Camel) beer and the little glasses of Abu Kadees (Father Cat) sherry in the outdoor cafes. Prohibition had been enforced with President Nimeiri's Islamic law reforms in 1983. Women students at the University of Khartoum still mingled with the young men, but more of them wore the modest *hijab* of the Islamists or gestured at it with their scarves and long-sleeved, long-skirted fashions.

These social changes, some resulting from the contemporary Islamic movement, others from policies of the political Islamist government, and others from labor migration and economic changes, have impacted tra-ditional practices affecting health, as I have noted above, especially re-ducing the practice of zar (at least in some areas)[3] and having some effects on female circumcision practices. In the late 1980s, public health programs achieved important successes in immunization programs, ma-laria control efforts, and programs to control diarrheal diseases, though many of these were not sustained into the 1990s.

The Khartoum conference helped make female circumcision practices also a target for change. Sociomedical research was undertaken in the early 1980s to assess more accurately the extent of circumcision practices and the correlates of its prevalence, which led to the studies by Asma El Dareer (1982) and Rushwan et al. (1982). Also as a direct result of the Khartoum conference, the Sudanese Ministry of Health adopted a policy against physicians conducting circumcisions of females. Although the medical profession as a whole did not promote female circumcision, the medicalization of it, it was feared, was contributing to acceptance of the practices.[4] The new policy effectively challenged that tendency.

In this context, I investigated the work of several people who were working for change.

[3] Because zar adepts use trance and other means to mollify possessing spirits, which are believed capable of causing their hosts physical and social ills, many Muslims consider this a manifestation of pre-Islamic beliefs that Muslims should discontinue once they have put their faith in God.

[4] Similarly, a recent evaluation by the Population Council of health personnel in Mali revealed that such medicalization was going on, with increased involvement of medical personnel and facilities in the practice of female circumcision. As a result, the minister of health issued a directive prohibiting the practice in health facilities (anonymous reviewer, personal communication, 1999).

Change Agent in Public Health: A Rural Medical Assistant

In the 1980s and 1990s, change efforts were already underway in some areas. Abdal Galil was one such place because of the advantageous situation of the Gezira with respect to educational opportunities, the cosmopolitan experiences of numerous families whose members worked in cities and in other countries, and the economic advantages. In Abdal Galil, one of the catalysts for change was the medical assistant in charge of Abdal Galil Health Center.

Jubara Ibrahim Ibed first came to the Health Center in 1986 and quickly impressed the local leadership with his abilities not only to treat the sick but to envision a healthier community and organize efforts to accomplish goals. By the time I first interviewed him in 1989, he had been working in the health field for forty-two years, including being part of the anti-smallpox campaign in the south many years before. A dynamic man with what could truly be described as a passion for health, his leadership helped Abdal Galil get government funding to hire a dental assistant and all the necessary equipment to set up a treatment service. The equipment arrived during my stay in 1992; it was a wonderful sight to see the enthusiastic unwrapping of gleaming stainless steel basins, the padded dental chair, the electric drill, and the numerous instruments.

What a contrast to my first stay in Abdal Galil back in 1977. Then I had visited the Health Center with one of the elders of the community, Siddig Dafalla, the president of the Village Council, and we sat on the veranda with the former medical assistant, overlooking the fenced garden where someone's calf was grazing. A pile of soiled cotton and gauze bandages had been swept out of the treatment room and off the veranda, into a corner of the garden. In the course of our conversation about the services offered, the Village Council president asked the medical assistant to have a look at his sore tooth. In the past most rural Sudanese had wonderful teeth because of good nutrition and the regular use of a type of fibrous stick that served like a toothbrush to keep the teeth and gums clean. After the advent of widespread use of refined sugar in tea and the spread of candy as treats for children in well-off families, things began to change. Children were having more tooth problems, and I had seen one teenage girl who had already lost her permanent molars to tooth decay. But even before such dietary changes, old people who had had no dental care during their lives were often troubled by toothaches and gum disease, and Siddig was one of them.

His tooth looked bad. "Stay right there," the medical assistant said, as he went inside. He returned with a pair of pliers. They had a good laugh about having this foreign visitor watch, but they didn't mind my photographing the procedure. Once the medical assistant got a good angle for pulling, it only took a minute and the troublesome tooth was yanked.

A decade later the clinic facilities had improved considerably. The new medical assistant Jubara pursued a high level of professionalism coupled with humanitarian values: he described himself as trying to be "a human being" about his practice. Sometimes he will drive a sick patient to the regional hospital in Mesellemiya (where he lives — about four kilometers away), rather than have them waste time looking for transportation, and he never wants anyone to go away without treatment or referral. It was a pleasure to observe his work. Having the only phone in the neighborhood, he was brusque and businesslike on the telephone because there were often calls from outside the village to his phone: "No, he's not here." Click. But with his patients, he showed great sensitivity. Although his office was quite open, with various people moving in and out unannounced, he did close the door when it was necessary to perform a physical examination behind the cloth screen that surrounded the examination table. He spoke softly and gently to a shy Hausa woman, so they could not be overheard. One needed to be especially careful, he said, because the "Fallata" were reluctant to come for treatment.

His advice included dietary suggestions and folk remedies. Avoid hot peppers and drink milk, he told someone with a stomach complaint. Rub the baby with sesame oil at bedtime to protect him from the chill (*sagat*) and the mosquitoes. For problems needing medications, he did not always have the ones he needed to prescribe. The preferred medicine for amoebic dysentery could only be had in the provincial capital, for instance. He sometimes had to give people prescriptions they could get filled only by traveling there. Sometimes he bought medicines that were available at the pharmacy in the Mesellemiya rural hospital to save the patients the trip. He usually had free medicine to treat some common diseases like schistosomiasis and malaria.

But clearly, the conditions for giving treatment were incredibly challenging, enough so that a fully trained physician would probably throw up his or her hands and say "How can anyone practice medicine like that?" Yet here was a man who put energy and good cheer into the task every day. His own wife was disabled by a severe chronic illness, which may have added to his understanding of suffering and the need for compassion.

Jubara had a clear sense of duty to educate the entire community, and not just about health care. "A doctor is not just for the needle," he said, referring to people's frequent expectation of getting shots. As an educated person, he should be "like a teacher of science and know something about economics, religion, and agriculture." It was his duty to enlighten the people about whatever he had knowledge of. He believed strongly in prevention and in promoting public health measures.

Circumcision was one example. One day he told me about an article he had read recently that discussed the pain boys feel when undergoing circumcision. The procedure is normally done there around the age of six or seven, but there was a trend toward earlier circumcision, on the assumption that children do not feel the pain when they are small. Learning that was erroneous, he concluded he should use anesthetic. But he also decided that early circumcisions should be promoted because in his clinical experience they seem to heal faster.

A few minutes after he told me this, a woman who had brought in her small son, who was about three years old, was treated to one of his jocular lessons.

"Has he had his circumcision (*tahur*) yet?" he asked her.

She looked a little surprised to be asked that about a boy so young. "No, not yet."

"No?" he joked. "What, are you going to wait till he gets married?" She smiled, but did not reply. The idea was planted, though. Boys should be circumcised early.

Acutely aware of the damage female genital cutting and infibulation can cause, Jubara decided to hold public meetings at the school in 1988, one separately for women and girls (including the junior high school students) and the other for men. There he strongly urged community residents to give up circumcision practices, especially infibulation. He stressed not only the harmfulness to health, including causing difficulties with intercourse and dangers in childbirth, but also said he considered it his duty as an educated person to speak out against the practice. From his religious knowledge he explained that the Qur'an does not require it.

I asked him whether many people had believed that female circumcision was not Islamic. He estimated only half; the rest thought Islam required the practice. In his talks, he mentioned that Islamist groups (he mentioned the Jebha Islamiyya, the Muslim Brothers, and the Ansar Sunna) all prefer sunna circumcision, as do the holy men at the shrines at Tayiba, the local pilgrimage destination where saints' graves are marked by domed *qubbas*.

Work on men's opinions is high priority, Jubara believes. Yet in the meeting with men, although many told him they were not happy with pharaonic circumcision, they considered it women's responsibility because it is done by the women. Many of the younger men, however, readily accepted the idea that it is better to marry a woman who is not circumcised. To help more young men be ready to promote change, Jubara undertook a program of school visits to explain to boys why it is better not to have female circumcision. He believes that if young men would refuse to marry pharaonically circumcised young women, the practice would stop quickly.

Jubara's community meeting approach seemed to have been effective. These meetings were well attended, and a large segment of the population heard his message firsthand or from others who went. Apparently he was very convincing, and many people mentioned these meetings as a turning point when the tide of public opinion had really begun to shift.

Besaina, the midwife I discussed earlier, summarized Jubara's message by saying that circumcision was "bad, sinful, not Islamic, and causes difficult birth." She noticed that the women listened, but most said nothing at the meeting, perhaps from embarrassment. Besaina thought the old women did not understand or accept what Jubara had to say. Others got the message that "sunna is better." Some said that people now "won't listen to the *habobas* (grandmothers)" who still think the pharaonic circumcision is necessary.

The mixed, though generally positive, response is based on some cultural readiness for change. Many people of Abdal Galil were aware of the changes being discussed in urban areas because of the long history of educational opportunity here, out-migration for urban and foreign jobs, and access to news, including television by the mid-1970s. Several women in the village were teachers and expressed notions of women's rights and responsibilities that seemed much more egalitarian than those of the older generation. As I discussed above, some of these women, like Suad, had already begun to question the pharaonic type of circumcision several years earlier but had done so quietly because it had entailed social risks. And even Besaina, the midwife who had been so proud of her pharaonic circumcision techniques back in the 1970s, was by 1989 saying that she preferred sunna. Besaina's attitude was the result not only of Jubara's influence, but also of the effects of her son's work in Saudi Arabia, where he was exposed to Islamic influences that were against female circumcision. Also her son had married an infibulated woman, and when he realized the damage done to women he asked his mother not to do pharonic circumcisions anymore. In my last interview with her in 1992, however, Besaina still had not completely stopped doing the pharaonics because people were still asking for them, but she reiterated her intention to do only sunnas in the future.

Surgical Innovation: An Urban Midwife

It was Jubara who first described for me a new type of female circumcision that was being tried, one that leaves the clitoris intact, sewn beneath a small flap of tissue. He said it had been invented by the trained nurse midwife, Sister Battool Siddiq, in the provincial capital, Wad Medani. (Sister Battool appears in the discussion in Chapter 5.) Because I was interested in linkages between the urban health educators and innovators and the rural population, I sought her out for an interview the next time I was in town.

Sister Battool, or "*Sitt* (lady) Battool" as some called her, operated a private practice at her home, which, though unmarked, was well known and centrally located, across the street from the provincial hospital. She also worked for UNICEF, training health workers. In her private practice, she was sought out by many, including the wealthiest families, to do circumcisions, attend childbirths, and perform small surgeries such as opening problem infibulations after marriage and repairing poorly done reinfibulations. One client who visited while I was there was a young mother who had delivered in Saudi Arabia, and the doctors there, un-familiar with postchildbirth reinfibulation, had done a poor job of get-ting the labia to rejoin. Upon urination, urine came out from several different openings. She arranged for Sister Battool to repair the area.

Being probably the most renowned circumciser in the province and beyond, Sister Battool is in a key position both to observe trends and to influence the type of circumcisions done. It was clear from the inter-view that although she has not enforced an absolute ban on pharaonic circumcision, she clearly has supported and popularized less harmful forms, including her innovation.

In Sister Battool's view, it is quite harmful to remove all the tissue; she prefers to remove only a small part of the prepuce, leaving the erectile tissue intact. Thus her "sunna" is far less severe than a clitoridectomy, thereby reducing the chances of the most common complications (hem-orrhaging, shock, septicemia) and preserving sexual sensitivity. Although she attempts to persuade clients to opt for minimal tissue damage, she said she does the operations however they wish. Although she said that some people still insist she "take it all," many more of her clients have now been willing to consider intermediate forms. During 1989, in fact, she noted a marked increase in the demand for sunna, estimating that it con-stituted perhaps 70 percent of the circumcisions. Even so, she reported that people who were ready to give up pharaonic circumcision were ask-ing for some degree of closure over the urethra, although calling it sunna, in order to avoid the spraying sound of urination, which is considered unfeminine.

Sister Battool did not claim complete originality. Many village mid-wives, she believed, were also avoiding clitoridectomy while still infibulat-ing, regardless of the terms they used. When they go too deep in their cutting, they hit major arteries and the bleeding is so profuse and hard to control that they soon learn to leave most of the clitoris in place beneath the infibulation. Presumably this would not interfere with sexual respon-siveness as much as other types of reduction operations.

Sister Battool finds the tenacity of people's desires to hold on to cir-

cumcision astounding. In one case, the parents of a girl who had a hemo-
philialike condition asked her to perform a pharaonic circumcision.
Their doctor had advised them not to circumcise her, but they were
adamant. She tried diligently to talk them out of it, but they believed that
circumcision was so necessary to their daughter's proper role in life that
they would even risk her death. Because she could not dissuade them and
they said they would go elsewhere if she did not agree to their request,
she reluctantly performed the surgery, knowing she could send them to
the provincial hospital right across the street if things went wrong. Indeed, before the bleeding was able to be controlled, the girl required the
transfusion of sixteen pints of blood.

Sister Battool told me that a major concern of parents considering
pharaonic circumcision is the expectation that their daughter's future
husband will not find sex with her pleasurable unless she is tightly infibulated. Indeed, according to Sister Battool, the main reason for social
resistance to abandoning circumcision is that the men want it to continue. She tries to convince parents to leave it up to their daughter when
she is older to decide whether to be infibulated.

Effects of the Islamist Movement

The large majority of people of the northern two-thirds of Sudan have
faithfully practiced Islam for many centuries. The spread and practice of
Islam has been particularly influenced by several *tariqas* (Sufi orders characterized by particular attention to the teachings and traditions of revered religious leaders, or shaykhs), so there are some variations in everyday practices of believers. Sudanese Islam in the 1970s displayed some
fascinating variations that were viewed as legitimate even by those who
did not engage in them: blessings by descendents of holy men at tombs;
joyful, musical worship with "whirling dervishes"; fervent communal
chanting of "al-Lah" (God) with drumming; treatment of the sick by
shaykhs who offered Qur'anic inscriptions in various forms to be worn,
imbibed, or inhaled. Followers of some orders need to see the crescent
moon with their own eyes to know that Ramadan has begun, while others
are content with the broadcast of reports of the sighting in Saudi Arabia.
As discussed earlier, in some areas many pre-Islamic beliefs and practices
have been syncretized and are considered part of the Islamic tradition,
whether mentioned in the Qur'an or not.

Muslims have long practiced pharaonic circumcision of females, venerated saints, and participated in zar spirit possession, despite occasional
criticism of these practices by some religious leaders. For many Muslims
who were more "secular" in their outlook, however, the prohibition of
alcohol seemed to be considered irrelevant and many intellectuals were

not too strict about fasting at Ramadan. Claims to orthodoxy by proponents of a particular interpretation of Islam were widely resented when they were imposed politically. Certainly the majority of the Sudanese, whether Muslim or not, were not pleased when the former president (Jaffar Nimeiri) attempted to Islamicize the political system by prohibiting alcohol and instituting *hudud* punishments like the amputation of the hands of thieves. Although Sudanese Muslims certainly considered themselves morally superior to non-Muslims, there was a tradition of tolerance toward Christians, who as "people of the book" were considered to accept the one God. This allowed Copts, people of other European and Middle Eastern ethnicities who had settled in Sudan, and educated non-Arab southern Sudanese to participate fully in Sudanese social life even though it was dominated by the Arabic-speaking Muslims of the central Nile Valley regions.

By 1989, though, following the coup d'état, the movement that propagated a particular version of political Islam referred to by analysts as "Islamism" achieved much more influence. It has produced a profound and divisive effect on the multiethnic, multifaith society of Sudan.

Many factors led to the Islamist movement in Sudan, and it would take me too far afield to try to account for them. The Nimeiri government (1969–87) put *Shari'a* (Islamic) laws into place in 1983, but other contributing factors were the experience of the large numbers of Sudanese migrants who had worked in the Gulf, the importing of Saudi and Kuwaiti television programs, the social influence afforded the external powers (especially Saudi Arabia) who held important economic control strings. Building upon the strong Sudanese history of allegiance to religious leaders, Islamist movement leaders seem to have succeeded in recruiting large numbers of Muslims who sincerely wish to improve their understanding of what God expects of them and live according to Islamic strictures.

Internationally, movements that are directed at political Islamicization have drawn a degree of inspiration from the example of Iran's dramatic transition to a theocratic government under the Ayatollahs, but for the most part that is not what individuals or parties are emulating. Islamist activists in many countries have not been followers of Iran but are seeking to transform their own societies according to their particular notions of orthodoxy. Arguing for Islamic universalism, Islamism has nevertheless found a variety of expressions. What has been most troubling about political Islam, from my perspective, has been a willingness to suspend civil debates and democratic institutions under the passionate belief that such earthly ideas are irrelevant to those who know what God wishes. Those who claim orthodoxy often draw on a particular conservative Arabian version of Islam (Wahhibist), dismissing the practices of other Muslims as incorrect. Some go further and pursue the Islamist goal by any means necessary, including force, prompting many other Muslims to oppose their tactics.

In Sudan, the Muslim Brotherhood–inspired National Islamic Front party has gained significant influence among urban young people (controlling, for example, the Student Union at the University of Khartoum for many years) and has managed to gain the upper hand in the political realm. The regime that came to power by military coup on June 30, 1989, put NIF policies into place and fired or arrested trade union leaders, government officials, and others opposed to the NIF. Although it may be only a small minority of Sudanese who support that party, they are extremely powerful and are in a position to use the tools of ideology to maintain their power and inculcate the next generation with their teachings.

This movement has had some influence on health in general and on the efforts to eradicate female circumcision in particular. While it has always been difficult to do medical work in a poor country with inadequate equipment, supplies, and facilities, the poor salaries and difficult living conditions (with frequent shortages of fuel and essential commodities) have in recent years made the situation even more stressful. Add to that the pressures of politicized Islam that many educated people have resisted, and you begin to understand why there are now so many Sudanese professionals working abroad.

Fortunately, the Islamist movement has not as yet had the effect of strict sex segregation in health services: every physician I asked believed that the respect for physicians as professionals who could, whether male or female, treat patients of either sex without compromise to anyone's morality was deeply established in Sudan. Even though there might be a few of the urban young women students allied with the Islamic movement who would say they were unwilling to be seen by male physicians, none of the university or medical people I spoke with believed this to be a problem. Two doctors even claimed the opposite was becoming a problem — that young women deprived of male company were seeking out male physicians for contrived complaints. The female physician discussed below, who was a conservative Muslim, told me that although she had chosen to specialize in maternal and child health (recognized as a highly appropriate medical specialty for Muslim women), even she saw no contradiction between her beliefs and either a physical examination by a physician of the other sex or the discussion of sexual matters (for her research) with both men and women.

With respect to the efforts to eradicate female circumcision, the Islamic movement has had some significant, though sometimes contradictory, impacts. First, many individuals who have experienced religious revitalization have questioned and abandoned practices considered by many religious leaders to be un-Islamic, especially spirit possession cults and pharaonic circumcision, in favor of more orthodox Islamic emphasis on the five pillars of Islam (expressions of faith, prayer, fasting, charity to the poor, and pilgrimage). Although zar has not been abandoned entirely in the villages I studied, the practice of it has definitely declined. As in the case of the spirit-possessed woman in Abdal Galil discussed earlier, who held twice-weekly healing clinics in the 1970s but now does not trance, other women have begun to abandon zar, some referring to it as a somewhat silly old custom that they say is dying out as the young women have become better educated and more knowledgeable about religion. For them, pharaonic circumcision is in the same category.

An Islamist Doctor

Claiming that pharaonic circumcision is a tradition of the pre-Islamic pharaohs, Islamist reformers have argued for modification to sunna circumcision as the appropriate Islamic alternative, though there seems to be no consensus on precisely what form of operation that entails. Yet there is another possible impact that is the result of educated women developing an interest in religious studies, as I learned from a religiously conservative woman physician who drew my attention to a possible new direction in circumcision change efforts.

This woman, who advocated the Islamist program but without the degree of compulsion the National Islamic Front government has sought to impose, dressed modestly but did not go to what the Sudanese considered the extremes of face veiling and black garments. She had received blanket permission from her husband to come and go as she wished, which enabled her to hold a part-time job (which she chose in preference to full-time employment for the benefit of her small children) and to travel to villages for her public health research.

I interviewed this woman in the modest apartment where she lived with her husband and child. Her husband was a well-educated professor who, in the Muslim Brother practice, politely declined to shake my hand. Like many of the younger urban couples, they did not own a house with the traditional separate entrances but occupied a small apartment in one of the multistoried buildings that had only recently begun to appear in Wad Medani. Some apartments have two separate entrances, but many have floor plans that do not allow for the usual degree of privacy between men (and their guests) and women, children, and other family members. This couple had arranged their apartment so that each could have a separate area when necessary; they had even divided their small living room down the center by a curtain on a ceiling track. She and I sat on the women's side of the curtain, while her husband did some paperwork on the other side. It was an unusual arrangement for Sudan, where most educated couples who live in small apartments simply share the space. Houses, too, usually have a larger area where both men and women mingle (yard, verandas, bedrooms, and kitchen), reserving if possible a formal room and some outdoor space with a separate entrance for the husband and his male guests. Although curtained off from us, the doctor's husband was there to respond if she asked him for any additional information we needed for our discussion of her research.

Through religious study of early Islamic writings, this doctor had begun to question the received interpretations of the Hadith concerning female circumcision. She concluded that the form of surgery to which the Prophet Mohammed gave his approval was not clitoridectomy but removal of the prepuce only.[5] Further, she concluded that later interpretations that claimed the purpose was to reduce female sexual desire — such as the Egyptian fetwa mentioned in Chapter 2 that said "We . . . sanction it in view of its effect on attenuating the sexual desire in women" — were simply wrong. Since the "proper sunna" (as she called it) is similar to experimental surgeries to increase clitoral stimulation for anorgasmic women, which she had read about in American medical journals, she came to believe that it is the enhancement of female sexuality rather than its suppression that was the original goal. Since all sex for Muslims should be within the bonds of marriage, there would logically be no reason to reduce either women's or men's pleasure. Indeed, as Kassamali has noted, "Muslim women not only have the right to sexual satisfaction within the context of a marriage but also can initiate sexual intercourse (Sura 4:1)" (1998:43). Therefore, in the view of this physician, not only pharaonic circumcision but also the clitoridectomies currently being called "sunna" would be against Islam, insofar as they might reduce a woman's God-given sexuality.

Because so many people in the rural areas where she hopes to do some community health work are strongly opposed to giving up female circumcision altogether, as the current Sudan Ministry of Health policy advocates, this physician is considering asking people to do the "proper sunna" in preference to the clitoridectomies if they are willing to give up pharaonic circumcision. Yet she worries that people might misunderstand and perform clitoridectomies, which she fears might harm the sexual desires of women for their husbands. If that were the case, she

[5] She cited an early Islamic text by Ibn Al-Qayyim Al-Joziya entitled *Tuhfat al Modud li Akham al-Moulud* (Gems of the Prophet Regarding Regulations of Birth [and the Newborn]).

believes strongly that she is enjoined both by Islam and by medical values to "do no harm," and she would in that case have to discourage all circumcisions.

In her research in a rural area east of the Blue Nile, this physician has encountered strong resistance in most communities to the idea of modifying female circumcision at all; she believes the current Ministry of Health policy will therefore fall on deaf ears, which is why she thinks it is realistic to consider an alternative approach. When I last spoke with her she had discussed these ideas with a surgeon to get help with developing information on the types of operations she recommended, but she had not decided when or how to move forward with her interpretation.

Sudanese Women Professors and Teachers

Finally, one of the most important categories of change agent is the dedicated women who have become involved in women's studies, development studies, and education in universities as well as at other levels. These dynamic women leaders have sometimes faced tremendous social obstacles but have managed to contribute their research, teaching, and social activism to improving the situation of women and girls. A woman like Belghis Bedri stands out as an example of someone who has contributed to social change, including circumcision change, by focusing on the development of the younger generations of women.

Belghis Bedri is one of a family of educators who are descendants of the much-respected Shaykh Babiker Bedri (1861–1954), who is considered the father of girls' education for his good-hearted and spirited support of providing educational opportunities for girls. The Bedri family is at the heart of the Ahfad University for Women located in Omdurman, across the Nile from Khartoum. As a private university, they have been able to work around some of the vicissitudes of Sudanese politics, utilize private and international sources of funds, and join with other institutions to achieve the goals of first-class education for girls at a reasonable cost based on pride in and service to Sudanese society.

Although Belghis Bedri was on the faculty of the University of Khartoum (I first knew her there in the 1970s, but she has since taken early retirement), she was also devoted to the development of programs at Ahfad of which she was justly proud. The Ahfad approach has been to try to find practical ways to help women through higher education, research, and outreach. Ahfad faculty were early advocates of what American universities call "service learning." All Ahfad students must participate in research and service activities in communities, and students are encouraged to publish findings of their research and to attempt to implement recommendations in projects. This keeps the students focused on social issues, so that even if they come from elite families, they can develop a social conscience to guide them into service.

Focusing on women's roles without conflicting with the Islamist government has at times presented a difficult challenge, but by emphasizing education, health careers, income-generating activities, and environmentally sound practices, Belghis Bedri and others have chosen to focus on practical issues that will help women get by in hard times while also raising their awareness of issues like female circumcision. Amazingly, despite economic hardship and political turmoil, the staff and students of Ahfad have continued for many years to publish the *Ahfad Journal*, which focuses on women's issues and features scholarly articles by faculty and students. This university is a powerful engine for change for women in Sudan, and although it is not targeted at a single issue, the topic of female circumcision can be very effectively addressed in the context of addressing the breadth of problems faced by women and their families.

Following the 1979 Khartoum conference, Ahfad University held a symposium that discussed the idea of undertaking a campaign to eliminate female genital mutilations in Sudan. A voluntary association called the Babiker Bedri Scientific Association for Women's Studies was formed, with circumcision reform as one of its major objectives. In coordination with the Ministry of Health, the organization sponsored workshops in 1981 that were well attended by leaders from across the spectrum of society, thanks to the superb organizing abilities of the Ahfad teachers and students. The discussion of the proposed campaign included public declarations of commitment to abolition by numerous educated women, which led many others to pledge support for the efforts; the production of many educational materials and organized efforts ensued (Sanderson 1982).

These educators clearly see that efforts to change require listening to the real problems women face. Thus, in the BBSAWS magazines, women get tips on economic efficiencies and self-sufficiency much needed in hard economic times, along with health education.

Social Movements for Change

In the past two decades, organized efforts for change have accelerated dramatically as international and nongovernmental organizations have become involved and as African women have moved into leadership positions in speaking out about female genital cutting. International organizations such as the Inter-African Committee have taken a lead role in conducting public health education by organizing discussion groups in towns and villages. The World Health Organization has taken on the anticircumcision work, as has the United States Agency for International

Development. It is also being addressed in human rights conventions (see Chapter 8). Can such a message be carried forward effectively, so that female circumcision might actually be eradicated soon?

Taking Risks

It has been my contention that without greater attention to analysis of the social conditions that act as barriers to parents taking the risk of leaving their daughters uncircumcised, change will not be rapid. No matter how clever the public health education message on the hazards of female circumcision or how authoritative the religious source that says it is unnecessary, parents know it is necessary if it is the prerequisite for their daughter's marriageability and long-term security. Although it is desirable for medical and public health experts to step forward to take a lead in reform, many parents are well aware of the medical risks and accept them, even if reluctantly. The religious authorities could speak unequivocally, however, and perhaps place this issue higher on their social agendas. But even when both medical and religious objections are voiced, it may not be a sufficient reason for parents to take the risk of not circumcising their daughters.

To counter that social risk, there are a number of possible issues for policymakers and change agents to address. One is the dependency of women. Better educational opportunities and employment opportunities would allow young women and their families to see delayed marriage as something other than a disaster. Daughters might even be encouraged more in their education and careers, knowing that although marriage may be desirable, failure to marry will not result in penury and dependence on male relatives.

This is indeed a part of the change process that I have observed in Sudan. The teacher Suad and Professor Belghis are not the only educated Sudanese women who are, as a result of their awareness, literacy, and cosmopolitan outlook, better able to state confidently that female circumcision can be left behind, that it is both dangerous and not Islamic. Such women can also be confident that they will be able to control the decision on the circumcision of their daughters and see that their daughters get the educational opportunities to be self-reliant.

But even educated and confident women cannot be certain their uncircumcised daughters will be marriageable. If the young men in the community are committed to marrying infibulated brides, a daughter's . education may preserve her from poverty, but it will not assure her of marriage and children. So there is a risk, one that is lightened if there are social and familial ties to progressive families where men prefer sunna or no circumcision. Although some of the most cosmopolitan educated men and women denied that very many people were doing female circumcision anymore and said it was dying out, the more common view was that the practices were still deeply entrenched, and some told me, "We will never give it up."

But it is true that a few young men are beginning to state preferences for uninfibulated brides, offering a glimmer of hope. One educated young man I knew in Khartoum told me he had insisted that the family not infibulate his sister, and he swore he would not marry an infibulated woman, even his cousin. But will he or others like him actually refuse to marry the proposed cousin who is infibulated or the young woman who has caught his eye? And can young men effectively prevent their sisters' circumcisions? How do families cope with the risk that there may not be men like this for their daughters to marry?

Footbinding

Gerry Mackie has offered a stimulating exploration of strategies for coping with risk in changing social practices in his comparison of the process of ending footbinding in China and what it would take to end infibulation in Africa (1996). Both practices, as Mackie notes, are or were widespread, persistent over several centuries (about ten centuries for footbinding, much longer for female genital cutting, and probably at least twenty centuries for infibulation), and are related to controlling the sexual access to females and ensuring their virginity and faithfulness. Both practices are associated with higher status but diffused widely, and certain ethnic groups do not practice them. Both are performed by women on young girls. "Both are said to properly exaggerate the complementarity of the sexes and both are claimed to make intercourse more pleasurable for the male" (Mackie 1996:1000).

Footbinding, the painful crippling of a girl's feet by bending and binding to prevent their proper growth between the ages of about six and eleven, was carried out by Chinese mothers seeking to assure their daughters' marriageability. "A mother can't love both her daughter and her daughter's feet at the same time" (Mackie 1996:1000) was a saying that a Sudanese mother might well understand if applied to the genitalia.

Mackie offers a fascinating account of the process of change that led to wholesale abandonment of footbinding in a single generation. An effort to abolish it in 1665 had no effect, and two centuries later another edict (1847) failed to bring any change. But with missionary activities in the 1870s, antifootbinding societies began to be founded for converts. Western women also founded a Natural Foot Society in 1895 to promote education on the disadvantages among the "non-Christian elite." According to Mackie, "The societies propagandized the disadvantages of footbinding in Chinese cultural terms, promoted pledge associations, and subtly conveyed international disapproval of the custom. By 1908, leading Chinese public opinion was opposed to footbinding, and the leadership of the Natural Foot Society was transferred to a committee of Chinese women" (Mackie 1996:1001).

The pledge society idea could work in Africa. In China it meant that groups pledged not to bind their daughters or let their sons marry brides whose feet had been bound. Pledges for other purposes are common in Africa; for example, there are rotating credit associations where members must be trusted to set aside the payment each month, no matter how difficult.

Just as groups of Sudanese fathers from single villages met at their mosque and agreed to minimal bridewealth payments for any marriages of their daughters to their sons as a way to counteract inflation and the resultant excessively delayed marriages, it should be possible for some members of a community to take a pledge regarding female circumcision. The teachers, health care workers, and religious leaders, for example, could pledge not to infibulate their daughters or allow their sons to marry infibulated brides. In Abdal Galil, for example, the greater openness of people like Suad the teacher who prefer minimal circumcision and of community members affected by medical assistant Jubara's lectures bodes well.

It would be particularly important to make this a women's pledge because the circumcisions are most often under women's control, and at least for the areas that I am most familiar with, mothers have significant roles in the choice of marital partners for their offspring. Fathers would also need to speak out and share the pledge, to enforce confidence that the men — despite the belief that it is men who want female circumcision to continue — are in support of this change.

Thus, despite the spread of female circumcision and its tenacity, there is no reason to conclude that it cannot change rapidly in the coming years, just as the practice of footbinding waned dramatically. According to Mackie one conservative rural area "went from 99 percent bound in 1889 to 94 percent bound in 1899 to zero bound in 1919" (1996:1001).

Such rapid change in China took effort, and it was preceded by some decades of discussion and organizing and international activity. With respect to infibulation in Africa, the conditions are ripe. The international activism, the efforts at culturally appropriate approaches, and the emergence of, and a degree of support for, indigenous leaders of the movement make this an excellent time for rapid change to occur, if the additional resources can be mobilized. Indeed, the World Health Organization, UNICEF, and the United Nations Population Fund have announced a joint plan to "significantly curb female genital mutilation over

the next decade and completely eliminate the practice within three generations" (Reaves 1997). The idea of pledge societies deserves the efforts
of change agents.

Mackie points out Boddy's observation of a shift in marriage preferences in the northern Sudanese village where she worked. Some of
the younger women who had been excised rather than infibulated had
married before their older infibulated sisters, suggesting "the local marriage convention had shifted from infibulation to excision around 1969"
(Mackie 1996:1014). An interesting problem is embedded in this observation, one that should not be overlooked. Where there is infibulation,
the result of a process of change might be to modify, rather than eliminate, female genital cutting. To mobilize the Islamic religious arguments
against infibulation can easily result in advocacy for sunna, rather than
total eradication of all forms. Certainly it would be easier to mobilize
Sudanese families for that change than to reject all forms immediately.
While such a change would constitute a definite improvement in the
health of women and girls, it might result, however, in even stronger
belief in the Islamic rightness of the remaining form.

Alternative Rites

Earlier I noted that even where circumcision continues, as in Abdal Galil,
the celebration of it has lessened. Whether that indicates a small decline
in the importance of the event or is merely the result of Sudan's severe
economic problems cannot be stated definitively, but it is probably both.
Even wealthy families, I was told, have curtailed the celebrations. If the
practice remains unchanged, reduction in celebrations offers only the
hope that the symbolic role is in the process of change and might in a few
years no longer hold its power.

An extremely positive development in the last few years has been even
more explicit changes in the way circumcision is celebrated in several
areas where activists have been at work. Recognizing that circumcision is
a rite of passage in many of the places where it is practiced, reformers
have begun to introduce alternative ways to mark these important life
transitions without the usual genital cutting. One good example comes
from Kenya, where rural families have been adopting an alternative rite
to circumcision over the last few years that is known as "Circumcision
Through Words" (*Ntanira na Mugambo*). As described by Malik Stan
Reaves (1997), groups of families have participated in bringing together
their daughters of an appropriate age to spend a week in seclusion learning their traditions concerning women's roles as adults and as future
parents, as well as being offered messages on personal health and hygiene, reproductive issues, communications skills, self-esteem, and deal-

ing with peer pressure. At the end of the week of seclusion, a community celebration of feasting, singing, and dancing affirms the girls' transition to their new status.

North American influence may be detected in the list of messages being taught—self-esteem, dealing with peer pressure, et cetera. Indeed, a nongovernmental international organization for women's and children's health based in Seattle called the Program for Appropriate Technology in Health provided technical facilitation and cooperated closely with the Kenyan national women's group, Maendeleo ya Wanawake Organization, in developing the program.

Such approaches recognize that female circumcision has deep cultural significance and if that significance can be preserved while the actual cutting is discontinued, there is strong hope that change can be rapid. Indeed, Reaves quotes the chair of the Maendeleo ya Wanawake Organization, Zipporah Kittonysaid, as saying she was "overjoyed" to see the positive response and believes it was a critical achievement toward the eradication of female circumcision (Reaves 1997). This project serves as an excellent example of combining local initiative, international expertise, preparatory research and community discussion, and private foundation support (including the Moriah Fund, Ford, Population Action International/Wallace Global Fund, and Save the Children–Canada) to accomplish a culturally sensitive alternative to female circumcision as a complement to other efforts to raise public awareness of the dangers.

Public Health Training

Poster campaigns, teachers on lecture tours, training for health workers, and public health announcements in the media have all been used at various times and places to spread the word on the dangers of female genital cutting. The movement has developed well in the past two decades, with more respectful and effective teaching tools and methods available.

The Inter-African Committee, for example, has developed a technique that involves sending a woman health worker into a marketplace where women are found to strike up a discussion. She asks questions like "What do you think, is female circumcision a good tradition?" Rather than preaching, she listens to what they have to say, what their beliefs are. "Are you aware of the hazards?" leads to a discussion of the short- and long-term complications. She encourages the women to bring up their beliefs and then discusses them respectfully. For example, the erroneous belief that if the clitoris touches the baby's head at birth the baby will die, was brought up in one such discussion filmed by the Inter-African Committee for its film *Female Circumcision: Beliefs and Misbeliefs* (1992), and the health worker explained that that was not possible. She also discussed potentially harmful traditional practices such as nutritional taboos and early marriages, encouraging the women to offer opinions and discuss their ideas with each other.

The work of national women's organizations in the countries affiliated with the Inter-African Committee appears to be having an effect through the facilitation of discussions, offering formal classes with anatomical teaching aids, and organizing in villages willing to undergo friendly "inspections" of their baby girls, to show the success of the message. In each participating country, a national committee is doing such work. The Sudan National Committee for Traditional Harmful Practices, for example, has many rural branches now, and although its efforts were met with resistance initially, its work is now better received. Rogaia Abusharaf has noted that the Sudan National Committee consistently avoids making female circumcision a separate issue and always discusses it as one among several reproductive health issues. By beginning with a discussion of child spacing, contraceptive use, and maternal and child health, the committee representatives find that people are better prepared to then consider the anticircumcision message (Abusharaf 1999).

Dr. T. A. Baasher, regional advisor on mental health for the World Health Organization, noted in 1977: "It is now obvious that the rate of progress in combating this practice is slow. . . . It is clear that a good 'push' is needed before certain communities are finally convinced to give it up" (quoted in Hosken 1978:151).

He was right. It has taken some time for momentum to build and strong leadership to arise. The "push" is now on.

Chapter 8
Involvement

It is unacceptable that the international community remain passive in the name of a distorted vision of multiculturalism. Human behaviours and cultural values, however senseless or destructive they may appear from the personal and cultural standpoint of others, have meaning and fulfil a function for those who practise them. However, culture is not static but it is in constant flux, adapting and reforming. People will change their behaviour when they understand the hazards and indignity of harmful practices and when they realize that it is possible to give up harmful practices without giving up meaningful aspects of their culture.
— Joint statement by the World Health Organization, UN Children's Fund (UNICEF), and UN Population Fund, February 1996

We live in a world of astonishing horrors juxtaposed with brilliant achievements. At the dawn of the new millennium, the citizens of planet Earth face some of the most horrible atrocities of which our species is capable, while many live in greater health, comfort, and security than our ancestors could have imagined. Our species has a long and sordid history of horrors of war, torture, economic exploitation, slavery, and callous disregard for the well-being of other people. We have failed to organize the world's resources to meet the basic human needs for nourishing food, clean water, and secure shelter, while simultaneously destroying the traditional means to solve survival problems by causing pollution, deforestation, overpopulation, and displacement. We see the persistence of patterns of behavior and practices that are harmful: domestic violence, drug abuse, and harmful traditional practices like female circumcision.

Our saving grace is our capability for the opposite. Societies have taken risks to bring peace. Struggles for basic human needs have sometimes brought progress, great or minimal. In the past century there have been tremendous improvements in human rights protection and recognition of rules of human decency in the conduct of conflict, economic relations, and social life. The Geneva Conventions, the Universal Declaration of Human Rights, the Convention on the Elimination of All Forms of Discrimination Against Women (CEDAW) — these are endorsed by scores of countries that are party to the agreements. More refined and progressive declarations have come out of successive international conferences such as the Vienna Conference of 1993 and the Fourth World Conference on Women in Beijing in 1995 (and its precursors).

And yet it seems that weekly we learn of new and more troubling actions against our fellow humans. Just in the late twentieth century we have seen mass rape and ethnic cleansing in Bosnia in 1992, forced evacuation for ethnic cleansing in Kosovo in 1999, civil war and enslavement in Sudan in the 1990s, genocide in Rwanda in 1994, terrorist attacks and bombings in places like Oklahoma City and Nairobi, assassinations, detention, kidnapping, and disappearances. Some events are the work of states, while others are out of the control of governments. While international political pressure can be brought on government-sponsored horrors, any potential action is often inhibited or restrained by other political and strategic factors — domestic political considerations, trade relationships, lack of awareness, and inadequate social and political analysis or intelligence.

Even those crises that seem "natural" have a degree of human culpability in their causes and handling. During the 1970s a drought that lasted for a few years devastated several countries in West Africa, causing crop failures, herd decimation, famine, and wholesale population dislocation. But the degree of devastation was the result of not just the lack of rainfall, but also the ways in which human agency had structured economic and social changes that eliminated the traditional provisioning and adaptation strategies that otherwise would have allowed the population to get through such periodic droughts (Watts 1983; Franke and Chasin 1980). The famine and economic devastation received almost no large scale media coverage in the United States. What might have stimulated human sympathies and mobilized earlier actions was presumably not judged to be of sufficient interest to more than a few readers. It was several years into the devastation before reporting and photographs were widely seen. The Ethiopian famine somewhat later did receive visual coverage and captured the sympathy needed to mobilize relief efforts on a larger scale.

Human Rights for Women

It is in this context that the struggle for human rights for women is taking place. "Human rights" are most commonly conceived as defending people against the actions of oppressive governments that forcefully suppress civil and political rights of citizens. Now the human rights movement has increasingly asserted that what have been thought of as "women's issues" ought to come under the same urgent agenda, even though many of the contemporary tragedies and atrocities affecting women are not caused by sovereign states and their policies but by groups and individuals. The cases of bride burning in India, made to look like accidents but usually directed at a woman's family for failing to complete a dowry payment, are one such example. While it is not a government that is carrying out these atrocities, the government's failure to provide effective deterrence and prosecute cases has been cause for protests by Indian feminist organizations.

Numerous atrocities against women fall into this category—criminal or other illegal activities that are difficult to predict or control. A 1999 article in *The Sowetan* (South Africa) reported the statement by the executive director of the United Nations AIDS organization, Peter Piot, that sexual violence has been a significant factor in the spread of AIDS to women and girls in South Africa. An estimated "9 out of 10 new HIV infections" are the "result of coerced sexual relations," according to the executive director of the UN Development Program, James Gustave Speth (1999). Rape, marital rape, trafficking in women, rapes relating to war crimes, "catch and rape" gangs of roving young men reported in South Africa, some of whom have HIV infections—the situation is truly horrific. In many countries, displaced war orphans and children of the poor are often forced into prostitution, where they are exposed to many risks to their safety and health, including AIDS, nutritional deprivation, and violence.

There are sulfuric acid attacks reported on girls and women in Bangladesh; the number is estimated to be approximately two hundred per year, most on girls under ten but many on girls in their teens. These attacks result in horrifyingly painful mutilations. Perpetrators commit these crimes as revenge for refusal of marriage, for dowry disputes, and because of domestic fights. The government passed legislation in 1995 authorizing the death penalty for these crimes, but activists note that police have not usually taken the reports seriously or have talked victims out of filing complaints (Sisterhood Is Global Institute 1999).

Particularly pernicious are social and economic restrictions placed on women that are claimed to be "justified" by divine will, something difficult to contest on the basis of human justice or international treaties. In Afghanistan, women have been confined by Taliban policies and prevented from enjoying freedom of movement; they have been denied education and prevented from taking advantage of economic opportunities outside the home.

Aggravated violence against women, as many more examples could attest, is rampant in our world, at home and abroad. Even in heavily policed societies with many prisons, like the United States, high rates of domestic violence, rape, kidnapping, and murders of women, young men, and children persist.

In this picture, where does the painful and unnecessary cutting and mutilation of girls and women fit? Female circumcision, too, provokes horrified revulsion in the international gaze. But because it is based on complex causality and done by loving parents in a context of celebration often with little knowledge of or ability to choose alternatives, female genital cutting is not commensurate with angry men throwing sulfuric acid on young girls. It is not similar at all to practices during periods of terror to force ethnic cleansing: rape, breast amputations and other mutilations, and torture directed at engendering ethnic hatred and fear to make people flee their homelands.

Female circumcision is not intended to hurt. It does not make one into a refugee shivering in a cold, open space in the rain with no government willing to take you in. It does not cause one to be pregnant with an enemy's child. It does not leave a child with nightmares of seeing her parents beheaded or her mother gang raped.

But good intentions do not make it harmless. From the experience of many young girls, female circumcision is a violent and frightening act. Yet we must approach the problem of female genital cutting in the larger, dismal context of the many terrible contemporary situations of abuses of human rights.

I see female genital cutting as connected to another, more basic form of "violence" embedded in the disparities of human well-being on the planet. Much unnecessary suffering and death is based on powerlessness and the inability to provide the means for health and survival. The world's governments and we as human actors have not succeeded in providing adequate economic opportunities or meeting health needs. There are many and disparate explanations for the gross inequality and human suffering: everything from the dynamics of capitalism to the work of the devil.

Are we who are not starving guilty of this "violence" because we have not effectively ameliorated the effects of poverty in Third World countries and at home? Most of us in the West have not understood the interconnections of our lives and those of impoverished people. Our failure thus far to figure it out or to arrive at a concerted direction for solving the problems is regrettable, though not surprising. But it is imperative that we become better informed. If we empathize with the young girls and women who are experiencing pain or harm from female genital alteration, that may be a first step toward developing greater understanding and empathy with the whole of their lives and struggles.

The means for working to ameliorate social problems have always been elusive. Is the answer socialism? Abolition of laziness? Should we let the market take full control of the world economy? Should we all adopt Islam? Or do Christian values need to be followed? Would things be better if women were in charge? If everyone immediately practiced birth control and limited childbearing to two per woman, would our descendants be able to live at peace and have enough food and security for all a century from now? Which is more important, individual rights or obedience to God? What will enable survival on the planet?

With questions like these swirling in powerful, sometimes destructive and depressing tornadoes of human thought and action, it is no wonder people are tempted to turn their consciousness toward escapist pursuits, to pretend all the problems are "over there" and perpetrated by "the other," or to explain the persistence of poverty by blaming its victims for creating their own problems. Even among social scientists who focus their energies on such things, our theories and beliefs lead us to varying conclusions about how to proceed.

For those of us who wish the world were different, wish each family had the opportunity to meet its basic needs, expect human decency to prevail, want conflicts to be settled through negotiation rather than bombing, expect prison guards not to rape prisoners—is there a reasonable approach that allows us not to be made insane by the sheer magnitude of it all? If one wishes to contribute to developing and realizing the right to bodily integrity for young girls, what might work?

Taking Action

Commenting on female circumcision, Jean Comaroff was quoted, "To us it looks barbaric. . . . Westerners are quick to be pejorative. But by and large, women in nations where this is done are not in revolt against this" (Joseph 1992:62). That situation could lead one to think urgent outside interference is necessary. But I discourage the idea that nothing will change without meddling by "enlightened" foreigners, not only because there are effective indigenous leaders working on the problem, but also because the track record for social change efforts instigated by outsiders has not always been encouraging.

But to some, this attitude is unduly cautious. It is as if one has gone too far in the direction of cultural relativism and shown an unwillingness to "draw the line" when it comes to female circumcision (Gordon 1991). Ernest Gellner, censuring extreme cultural relativism, upbraided Clifford Geertz for encouraging the " 'metatwaddle' of a fashionable relativism: the idea that every culture's practices, from child sacrifice to clitoridectomy to mutilation for thieves, must get equal respect" (quoted in

Berreby 1995:46). Geertz responded: "Look, I think clitoridectomy is a horrible business. But what are we going to do? Invade the Horn of Africa and arrest everybody? If you're serious about addressing this, you ask people there about the practice and you listen to them. You listen to women from there who justify the practice. [If] you want to change things, you don't start by proclaiming that you possess the truth. That's not very helpful" (Berreby 1995:46).

Precisely. Talking, listening, and writing about people's experiences are important contributions to change, helping to refine the approach, to avoid pious pronouncements, and instead to offer some form of meaningful assistance to indigenous change efforts. How can that be achieved, short of seeming to interfere inappropriately?

Unwelcome Interference and Ineffective Interference

Agitation for change to deeply held beliefs and for modification or elimination of practices that define or reinforce important elements of identity is sure to encounter obstacles, not only from those who defend the practices, but also from those who have a different analysis of when and how to approach the issue and what the priorities should be. This explains the backlash reaction this issue has often provoked. At the Copenhagen Conference in 1980, the anger of African women toward European and North American women who pressed for the elimination of female circumcision flared. The message the African women conveyed, in essence, was that the matter of changing or ending genital cutting should be in the control of those affected, not outsiders passing judgment. Illuminating the gulf between viewpoints, Angela Gilliam characterized that 1980 debate in Copenhagen as a division between those who believe "the major struggle for women is increasing their access to, and control over, the world's *resources* and those who believe that the main issue is access to, and control over, *orgasms*" (emphasis added, 1991:217).

I witnessed a similar exchange at the Sisterhood Is Global Institute's 1994 conference on Women's Human Rights in the Muslim World. One presenter, a professor who had immigrated to the United States from Lebanon, said she had "found family" within the American feminist movement in the 1960s and valued their sisterly support during the bombing of Beirut in the early 1980s. But she vehemently denounced the way "white Western feminists" have defined Third World problems. She accused the "neo-feminist movement" of having "become patriarchal" by no longer adequately questioning authority when it comes to international matters. Instead of concern about basic human needs for Third World women, like water supply, economic development, and peace, Western feminists seem more concerned about veils, clitorises, and so on. I recorded her words in my notes, "What good is all this without our *lives?*"

Not only do these Western definitions of priorities seem to the speaker to be off the mark, but also this image of women's rights as being equated with struggles against veils and circumcision has had the effect of "poisoning the well" between Muslim women and Muslim men. "I want to handle them my own way," not according to the agendas of others, she said.

An African woman from the audience, who identified herself as a non-Muslim, commented that "it *is* important to save clitorises and save lives." Others agreed. The presenter's response was to say that outsiders should stay "off our backs. . . . You'll get your chance. We'll tell you how we'd like you to support us."

According to this view, unsolicited interference on issues not at the top of women's agendas is divisive in the women's movement. This view extends Egyptian feminist writer Nawal El Saadawi's criticism of the " 'them' helping 'us' " approach of so many foreign groups concerned about female circumcision: "That kind of help, which they think of as solidarity, is another type of colonialism in disguise. So we must deal with female circumcision ourselves. It is our culture, we understand it, when to fight against it and how, because this is the process of liberation" (1980a).

For some researchers who are from Middle Eastern or African countries, outsiders taking up the issue of female circumcision is offensive because of the lesson it teaches in the West. I once was asked to change a paper title and revise its contents before publication (Gruenbaum 1991) — to make circumcision just one of several health issues covered, rather than the main focus — because the person who was to write an introductory piece to a planned collection of articles on Middle Eastern women's health thought she could not do so if female circumcision was in one of the titles. Even though she did not substantially disagree with my viewpoint, she wanted no part of the tendency in the West to focus on this image of Middle Eastern and African women. In her experience, many people know little about the Middle East except the topics of veils and circumcision. We should be writing about many other topics important to women's health in these regions, she argued, lest unflattering North American and European stereotypes of Arabs, Muslims, and Africans be reinforced and allowed to fuel hostile political and economic policies.

While interference may be unwelcome, I am also concerned about the ineffectiveness of much of the outside interference that has been attempted.[1] For example, Alison Slack notes that one of the main reasons

---

[1] "Involvement" is the more positive conception of this activity, but the word "interference" is used here merely to accentuate how it is perceived by some insiders. "Cultural

that laws or attempts to legislate against female circumcision in Egypt, Kenya, and Sudan have not been effective is that "the laws were the by-products of external pressure and did not reflect the desire of the local people to suppress the tradition" (1988:478).

Thus it is not only respect for cultural difference or rights, but also the desire for effectiveness that demands assessment of the questions: Who owns the problem? Who sets the agenda? Sondra Hale's comment upon her return from the NGO Forum at the Fourth World Conference in Beijing was trenchant. Noting the "international trend (read hysteria) [concerning] what is now ubiquitously referred to as 'Female Genital Mutilation' (FGM)," she reported that it was both a prominent workshop theme and that "most of the workshops were staffed by women from countries where female circumcision is common or prevalent, perhaps sending a message to western feminists that women living in the countries affected by the custom are taking the lead in its eradication and that we might want to mind our own affairs" (1995:5).

In the earlier days of the new international awareness of female genital cutting, dating most dramatically from Fran Hosken's publication of *The Hosken Report: Genital and Sexual Mutilation of Females* (1979; 3d ed. 1982) and *Female Sexual Mutilations: The Facts and Proposals for Action* (1980), it was decidedly outsiders who trumpeted the outrage. Hosken worked to spread awareness further with her self-published periodical *Women's International Network News* (*WIN News*, still publishing at the turn of the millennium) and conference appearances. A professional architect and planner with a devotion to international investigation of the issue of female genital mutilation, Fran Hosken is well known among activists and scholars for her fire and sometimes for her ire. On a personal crusade to eliminate these practices, her publications have regularly lambasted individuals and organizations in the United States and the affected countries that were not putting this issue into an urgent agenda. And over the years she has denounced numerous younger academic writers struggling to do their research on the topic in academically acceptable ways.

But even though professional disagreements and rivalries may occasionally surface, more significant are the dramatic differences in the perspectives of research, the political clout, and the effectiveness of change efforts depending upon who is perceived as a spokesperson: the insider/outsider divide. The backlash reactions at the Copenhagen conference and other venues—which seemed to be a reaffirmation of the right to

---

brokers" who seek roles as authorities who can speak for a group (among whom elite educated immigrants from other regions of the world play a valuable, but also contradictory, role) also use such terminologies, apparently to discourage outsiders from trespassing on a process that should be controlled by insiders.

circumcise girls and women — were probably a necessary step toward establishing African ownership of the issue. In subsequent years, the "Stay out of our business" sort of responses have changed to "We're working on it. Here's what you can do to help."

A large number of African women have taken leadership, removing the issues to a large extent from the accusation of being only a white women's agenda. Those African women with best access to facilities, research assistance, and high profile roles are not usually the rural women or poor women themselves, of course. Indeed, it is far more likely that the African women most heard will be educated, elite women who have migrated to North American or European countries. Some of these may have relatively little firsthand experience with poverty or isolated rural areas of their home countries. Nevertheless, their greater effectiveness in leading the change efforts is unquestionable, and their role in organizations like the Inter-African Committee on Traditional Practices Affecting the Health of Women and Children and other nongovernmental and international organizations is instrumental to the movement to end female circumcision.

The process of change utilizes various approaches, offering a variety of opportunities for involvement.

Tools for Change: Legislation

The enactment of laws prohibiting female circumcision practices has proven in the past to be not very effective at actually stopping the practices because these laws flew in the face of a very important, socially accepted practice. Sudan's legislation has been in place since 1946, when the Ministry of Health under the British colonial control of the Anglo-Egyptian Condominium Government pushed for a law that prohibited infibulation but stated, "It is not an offense against this section merely to remove the free and projecting part of the clitoris" (Sudanese Penal Code, quoted in Slack 1988:477; El Dareer 1982:95). The punishment prescribed for midwives was unusually severe in a country with no tradition of criminal punishment of women: up to seven years' imprisonment.

When the law was first enacted, the British-controlled government made some attempts to enforce it, but the efforts failed completely. In 1977, when I visited the town of Rufa'a on the Blue Nile in central Sudan, residents told me about what they called "our Revolution" — the local citizens' response to one attempt at enforcement immediately after the law was enacted in 1946. The police took a midwife into custody for circumcising a girl and put her in the local jail. Outraged at this affront to their customs and abuse of their midwife, an angry crowd of Rufa'a citizens attacked the jail and "tore it to the ground" to free the midwife. Government troops fired on the crowd, and there were injuries.

One of the leaders of this resistance in Rufa'a was the religious leader Mahmoud Mohammed Taha, who is credited with being the first Muslim reformer in Sudan to advocate women's equality in Islam. Although he did not advocate female circumcision as the majority of citizens did, he led opposition to the law based on the conviction that education should come first, before a law was imposed.

Clearly the citizens won — the government seldom again attempted to enforce this law. A law against infibulation could not be enforced where there was deep public opposition because the activity was done in homes, with family consent, outside the purview of law enforcement by troops commanded by a foreign power (Slack 1988:478), so the practice continued as before. The fact that the Sudanese law did allow sunna circumcision also left people with an easy response to any potential accusation: whatever type of cutting was done, if people claimed it was sunna, it would have to be allowed. In my research, health workers and other educated people were aware of the law, but they ignored it because there was no enforcement.

In other countries in which externally inspired laws or government policies against female circumcision were initiated, they proved similarly unenforceable. In Kenya there were attempts at legal prohibition as early as 1906 (under the influence of Church of Scotland missionaries and the British colonial government), but again these laws were difficult to enforce (Slack 1988:477). In the 1920s, the missionaries campaigned with "native councils" of the Gikuyu to get them to pass resolutions to outlaw female circumcision, including clitoridectomy, or at least to reduce the severity, and to ensure more hygienic conditions and regulation of midwives, trying thereby to use tribal enforcement procedures to make severe forms illegal. But the tribal councils balked, with the opposition drawing on Gikuyu opposition to other British policies such as the land and population control policies that were allowing the settler colonies to flourish at the expense of the indigenous people. Even the Christian Gikuyu split over whether to preserve clitoridectomy and polygyny, some forming separate churches (Davison 1989:21–23, Browne 1991).

Later Kenyan governments, after independence, actually supported female circumcision for a time (e.g., during Kenyatta's presidency) as part of their opposition to British policies. Kenyatta supported the practices as having positive social value as well as being a symbol of national identity. Although Kenyan policies later changed, when President Moi initiated a ban on female circumcision in 1982, these policies still did not result in formal laws against it (Davison 1989:202).

Egypt had the interesting situation that for years many educated people believed there was a law against female circumcision, but researchers were unable to find it. A resolution from the Ministry of Public Health dating to 1959 has therefore been the practical guide, and subsequent controversies over health policies (rather than law) have been the venue for debate. The 1959 policy invoked religious, rather than legal, bases for its determination that total clitoridectomy was prohibited, while partial clitoridectomy was allowed, noting that the Islamic jurists were divided on whether *Khafd* was a duty in Islam (i.e., a sunna) or only a practice considered ennobling (*makrama*, Assaad 1980:5). Policymakers also decreed that only doctors be allowed to perform circumcisions. In 1978 the operation was forbidden to be performed in the health units of the Ministry of Public Health, and traditional midwives were specifically forbidden to perform it (Assaad 1980:5). However, according to ethnographic reports, midwives still continue the practices in Egypt (e.g., Inhorn 1994; Jennings 1995:48; Ahmed 1992:175–76).

In the 1990s further problems arose in Egypt when the practices were disputed by religious leaders. In October 1994, the mufti of Egypt (Muhammad Sayyid Tantawi) took a stand that the Hadith used to justify female circumcision were unreliable and that the Prophet Mohammed's own daughters were evidently not circumcised (Kassamali 1998:43). Days later, however, a religious ruling from Al-Azhar University by Shaykh Gad al-Haq Ali stated that "female circumcision is a part of the legal body of Islam and is a laudable practice that does honor to the women" (quoted in Kassamali, 1998:43). A lawsuit by the Egyptian Organization of Human Rights ensued. In the Ministry of Health, too, there were contradictory policies issued during the 1990s that bounced back and forth the issue of whether the procedures would be allowed in the more hygienic environment of the hospitals and clinics.

Nahid Toubia reviewed the existing laws and policies of countries affected by FGM for a chart in her publication *Female Genital Mutilation: A Call for Global Action* (1993:44).[2] The majority of the thirty-four countries listed (including ten outside Africa) did not have specific legislation addressing female genital cutting; indeed only five (including the United Kingdom and Sweden) had explicit anti-FGM laws, but officials from a significant number of countries consider the existing legislation and case law to be adequate to prosecute female circumcision cases as child abuse, assault, or battery causing bodily harm (Toubia 1993:44). In the United States, the federal government criminalized female genital mutilation in 1998 and expressly prohibited any defense based on beliefs. Ameri-

---

[2] See also the new guide to worldwide laws and policies on female genital mutilation by Toubia and Rahman 2000.

can consulates abroad are required to inform applicants for immigration that female circumcision is not tolerated. Individual states in the United States have begun to enact laws or attach specifications about female circumcision to existing laws on child abuse.

A concerted effort to draw attention to the issue through bringing legal cases might be a route for activists. One problem with this approach, however, is that the people likely to be harmed would be midwives and parents trying to follow their ideas of doing the right thing. A well-funded public health education campaign would be far superior to a punitive approach. California's act is punitive, adding an additional year's punishment to the sentence mandated for child abuse, but it also compels health departments to provide educational services.

Although legislation and case prosecution may well have a place, it is also conceivable that defense attorneys might utilize cultural defenses, unless there has been an effort to establish public commitment to the principles of bodily integrity and the rights of the child. Almost all the countries Toubia surveyed do have official statements and policy against female genital cutting as well as being signatories to international conventions that take positions against the practices (Toubia 1993:44). Although these international conventions do not usually have the force of law, it is an important arena for debate, offering the potential to raise awareness, influence public opinion, and provide additional policy tools for reformers. These international convenants and the embedding of female circumcision in human rights discourse may prove to be more effective than national or local laws as tools for change.

The International Arena

One of my favorite purchases at the NGO Forum at the Fourth World Conference on Women in China in 1995 was a T-shirt being hawked by an earnest and enthusiastic young man from Ethiopia. Depicted on the shirt was a red rosebud, just about to open into full flower, but about to be stopped by a double-edge razor poised just below the bud, ready to slit its stem. "Fight against female genital mutilation!" the shirt declared in English, with a gentler Amharic message: "Female circumcision is harmful: don't do it!" Earlier that day, this man and another male colleague had led a workshop on their public health efforts to end female circumcision in Ethiopia. Evidently schooled in marketing, they handed out ballpoint pens with anticircumcision messages to attendees.

That men are becoming more involved is encouraging, and like other activists against female circumcision, their insider status is a significant factor in their effectiveness. And yet there is a clear role for outsiders in their efforts. Silk-screened at the bottom of the image of the rosebud on the T-shirt appears the logo not only of the national committee involved, but also the logo of "Radda Barnen" ("Save the Children"), a figure with up-stretched arms. An international organization's funds, facilitation, and direct efforts have come together with Ethiopian public health efforts in a powerful model of international collaboration to accomplish a humanitarian goal.

Resolutions, Declarations, and Platforms for Action

Putting words on paper, debating positions, reacting to nuances, and hammering out compromises so that officials representing the governments of large numbers of sovereign countries can agree — this is the process of making international agreements. The degree to which this activity, which has gained much ground in the twentieth century, can produce rapid change is debatable: enforcement of international agreements has never been highly effective. But in spite of the limitations, the efforts to forge such declarations and platforms, the words themselves, and their use by activists and educators in selective legal efforts, can have a tremendous effect on developing consensus and promoting changes in laws, policies, and programs. Declarations are developed in a process of convening regional, national, and international conferences to debate their wording, and the process itself promotes networks and cross-cultural discussions and information sharing that can be valuable to activists.

The major step in the internationalization of the human rights movement was the 1948 Universal Declaration of Human Rights, which was established through United Nations efforts. Despite criticism of its particularly Western and individualist flavor, the Universal Declaration of Human Rights has long served as the foundation for efforts to develop international consensus on what we wish to recognize as the basic rights of humans in the contemporary world. People, it holds, should have security for their person and not be subjected to degrading or cruel treatment. As Amnesty International literature points out, "The traditional interpretation of these rights has generally failed to encompass forms of violence against women such as domestic violence or FGM" (ACT 77/14/1997). Thus as activism by individuals, efforts by nongovernmental organizations, and campaigns by international organizations on the issue of female genital cutting accelerated, it was necessary to pursue more explicit statements against the practices and attempt to generate more concerted efforts by governments.

Violence and discrimination against women are prohibited under the sweeping provisions of the 1979 United Nations Convention on the Elimination of All Forms of Discrimination Against Women, which took effect in 1981 and has now been ratified by 163 countries.[3] In this agreement, commonly known as CEDAW, more assertive statements challenged governments who ratified the document to "take all appropriate measures to modify the social and cultural patterns of conduct of men and women, with a view to achieving the elimination of prejudices and customary and all other practices which are based on the idea of the inferiority or the superiority of either of the sexes or on stereotyped roles for men and women." The United Nations Committee on the Elimination of Discrimination Against Women, drawing recommendations from CEDAW for governments to follow, was even more explicit, calling on the governments that had signed the Convention to undertake effective measures to eliminate FGM, including educational and health care measures.

CEDAW poses a revolutionary challenge, taking on culture as well as law and prodding signatories to initiate programs to change practices of many types, covering everything from equal employment and educational opportunities to the suppression of prostitution and other trafficking in women, from nationality rights to access to health care, including family planning services. The convention requires states to set a minimum age and consent requirement for marriage and mandates equality before the law and women's equal rights to their children.

Yet many of the signatory states signed CEDAW only with "reservations," that is, explicit limitations they intend to impose on the implementation of certain articles or clauses that they consider inconsistent with their religious and cultural traditions or legal structures. For example, a theocratic government might hold that these principles are in some specific areas in contradiction to their religious values, as in the case of countries where shari'a law governs family matters. For some cultures, the term "equal" rights (commonly taken to mean "the same") seem anathema because each sex is viewed as having a different and respected role ordained by God. As we saw in the Beijing Conference in 1995, it was necessary to use words like "equitable" rather than "equal" to allow for that difference. Where careful wording has not resolved a difference, reservations have often been stipulated by a signatory state, and these reservations on key clauses can virtually negate the provisions of the Convention.

There are also complaints that the agreement has "no teeth" even

---

[3] Although President Carter signed the Convention, the United States Congress did not ratify it because of a concern that the federal government would thereby violate the principle of states' rights because CEDAW includes issues normally determined by state laws in the United States. A carefully crafted "reservation" might allow the United States to sign, but at the time of this writing, the political impetus remains to be sufficiently developed. In response, individual U.S. cities such as San Francisco have begun to consider ratification of CEDAW and implementation of its provisions.

where it has been ratified. Indeed, there was much discussion at the Beijing Conference of the need for what has been termed a "strong and effective optional protocol" to CEDAW that would give women the right to complain to the UN's Committee on the Elimination of Discrimination against Women about violations of the Convention by their governments. A draft of such a protocol was prepared by the U.N. Commission on the Status of Women in 1999. That draft, which specifies complaint and inquiry procedures, is still being revised at the time of this writing, but it is seen by many as an essential tool if CEDAW is to effect change. One of the organizations most actively pushing for it is Equality Now (see Appendix).

The word "optional" is significant. Thus far, the provisions of CEDAW have proven easy to get around. So what can it achieve, if governments wish to ignore it? In this respect it is similar to a law that does not have popular consensus, like colonial impositions. Although the treaty should have the force of law, it is up to some jurisdiction to enforce it. But because each government ratifying CEDAW has thereby stated support for the agreement, even if it is not prepared to enforce its provisions, the existence of CEDAW can be useful to activists who want to work on the issues addressed. Some have planned to sue governments to enforce provisions, and it offers a moral cudgel and an educational tool for those who are working to develop women's rights in their countries.

I began to understand the educational value of CEDAW when I attended a session at the NGO Forum in Beijing in 1995. A large room full of women from every continent gathered to discuss the implementation of CEDAW in their countries. Among the stories of frustration about ways in which some governments were ignoring CEDAW's provisions — despite having ratified it — were other stories of how women were taking the agenda to the grassroots and using it to fertilize the growing women's rights movements in their countries.

A woman from Nepal described how village women and girls her group met with did not have any idea what rights they could claim. They were illiterate and had not traveled far from their villages to be influenced by international ideas. So the Nepalese feminists joined with them in making up songs about rights. She described how girls and young women in some of the villages now sing songs with lyrics about rights such as, "I have the right to choose my own husband and decide for myself when to marry." A girl entertaining herself with this song not only strengthens her own confidence in the message, making it less likely she will be forced into early marriage against her will, but she is also spreading the word to others who hear her song or join her in singing. The Nepalese woman who told us the story was pressed to sing this song for us, which she did. It was a simple tune, like a folksong, that could be easily learned and used. The international crowd in the room applauded enthusiastically.

This idea, spreading messages through creative cultural means — songs, entertainment, poster art — clearly has a place in the dissemination of messages against female circumcision practices. Girls' songs are quite popular in Sudan, and women's stories and poetry that allude to strong feelings are popular throughout the Middle East (e.g., Abu-Lughod 1986) and could prove fine vehicles for such messages.

Other International Statements

When consensus can be achieved by representatives of diverse governments, even when the documents do not have the force of a treaty, they can carry moral authority to be wielded by government agencies, nongovernmental organizations, and other activists as they seek grants, solicit donations, and develop programs. Several important and well-publicized international conferences, particularly since CEDAW, have resulted in such useful statements, which seem to have become increasingly explicit about the need to eliminate FGM.

The UN Declaration on the Elimination of Violence Against Women, adopted in 1993, the year of the Vienna Conference on this topic, addressed gender-based violence in both public and private life. This declaration calls upon governments to take measures to prevent and punish violence and to exercise "due diligence" in investigation and prosecution. It explicitly states that they should not avoid their responsibilities in this matter by invoking customs, traditions, or religious considerations, the latter clearly applicable to female genital cutting.

In 1994 the United Nations' International Conference on Population and Development, which was held in Cairo, Egypt, garnered a high level of press coverage focusing especially on reproductive rights and technology issues and the role of the Vatican in these debates. The "Programme of Action" that emanated from the conference included in the section on "the girl child" an explicit statement on FGM: "Governments are urged to prohibit female genital mutilation wherever it exists and to give vigorous support to efforts among non-governmental and community organizations and religious institutions to eliminate such practices" (United Nations 1994: B.4.22, p. 29).

The very title of the conference underscores another key development in international thinking on social issues — the growing recognition of the economic context in which policies and rights are to be pursued. Particularly in the case of "population," in which previous international efforts have been directed at "control" in those Third World countries where high reproductive rates have been the norm, a new perspective has clearly emerged. No longer do you hear of coercive "vasectomy fairs" such as were held in India where uninformed rural men were offered transistor radios in exchange for their reproductive potential with only minimal understanding and consent, though some national governments still pursue rather aggressive birth control policies. But the theme in international literature these days shows clear recognition that the key to population balance is improving women's status, providing adequate health care, including family planning, and ensuring economic development so that people have options.

It is a widely held misconception in the industrial countries that people are poor because they have so many children. Now researchers are arguing that people have so many children because they are poor.

This was certainly my experience in looking at families in Sudan. Without old age security systems and with economic production dependent on family labor, people need many children to provide for their own economic well-being. If, on top of that, the health conditions are so abysmal that you can expect that as many as four out of ten of your children might not survive their first five years of life and that daughters will not have the means to support you in your old age, then you had better have as many children "as God gives you," to use the phrase I so often heard in Sudan. It is rare for child mortality to be that high, particularly where vaccination programs and improved water supply are found. But 40 percent child mortality (i.e., four hundred deaths in the first five years of life per thousand live births) is what our eighty reproductive histories taken in the mid-1970s in southern Sudan revealed. Without reliable demographic studies or vital statistics, these data can only be taken as suggestive, but it is an extraordinarily high rate of loss that rural families face.[4] The infant and child death rates may well be even higher today in some areas of Sudan because of the conditions of civil war and population displacement. In short, poor people in poor countries, dependent on their children's help to contribute to subsistence work now and for old-age support later, often choose to have numerous children for reasons of economic well-being and because they lack other options.

This recognition is important to the struggle against female circumcision as well. Without options and opportunities for economic development, education, and women's empowerment, female subordination

[4] Conducted with a translator, the interviews had to rely on mothers' retrospective recall and highly imprecise age estimates (mothers did not know ages or years of birth or death), and we did not measure events in a single year as demographic studies would require. See Gruenbaum 1990.

persists, and families cannot protect all of the rights their daughters ought to have.

The series of international conferences focusing on women's issues that began with the United Nations Decade for Women have contributed much to the development of international thinking on these issues and have added to the momentum for CEDAW. The series began with the Mexico City conference in 1975 and continued with the Copenhagen conference in 1980 and the Nairobi Conference in 1985. Out of the Nairobi Conference came a document called "Forward-looking Strategies for the Advancement of Women," which was used extensively to guide the development of the programs of the United Nations and its agencies (UNICEF, UNIFEM, etc.) The goal of the framers of the declaration that came out of the Fourth World Conference on Women held in Beijing in 1995 was to take the previous declarations forward into a new stage of action — hence its title "Beijing Declaration and Platform for Action." Preparatory conferences were held in home countries, where proposals were developed. The preliminary document that came out of Sudan called for the "eradication of harmful traditional practices that affect girls' and women's health" (Sudanese Women NGO Preparatory Committee 1995:11). The Beijing Platform for Action also contains clear language condemning FGM and urging member nations of the UN to take measures to prevent this form of violence against females.

Similarly, several other conventions and declarations can be invoked to limit any nation's use of "culture" as an excuse not to address female genital cutting: the UN Convention on the Rights of the Child, the UN Declaration on the Elimination of All Forms of Intolerance and of Discrimination Based on Religion or Belief, and the International Covenant on Economic, Social, and Cultural Rights. In the region most affected, the Organization of African Unity adopted the African Charter on the Rights and Welfare of the Child (1990), which is intended to protect the welfare and health of children and eliminate discriminatory practices based on sex. It contains the extraordinary statement that "any custom, tradition, cultural or religious practice that is inconsistent with the rights, duties and obligations contained in the present Charter shall . . . be null and void" (quoted in Amnesty International, ACT 77/14/97). Nullifying cultural practices sounds highly oppressive and normally would not be undertaken by countries of a region that for centuries had the cultural will of outsiders imposed upon it. This statement demonstrates that FGM is increasingly regarded as sufficiently noxious not to merit the protections of cultural self-determination traditionally accorded countries and communities in the area.

But lest I sound too enthusiastic about these agreements, I must point out that there remain many obstacles to implementing women's rights, including spreading awareness about such agreements. Human rights pronouncements hold limited applicability in a country where there is pervasive poverty, illiteracy, and hunger, where there are situations of conflict, and where leaders believe that "development comes first." These leaders may argue that they cannot hope to implement improvements in health care or girls' education if there is insufficient economic production to meet the population's basic needs. As Alison Slack has noted, "Can the government of a country in which female circumcision is practiced be expected to wage a campaign against this practice when the majority of the people within the country are struggling merely to feed their families and find work?" (1988:475). Indeed, individual African women usually do not have this matter at the top of their list of urgent priorities and would question government or NGO policies that neglect the community's need for clean water and adequate economic opportunities to prevent their children from dying.

Asylum Cases

As the rhetoric of women's human rights in the international arena has received greater attention and become more explicit about eliminating mutilating practices, individuals have been able to argue that these principles should be applied to cases of political asylum. Claims for political asylum to avoid coercive female circumcision are still few in number, but they have received much attention. In one case reported in the *Washington Post*, a Nigerian woman who had come to the United States with her husband on a student visa stayed on for several years after his death because she feared that her eleven-year-old daughter would be circumcised if they returned. Not wanting the daughter, an American citizen, to be forced to undergo the "barbaric custom" that she herself had experienced as a child, she submitted an asylum petition to the U.S. Immigration and Naturalization Service so she would not be forced to return and "become property" of her late husband's family. Similar cases have been successful in Canada, Australia, Sweden, and other countries.

One of the more well-known cases was Fauziya Kassindja, from Togo, who was imprisoned in the United States for some time before resources were mobilized to press her case for political asylum. It was necessary to overcome an initial ruling that her story was "not credible" before she eventually won asylum status in 1996 (see the review of her book with Layli Miller Bashir, Shapiro 1998:57). Kassindja, like Aminata Diop from Mali who had earlier fled to France (Joseph 1992:62), left her family and home to resist circumcision that was to be forced on her prior to a marriage arranged by her family. Diop had found support from French feminists in her efforts to be granted asylum, and Kassindja also eventually received women's support.

The use of asylum provisions for cultural, rather than strictly political, risks is a remarkable development, giving new stature to the human rights of women and children to be protected from the effects of their social and economic disempowerment. The basis for such claims to asylum is the 1951 UN Refugee Convention, on the grounds that these women would be at risk of grievous harm in the form of FGM if they were to return home. The French case was accepted on the basis of classifying FGM as persecution, and the Australian government's 1996 publication *Guidelines on Gender Issues of Decisions Makers* came to a similar position (Amnesty International, ACT 77/13/97).

Only those who are privileged enough to be in one of the industrial countries, perhaps on a student visa or other visa, and to be able to pay for or obtain through activists some legal services will be in a position to bring such cases to court. But as precedent is established, this could become a new route to immigration for larger numbers. Amnesty International noted that the size of the persecuted group of which one is a member is irrelevant to the legal determinations (Amnesty International, ACT 77/13/97), but if a large number of cases began to be seen one could anticipate changes in the interpretations of the Refugee Convention. Meanwhile, asylum cases offer a new arena for active involvement in preventing FGM and for raising public awareness of the issue.

What Can Be Done? Organizations and Activities

Human rights and declarations about them are only as valuable as their implementation. Implementation requires the spread of information and the development of resources, organizations, and programs that will be able to accomplish something concrete. For those who decide that they want to play a role in social change on these issues, there are numerous opportunities to be involved, some demanding career commitments, others smaller tasks.

Making oneself a resource to answer the questions of others is valuable. Many students, for example, have written term papers or done other sorts of class projects (reporting on web sites, conducting interviews, taking surveys on attitudes, etc.) that enrich their knowledge of the practices and their contexts, the change efforts, and the experiences of women who have been circumcised. This enhances their sophistication in analyzing the phenomenon and makes them available as resources to their social networks, co-workers, and family. A better informed public can offer a more sympathetic response.

Nongovernmental organizations (NGOs) often need volunteers, interns, or writers to help with their work. There are several with long-standing interest in this issue: RAINBO (Research Action Information Network for Bodily Integrity of Women), Equality Now (New York), Amnesty International's program on women (branches in several countries), Minority Rights Group, and Forward International (London) (see the Appendix). The Inter-African Committee on Traditional Practices Affecting the Health of Women and Children, based in Geneva, Switzerland, with affiliates in the majority of affected African countries, is doing important direct activism, including conferences, action platforms, educational campaigns, and media projects (e.g., Inter-African Committee 1987, 1992). Population Action International is based in Washington, D.C. Several activist and professional organizations have useful web sites for data, advice on activities and approaches, and discussion. A couple of examples are those of the American Academy of Pediatrics (www.aap.org/policy/re9749.html) and RAINBO, but search engines do well with "female circumcision" and "female genital mutilation."

There are also local groups and individuals working with immigrant women, particularly in cities with large immigrant populations such as Los Angeles, New York, Seattle, Toronto, and London. One such activist, a California nurse named Mimi Ramsey who is an immigrant from Ethiopia, approaches other immigrants and spends time discussing the issue with them, offering them information about the medical advice against female circumcision and pressing them to join her in trying to end it. Catherine Hogan, founder of the Washington Metropolitan Alliance Against Ritualistic FGM, argues that we should "warn [immigrant] families that we consider this child abuse. . . . It's a form of reverse racism not to protect these girls from barbarous practices that rob them for a lifetime of their God-given right to an intact body" (quoted in Burstyn 1995:30).

Legislative aides have worked with Congress and some state legislatures to put together bills to outlaw female circumcision in the United States. In the case of California, anticircumcision activist Mimi Ramsey played a key role in pressing legislators for action. Other such work by volunteers, interns, or staff to prepare legislation and ordinances for other jurisdictions might be welcomed by legislators. Also, once enacted, such legislation requires implementation of programs in local areas, such as the educational programs against female circumcision mandated for local public health agencies. Where such programs are not yet in place, volunteers or collaborative efforts of local organizations could be helpful. Police training and victim services training should include information on female circumcision to sensitize practitioners to be able to handle situations involving these practices well. Training for health care providers and counselors is also needed (e.g., Shaw 1985) so that they can be prepared for the concerns of their patients. The American College of

Obstetrics and Gynecology has now issued guidelines to assist doctors in caring for circumcised patients, and a technical manual by Dr. Toubia titled *Caring for Women with Circumcision* (1999) is being distributed by the U.S. Department of Health and Human Services.

Dissemination of referral lists to help immigrant women find sensitive and knowledgeable health care providers would be useful, particularly in light of the reported tendency for obstetricians unfamiliar with infibulations (and anterior episiotomies) to resort to caesarian section deliveries (e.g., El Dareer 1982:39). Also, there have been relatively few surgeons doing reconstructive surgery for circumcised women — one was interviewed in the film *Fire Eyes* by Los-Angeles-based Somali filmmaker Soraya Mire — and referrals will be needed.

Publications and nonprofit organizations often must operate with a small budget and little assistance. Making documentaries, arranging public programs, writing opinion pieces for local news media, developing web sites and links, and engaging others in discussions in whatever venue is available (a community women's resource center, church group, service club) may help to bring about cooperation with organizations that are supporting change efforts. As one example of an effective discussion piece, Soraya Mire's film brilliantly conveys varying viewpoints that can serve as a stimulus for discussion, especially among immigrants. Efforts to show, discuss, or make other such documentaries deserve support.

When approaching this topic with an audience, though, my recommendation is always to try to elicit more than just reactions of shock and horror. Always include contexts and stretch people beyond their ethnocentric first reactions. Mitigate shock with comparisons of other culturally impelled harmful practices that are familiar in Western culture, like the wearing of corsets or the risks of liposuction. Your discussion group may still conclude that nothing is as bad as female genital cutting, but the exercise of thinking about the ways that culture frames our interpretations of what is acceptable helps people to see that a woman who lets her daughter be circumcised may be just as loving and devoted as the one who takes her daughter to soccer practice. Be sure to include information about the activism that is already going on that is led by African and immigrant women.

Promoting dialogue among religious groups is also valuable. Often Christians who learn that female circumcision is practiced by some Muslims assume it is Islamic. As we have seen, the practices cross the lines of religious communities, and theologians find no requirement in any of the monotheistic religions to circumcise females. Discussions that break down misconceptions and prevent the anger at female circumcision from being directed inappropriately at Muslims help to develop greater religious and cultural tolerance.

I have argued that a major factor inhibiting change is the inadequacy of educational and economic opportunities for women and girls, so support for the work of international organizations like UNICEF and UNIFEM that promote education and development is an appropriate action. Involvement in influencing the agendas of organizations can be a fruitful activity. For example, human rights organizations have increasingly become more focused on women's human rights issues, including FGM, because of the involvement of knowledgeable people who have pushed these agendas. As an example, Amnesty International began in the early 1990s to move beyond the concept that it was only governments that had legal obligations under international human rights standards and began to address the abuses of other armed political groups. Later Amnesty International began moving in the direction of addressing governments' failures to prevent abuses by private individuals "as a breach of their international legal obligations" (ACT 77/11/97). With the evolution of this thinking, the FGM issue, which had been brought to the table some fifteen years earlier, has now become a clearer agenda for Amnesty International.

Questions at the Heart

Whatever condemnation people might feel for those who perpetuate human injustices or cause harm with their actions needs to be tempered by an understanding of their purposes. Enculturation, life experiences, and spiritual beliefs contribute to human actions over which reasonable people will differ. So it is important to understand people's reasons for their actions. Is an action based on love and a desire to do the right thing? Or is it defined by anger, hatred, or evil and destructive intent?

High mortality rates have wrenched so many infants and children from their African mothers. Clean water, immunizations, economic opportunities, and the cessation of warfare are certain routes to ameliorating this suffering. Yet the world wears cultural blinders about the causes of poverty that make it difficult to understand how to prevent these tragedies of child deaths and stunted lives. Are we inured to the suffering of poverty? Is it easier to focus on female circumcision because it seems so much starker and occurs as a single event?

Joyce Russell-Robinson denounces the "Western missionaries" like Alice Walker and Congresswoman Pat Schroeder for "harping on the ritual of female circumcision." Instead, she says, "Let them save Africans from malnutrition, unhealthy environments and diseases. Let them save Africans from poverty and violence, themselves responsible for malnutrition, poor sanitation, lack of clean drinking water and infant mortality" (1997:56).

In part, this is a question of sequence. Perhaps working on poverty must precede working on ignorance. Perhaps changes in beliefs about how to preserve sexual morality must precede abandonment of a marker of virginity. Will that be any easier than changing beliefs about the right of the wealthy to neglect the poor? Is improvement in nutrition more urgent than improvement in women's rights? If beliefs are sanctioned by one's religion, who but another follower of that faith can effectively engage in theological disputation? Will we be able to persuade one another of our views of justice by reference to shared human values? Or are we too far away from consensus, firmly rooted in opposing cultural beliefs? If some of us feel "enlightened" about footbinding and female genital cutting and others consider themselves "enlightened" about humans' duties to God and to one's elderly parents, where will our dialogue take us?

We need dialogues about priorities. Is ending the pain of female circumcision high on everyone's list? Or is it perhaps lower on the list than clean water, economic opportunities, clinics, and schools? In struggling to understand the insider's view, are we at risk of succumbing to metatwaddle, failing to take up the sword in an important crusade? Or is seeing the spectacular kaleidoscope of human experience the prerequisite for a calmer, more effective human movement toward a future vision of a healthy life on this planet?

While students and the general public engage in disputes about female circumcision, I hope that they, like my son and his fellow philosophy students, include the questions of context, motive, perspective, and persuasion. The world needs some deep thinkers with passionate hearts and caring words.

It is a good thing that the sunna-circumcised girls of Garia Wahid can laugh back at their infibulated taunters, that Kenyan families can embrace "circumcision through words" without cutting, and that the infibulated mothers can transcend their painful experiences to love their children, grow their crops, carry their water, sing their songs, and consider new ways of doing things when the risks no longer seem too great.

Appendix
Organizations That Focus on Female Genital Cutting Issues

Equality Now. An international human rights organization that is dedicated to action for the civic, political, economic, and social rights of girls and women. ‹www.equalitynow.org›

The Female Genital Mutilation Education and Networking Project. Dedicated to stopping female genital mutilation. Site contains many links and much on-line information. ‹www.fgmnetwork.org›

Forward and **Forward UK.** Promotes awareness to counter traditional practices prejudicial to the health of women and children. ‹www.forward.dircon.co.uk›

NOCIRC: National Organization of Circumcision Information Resource Centers. FGM awareness and education project. ‹www.nocirc.org›

Population Council. An international nonprofit organization whose mission is to improve the well-being and reproductive health of current and future generations and to help achieve a humane, equitable, and sustainable balance between people and resources. ‹www.popcouncil.org›

RAINBO: Research, Action, and Information Network for Bodily Integrity of Women. A nonprofit organization headed by Dr. Nahid Toubia. ‹www.rainbo.org›

Rising Daughters Aware. A website dedicated to the existence of support and culturally sensitive, qualified medical and advocacy assistance for women who are seeking to avoid, or have already been subjected to, female genital mutilation. Site contains many links and much on-line information. ‹www.fgm.org›

Tostan. An international nongovernmental organization based in Senegal (West Africa) that has developed a basic education program run by local people and funded primarily by UNICEF. ‹www.townonline.koz.com/visit/Tostan›

Women's International Network. A nonprofit, worldwide, open participatory communication system by, for, and about women. Fran Hosken's organization. Publishes *WIN News.* ‹*www.feminist.com/win.htm*›

Many other organizations now include female genital cutting issues on their agendas and can be found on the Internet: Feminist Majority Foundation, Physicians for the Rights of the Child, United Nations Division for the Advancement of Women, UNICEF (United Nations Children's Emergency Fund), the Office of Women in Development at USAID (United States Agency for International Development), and the World Health Organization.

Glossary

All terms are renderings of Sudanese colloquial Arabic, unless otherwise noted.

Al-Lah, or Lah	God
bumber	a stool made of a wooden frame joined by rope or hide webbing
enkishon	A blessed state of well-being (Maasai)
Fallata	Sudanese term for West Africans, primarily the Hausa living in Sudan
fatwa, fetwa	an authoritative religious decree or determination
Hadith	recorded accounts about the traditions of the Prophet, a second source of religious guidance (after the Qur'an) for Muslims
haram	that which is forbidden or sinful
irua	Female initiation ritual that includes circumcision (Gikuyu)
jalabiya	kaftan, usually white or a light, plain color, commonly worn by men; women wear similar garb at home, in colorful fabrics
juwaniya	a type of infibulation, or closure, in which the inner labia, rather than the outer labia, are joined
khawajiya	female foreigner, applied mostly to Europeans and North Americans
makrama	a practice considered ennobling
ma'leysh	a calming or consoling expression, roughly equivalent to "never mind, it's okay"
mesjid	Muslim place of prayer, usually smaller and less formal than a mosque

mihaya	traditional healing practices that rely on Qur'anic writings from holy men
mufti	a senior religious leader
mushahara	cultural practices related to protection from illnesses, especially related to blood and female fertility
nuss	half; term for intermediate type of female circumcision operation
Qur'an	Muslim holy book, the word of God revealed to the Prophet Mohammed
salaam	peace, used in greeting; a short form of *salaam al-eykum*, peace be with you
shari'a	Islamic law
shaykh	leader; often connotes religious teacher, but also can refer to a local political leader (also spelled *sheikh*)
shaykha	female leader or healer in the *zar* traditions (also spelled *sheikha*)
sunna	practices based on the traditions of the Prophet Mohammed; religious obligations or recommended practices
sunna circumcision	The form of circumcision considered acceptable or desirable by Muslims, involving minimal tissue removal
tahur	circumcision; literally, purification
tariqa	Sufi brotherhood or order, religious fraternity
tobe	Sudanese women's modesty garment — nine meters of lightweight cloth sewn in a rectangle and worn wrapped around the body over other clothing and over the head
tobe al sharaf	cloth of honor, i.e., the cloth spotted with blood that some Western Sudanese ethnic groups, for example, place on display after the consummation of a marriage as evidence of virginity
zar	spirit possession practices aimed at mollifying mischievous or harmful spirits; found widely in the Middle East and North Africa and practiced primarily by women

Bibliography

Abdal Rahman, Awatif. 1997. Member of the Sudan National Committee on Harmful Traditional Practices, quoted in Reuter report, "Sudan Tackles 'Silent Issue' of Female Circumcision," February 20.

Abdalla, Raqiya Haji Dualeh. 1982. *Sisters in Affliction: Circumcision and Infibulation of Women in Africa.* London: Zed Press.

Abu-Lughod, Lila. 1986. *Veiled Sentiments: Honor and Poetry in a Bedouin Society.* Berkeley: University of California Press.

——. 1990. "The Romance of Resistance: Tracing Transformations of Power Through Bedouin Women." *American Ethnologist* 17:41–55.

Abusharaf, Rogaia. 1998. "Unmasking Tradition." *The Sciences* (March–April): 22–27.

——. 1999. Personal communication, November 18.

Accad, Evelyne. 1989. *The Excised.* (First published in French as *L'Excisée*, 1982.) Colorado Springs: Three Continents Press.

Afkhami, Mahnaz, ed. 1995. *Faith and Freedom: Women's Human Rights in the Muslim World.* Syracuse: Syracuse University Press.

——. 1996. "Building on Indigenous Concepts of Human Rights: A Conversation with Dr. Mahnaz Afkhami." *Al-Raida* 13, nos. 74–75:13–18.

Ahmed, Leila. 1992. *Women and Gender in Islam: Historical Roots of a Modern Debate.* New Haven: Yale University Press.

Ali, Taisier, and Jay O'Brien. 1984. "Labor, Community, and Protest in Sudanese Agriculture." In *The Politics of Agriculture in Tropical Africa,* ed. J. Barker, pp. 205–38. Beverly Hills, Calif.: Sage.

Al-Safi, Ahmad. 1970. *Native Medicine in the Sudan: Sources, Conception, and Methods.* Khartoum, Sudan: University of Khartoum, Faculty of Arts, Sudan Research Unit, Salabi Prizes Competition Series No. 1.

Amnesty International. 1997. *Female Genital Mutilation: A Human Rights Information Pack.* ACT 77/12/97, 77/13/97, 77/14/97, 77/15/97, 77/16/97. London: Amnesty International.

Anderson, Kenneth. 1997. "Where No Man Has Gone Before." *Times Literary Supplement,* January 3, pp. 18–19.

An-Na'im, Abdullahi Ahmed. 1990. *Toward an Islamic Reformation: Civil Liberties, Human Rights, and International Law.* Syracuse, N.Y.: Syracuse University Press.

Asad, Talal. 1970. *The Kababish Arabs: Power, Authority, and Consent in a Nomadic Tribe.* London: C. Hurst.

Assaad, Marie Bassili. 1980. "Female Circumcision in Egypt: Social Implications, Current Research, and Prospects for Change." *Studies in Family Planning* 11, no. 1:3–16.

Baashar, T. A., M. Badri, G. Price, G. Badri, and Y. Ownallah. 1979. "Psycho-social Aspects of Female Circumcision." Presentation at Seminar on Traditional Practices Affecting the Health of Women. World Health Organization, Regional Office for the Eastern Mediterranean.

Badran, Margot, and Miriam Cooke, eds. 1990. *Opening the Gates: A Century of Arab Feminist Writing*. Bloomington: Indiana University Press.

Bamberger, Joan. 1974. "The Myth of Matriarchy: Why Men Rule in Primitive Society." In *Woman, Culture and Society*, ed. Michelle Zimbalist Rosaldo and Louise Lamphere, pp. 263–80. Stanford, Calif.: Stanford University Press.

Berreby, David. 1995. "Unabsolute Truths: Clifford Geertz." *New York Times Magazine*, April 9, pp. 44–47.

Boddy, Janice. 1982. "Womb as Oasis: The Symbolic Context of Pharaonic Circumcision in Rural Northern Sudan." *American Ethnologist* 9:682–98.

———. 1989. *Wombs and Alien Spirits: Women, Men and the Zar Cult in Northern Sudan*. Madison: University of Wisconsin Press.

———. 1991. "Body Politics: Continuing the Anticircumcision Crusade (Commentary to Gordon)." *Medical Anthropology Quarterly* 5, no. 1:15–17.

———. 1998a. "Remembering Amal: On Birth and the British in Northern Sudan." In *Pragmatic Women and Body Politics*, ed. Margaret Lock and Patricia A. Kaufert, pp. 28–57. Cambridge: Cambridge University Press.

———. 1998b. "Violence Embodied? Female Circumcision, Gender Politics, and Cultural Aesthetics." In *Rethinking Violence Against Women*, ed. R. Emerson Dobash and Russell P. Dobash, pp. 77–110. Thousand Oaks, Calif.: Sage.

Boserup, Esther. 1971. *Woman's Role in Economic Development*. New York: St. Martin's.

Boston Women's Health Book Collective. 1984. *The New Our Bodies, Our Selves*. (Original *Our Bodies, Our Selves* published in 1973.) New York: Simon and Schuster.

Brecher, Ruth, and Edward M. Brecher. 1966. *An Analysis of Human Sexual Response*. New York: Signet Books, New American Library.

Brodie, Fawn M. 1967. *The Devil Drives: A Life of Sir Richard Burton*. New York: W. W. Norton.

Brown, Isaac Baker. 1866. "Correspondence." *British Medical Journal*, 15 December, p. 676.

Browne, Dallas. 1991. "Christian Missionaries, Western Feminists, and the Kikuyu Clitoridectomy Controversy." In *The Politics of Culture*, ed. Williams Brett, pp. 243–72. Washington, D.C.: Smithsonian Institution Press.

Brownworth, Victoria. 1994. "Battling the Butchers: The Fight Against Female Sex Mutilations." *Lesbian News* 19, no. 7:46–47, 59–61.

Burstyn, Linda. 1995. "Female Circumcision Comes to America." *Atlantic Monthly*, October, pp. 28–35.

Chagnon, Napoleon. 1983. *Yanomamo: The Fierce People*. 3d ed. New York: Holt, Rinehart and Winston.

Cloudsley, Anne. 1983. *Women of Omdurman: Life, Love, and the Cult of Virginity*. London: Ethnographia.

Constantinides, Pamela. 1982. "Women's Spirit Possession and Urban Adaptation in the Muslim Northern Sudan." In *Women United, Women Divided: Comparative Studies of Ten Contemporary Cultures*, ed. Patricia Caplan and Janet M. Bujra, pp. 185–205. London: Tavistock.

Cook, R. 1976. "Damage to Physical Health from Pharaonic Circumcision (Infibulation) of Females: A Review of the Medical Literature." World Health Organization, September 30.

Culwick, Geraldine Mary. 1951. *Diet in the Gezira Irrigated Area, Sudan.* Khartoum: Sudan Government Printing Press.

Cunnison, Ian. 1966. *Baggara Arabs: Power and the Lineage in a Sudanese Nomad Tribe.* Oxford: Clarendon Press.

Davison, Jean. 1989. *Voices from Mutira: Lives of Rural Gikuyu Women.* Boulder, Colo.: Lynne Rienner.

Deen, Thalif. 1999. Untitled article in *The Sowetan.* Africa News Online, Johannesburg (www.africanews.org), March 9.

Dirie, Mahdi A., and Gunilla Lindmark. 1991. "Female Circumcision in Somalia and Women's Motives." *Acta Obstet Gynecol Scand* 70:581–85.

Dorkenoo, Efua. 1994. *Cutting the Rose: Female Genital Mutilation: The Practice and Its Prevention.* London: Minority Rights Group.

Dorkenoo, Efua, and Scilla Elworthy. 1992. *Female Genital Mutilation: Proposals for Change.* London: Minority Rights Group.

Drewal, Henry John, and Margaret Thompson Drewal. 1983. *Gelede: Art and Female Power Among the Yoruba.* Bloomington: Indiana University Press.

Duffield, Mark R. 1988. "The Fallata: Ideology and the National Economy in Sudan." In *Economy and Class in Sudan,* ed. Norman O'Neill and Jay O'Brien, pp. 122–56. Aldershot, U.K.: Avebury/Gower.

Dugger, Celia. 1996. "African Ritual Pain: Genital Cutting." *New York Times,* October 5, pp. 1, 4–5.

Ehrenreich, Barbara. 1984. *The Hearts of Men: American Dreams and the Flight from Commitment.* Garden City, N.Y.: Anchor Press.

Ehrenreich, Barbara, and Dierdre English. 1973. *Complaints and Disorders: The Sexual Politics of Illness.* Old Westbury, N.Y.: Feminist Press.

Eisler, Riane Tennenhaus. 1987. *The Chalice and the Blade: Our History, Our Future.* San Francisco: Harper and Row.

El Dareer, Asma. 1982. *Woman, Why Do You Weep? Circumcision and Its Consequences.* London: Zed Press (with Babikr Bedri Scientific Association for Women's Studies, Sudan).

El Nagar, Samia El Hadi. 1987. "Women and Spirit Possession in Omdurman." In *The Sudanese Woman,* ed. Susan Kenyon, pp. 92–115. Khartoum: University of Khartoum Graduate College Publications No. 19.

El Saadawi, Nawal. 1980a. "Creative Women in Changing Societies: A Personal Reflection." *Race and Class* 22, no. 2:159–82.

———. 1980b. *The Hidden Face of Eve: Women in the Arab World.* London: Zed Press.

Fernea, Elizabeth, and Marilyn Gaunt. 1981. *Some Women of Marrakech* (film, Odyssey series).

———. 1989. *A Veiled Revolution* (film, First Run Icarus).

Fleuhr-Lobban, Carolyn. 1994. *Islamic Society in Practice.* Gainesville: University Press of Florida.

———. 1995. "Cultural Relativism and Universal Rights." *Chronicle of Higher Education* 41, no. 3a (June 9): B1–B2.

Ford, Clellan S., and Frank A. Beach. 1951. *Patterns of Sexual Behavior.* New York: Harper & Row.

Franke, Richard W., and Barbara H. Chasin. 1980. *Seeds of Famine: Ecological Destruction and the Development Dilemma in the West African Sahel.* Totowa, N.J.: Rowman and Allenheld.

French, Howard W. 1997. "The Ritual: Disfiguring, Hurtful, Wildly Festive." *New York Times,* January 31, International, p. A4.

Giddings, Paula. 1992. "Alice Walker's Appeal" (interview with Alice Walker). *Essence* (July): 59–60, 62, 101.

Gilliam, Angela. 1991. "Women's Equality and National Liberation." In *Third World Women and the Politics of Feminism,* ed. Chandra T. Mohanty, Ann Russo, and Lourdes Torres, pp. 215–36. Bloomington: Indiana University Press.

Gimbutas, Marija A. 1989. *The Language of the Goddess: Unearthing the Hidden Symbols of Western Civilization.* San Francisco: Harper and Row.

Goldberg, Daniel C., et al. 1983. "The Grafenberg Spot and Female Ejaculation: A Review of Initial Hypotheses." *Journal of Sex and Marital Therapy,* pp. 9, 27–37.

Gordon, Daniel. 1991. "Female Circumcision and Genital Operations in Egypt and the Sudan: A Dilemma for Medical Anthropology." *Medical Anthropology Quarterly* 5, no. 1:3–14.

Gosselin, Claudie. 2000. "Handing Over the Knife: Numu Women and the Campaign Against Excision in Mali." In *Female "Circumcision" in Africa: Culture, Controversy, and Change,* ed. Bettina Shell-Duncan and Ylva Hernlund, pp. 193–214. Boulder, Colo.: Lynne Rienner.

Greenbaum, Dorothy. 1997. "Intellect Without Morality?" (Letter to the Editor), *Anthropology Newsletter,* February, p. 2.

Grotberg, Edith. 1990. "Mental Health Aspects of *Zar* for Women in Sudan." *Women and Therapy* 10, no. 3: 15–24.

Gruenbaum, Ellen. 1979. "Patterns of Family Living: A Case Study of Two Villages on the Rahad River." Development Studies and Research Centre Monograph Series No. 12. Khartoum: Khartoum University Press.

———. 1982a. *Health Services, Health, and Development in Sudan: The Impact of the Gezira Irrigated Scheme.* Ph.D. diss., University of Connecticut. (University Microfilms.)

———. 1982b. "The Movement Against Clitoridectomy and Infibulation in Sudan: Public Health Policy and the Women's Movement." *Medical Anthropology Newsletter* 13, no. 2:4–12. (Reissued in 1997 in *Gender in Cross-Cultural Perspective,* 2d ed., ed. Caroline Brettell and Carolyn Sargent, pp. 441–53. Upper Saddle River, N.J.: Prentice Hall.)

———. 1988. "Reproductive Ritual and Social Reproduction: Female Circumcision and the Subordination of Women in Sudan." In *Economy and Class in Sudan,* ed. Norman O'Neill and Jay O'Brien, pp. 308–25. Aldershot, U.K.: Avebury/Gower.

———. 1990. "Nuer Women in Southern Sudan: Health, Reproduction, and Work." Women in International Development Working Papers Series, no. 215. East Lansing: Michigan State University.

———. 1991. "The Islamic Movement, Development, and Health Education: Recent Changes in the Health of Rural Women in Central Sudan." *Social Science and Medicine* 33, no. 6:637–46.

———. 1994. "Female Circumcision: Beliefs and Misbeliefs." (Film review.) *American Anthropologist* 96, no. 2:488–89.

———. 1996. "The Cultural Debate Over Female Circumcision: The Sudanese Are Arguing This One Out for Themselves." *Medical Anthropology Quarterly* 10, no. 4:455–75.

———. 1998a. "Resistance and Embrace: Sudanese Rural Women and Systems of Power." In *Pragmatic Women and Body Politics,* ed. Margaret Lock and Patricia Kaufert, pp. 58–76. Cambridge: Cambridge University Press.

———. 1998b. "Transition Rites: Clitoridectomy and Infibulation." *The Encyclopedia of Africa South of the Sahara,* ed. John Middleton. New York: Charles Scribner's Sons.

———. 2000. "Is Female Circumcision a Maladaptive Cultural Pattern?" In *Female "Circumcision" in Africa: Culture, Controversy, and Change,* ed. Bettina Shell-Duncan and Ylva Hernlund, pp. 41–54. Boulder, Colo.: Lynne Rienner.

Hale, Sondra. 1987. "Women's Culture/Men's Culture: Gender, Separation, and Space in Africa and North America." *American Behavioral Scientist* 13, no. 1:115–34.

———. 1994. "A Question of Subjects: The 'Female Circumcision' Controversy and the Politics of Knowledge." *Ufahamu* 22, no. 3:26–35.

———. 1995. "The Year of the Muslim Woman." *Association for Middle East Women's Studies Newsletter* 10 (November): 3, 5–6.

———. 1996. *Gender Politics in Sudan: Islamism, Socialism, and the State.* Boulder, Colo.: Westview Press.

Hall, Marjorie, and Bakhita Amin Ismail. 1981. *Sisters Under the Sun:The Story of Sudanese Women.* New York: Longman.

Hayes, Rose Oldfield. 1975. "Female Genital Mutilation, Fertility Control, Women's Roles, and the Patrilineage in Modern Sudan: A Functional Analysis." *American Ethnologist* 2: 617–33.

Hicks, Esther K. 1993. *Infibulation: Female Mutilation in Islamic Northeastern Africa.* New Brunswick, N.J.: Transaction.

Hosken, Fran P. 1978. "The Epidemiology of Female Genital Mutilation." *Tropical Doctor* 8: 150–56.

———. 1980. *Female Sexual Mutilations: The Facts and Proposals for Action.* Lexington, Mass.: Women's International Network News.

———. 1982. *The Hosken Report: Genital and Sexual Mutilation of Females,* 3d ed. Lexington, Mass.: Women's International Network News.

———, ed. 1998. *WIN News* (Periodical). Lexington, Mass.: Women's International Network.

Hossain, Rokeya Sakhawat. 1988. *Sultana's Dream and Selections from the Secluded Ones.* Ed. and trans. Roushan Jahan. New York: Feminist Press.

Huelsman, Ben R. 1976. "An Anthropological View of Clitoral and Other Female Genital Mutilations." In *The Clitoris,* ed. Thomas Lowry and Thea Snyder Lowry, pp. 111–61. St. Louis: W. H. Green.

Hutchinson, Sharon E. 1996. *Nuer Dilemmas: Coping with Money, War, and the State.* Berkeley: University of California Press.

Hyde, Janet Shibley. 1994. *Understanding Human Sexuality.* 5th ed. New York: McGraw-Hill.

Inhorn, Marcia C. 1994. *Quest for Conception: Gender, Infertility, and Egyptian Medical Traditions.* Philadelphia: University of Pennsylvania Press.

———. 1996. *Infertility and Patriarchy: The Cultural Politics of Gender and Family Life in Egypt.* Philadelphia: University of Pennsylvania Press.

Inhorn, Marcia C., and Kimberly A. Buss. 1993. "Infertility, Infection, and Iatrogenesis in Egypt: The Anthropological Epidemiology of Blocked Tubes." *Medical Anthropology* 15:1–28.

Inter-African Committee. 1987. *Report on the Regional Seminar on Traditional Practices Affecting the Health of Women and Children in Africa* (Addis Ababa, Ethiopia, 6–10 April 1987). Organized by the Inter-African Committee on Traditional Practices Affecting the Health of Women and Children, cosponsored by the Ministry of Health of Socialist Ethiopia, UNECA, OAU, UNICEF, and WHO.

———. 1992. *Female Circumcision: Beliefs and Misbeliefs.* Documentary film, 18 min., color.

Jennings, Anne M. 1995. *The Nubians of West Aswan: Village Women in the Midst of Change.* Boulder, Colo.: Lynne Rienner.

Johnson, B. C. A. 1979. "Traditional Practices Affecting the Health of Women." Paper presented at the Seminar on Traditional Practices Affecting the Health of Women, Khartoum, February 10–15.

Johnson, Michelle C. 2000. "Excision and Girls' Initiation Among the Mandinga of Guinea-Bissau: Local Dynamics of a Global Debate." In *Female "Circumcision" in Africa: Culture, Controversy, and Change,* ed. Bettina Shell-Duncan and Ylva Hernlund, pp. 215–34. Boulder, Colo.: Lynne Rienner.

Joseph, Toni. 1992. "One Who Defied Tradition." *Essence,* July, p. 62.

Kapteijns, Lidwien. 1983. "Islamic Rationales for the Changing Social Roles of Women in the Western Sudan." Paper presented to the conference Women in Muslim Societies: Is Feminism Possible? Brooklyn College, City University of New York.

Kassamali, Noor J. 1998. "When Modernity Confronts Traditional Practices: Female Genital Cutting in Northeast Africa." In *Women in Muslim Societies: Diversity Within Unity,* ed. Herbert L. Bodman and Nayereh Tohidi, pp. 39–61. Boulder, Colo.: Lynne Rienner.

Kennedy, John. 1970. "Circumcision and Excision in Egyptian Nubia." *Man* 5:175–90.

Kenyatta, Jomo. 1965 [1938]. *Facing Mount Kenya.* London: Secker and Warburg.

Kenyon, Susan. 1991. "The Story of a Tin Box: *Zar* in the Sudanese Town of Sennar." In Lewis et al., eds., *Women's Medicine,* pp. 100–117.

Koso-Thomas, Olayinka. 1987. *The Circumcision of Women: A Strategy for Eradication.* London: Zed Press.

Ladas, Alice K., Beverly Whipple, and John D. Perry. 1982. *The G Spot and Other Recent Discoveries About Human Sexuality.* New York: Holt, Rinehart, and Winston.

Lane, Sandra, and Robert A. Rubinstein. 1996. "Judging the Other: Responding to Traditional Female Genital Surgeries." *Hastings Center Report* 26, no. 3:31–40.

Leacock, Eleanor. 1972. Introduction to *The Origin of the Family, Private Property, and the State,* by Friedrich Engels (Original 1884). New York: International.

Lewis, I. M. 1991. Introduction to Lewis et al., eds., *Women's Medicine,* pp. 1–16.

Lewis, I. M., Ahmed Al-Safi, and Sayyid Hurreiz, eds. 1991. *Women's Medicine: The Zar-Bori Cult in Africa and Beyond.* Edinburgh: Edinburgh University Press for International African Institute.

Lightfoot-Klein, Hanny. 1989. *Prisoners of Ritual: An Odyssey into Female Genital Circumcision in Africa.* New York: Harrington Park Press.

Llewellyn-Davies, Melissa. 1983. *Maasai Women.* (Film.)

Lock, Margaret, and Patricia Kaufert. 1998. Introduction to *Pragmatic Women and Body Politics,* ed. Margaret Lock and Patricia Kaufert, pp. 1–27. Cambridge: Cambridge University Press.

Lowry, Thomas, and Thea Snyder Lowry, eds. 1976. *The Clitoris.* St. Louis: W. H. Green.

Mackie, Gerry. 1996. "Ending Footbinding and Infibulation." *American Sociological Review* 61: 991–1017.

Mascia-Lees, Frances E., and Patricia Sharpe, eds. 1992. *Tattoo, Torture, Mutilation, and Adornment: The Denaturalization of the Body in Culture and Text.* Albany: State University of New York Press.

Meinardus, Otto. 1967. "Mythological, Historical, and Sociological Aspects of the Practice of Female Circumcision Among the Egyptians." *Acta Ethnographica Academiae Scientiarum Hungaricae* 16:387–97.

Mernissi, Fatima. 1991. (original publication 1987). *The Veil and the Male Elite: A Feminist Interpretation of Women's Rights in Islam.* Trans. Mary Jo Lakeland. Reading, Mass.: Addison-Wesley.

Messer, Ellen. 1993. "Anthropology and Human Rights." *Annual Review of Anthropology* 22:221–49.

Mire, Soraya. 1994. *Fire Eyes.* (Film.) New York: Filmmakers Library.

Morsy, Soheir. 1991. "Spirit Possession in Egyptian Ethnomedicine: Origins, Comparison and Historical Specificity." In Lewis et al., eds., *Women's Medicine,* pp. 189–208.

———. 1991. "Safeguarding Women's Bodies: The White Man's Burden Medicalized (Commentary to Gordon)." *Medical Anthropology Quarterly* 5, no. 1:19–23.

———. 1993. *Gender, Sickness, and Healing in Rural Egypt: Ethnography in Historical Context.* Boulder, Colo.: Westview Press.

Mudawi, Suliman. 1977. "The Impact of Social and Economic Changes on Female Circumcision." In *Sudan Medical Association Congress Series,* no. 2.

Nagengast, Carole. 1997. "Women, Minorities, and Indigenous Peoples: Universalism and Cultural Relativity." *Journal of Anthropological Research* 54:349–69.

Ngugi wa Thiong'o. 1965. *The River Between.* London: Heinemann.

Nordenstam, Tore. 1968. *Sudanese Ethics.* Uppsala, Sweden: Scandinavian Institute of African Studies.

Oberman, Michelle. 1998. "Coming to Terms with Modern American Infanticide." Paper presented at the Gender, Health and History conference, University of Illinois at Chicago, April.

Obermeyer, Carla Makhlouf. 1999. "Female Genital Surgeries: The Known, the Unknown, and the Unknowable," *Medical Anthropology Quarterly* 13, no. 1:79–106.

O'Brien, Jay. 1980. "Agricultural Labor and Development in Sudan." Ph.D. diss., University of Connecticut.

———. 1984. "The Political Economy of Semi-Proletarianisation Under Colonialism: Sudan 1925–50." In *Proletarianisation in The Third World,* ed. Barry Munslow and Henry Finch, pp. 121–47. London: Croom Helm.

———. 1986. "Toward a Reconstitution of Ethnicity: Capitalist Penetration and Cultural Dynamics in Sudan." *American Anthropologist* 88, no. 4:898–907.

———. 1987. "Differential High Fertility and Demographic Transitions Under Peripheral Capitalism in Sudan." In *African Population and Capitalism: Historical Perspectives,* ed. Dennis Cordell and Joel Gregory, pp. 173–86. Boulder, Colo.: Westview Press.

O'Brien, Jay, and Taisier M. Ali. 1984. "Labor, Community and Protest in Sudanese Agriculture." In *The Politics of Agriculture in Tropical Africa,* ed. Jonathan Barker, pp. 205–38. Beverly Hills: Sage.

Perry, John D., and Beverly Whipple. 1981. "Pelvic Muscle Strength of Female Ejaculators: Evidence in Support of a New Theory of Orgasm." *Journal of Sex Research* 17, no. 1:22–39.

Price, Sally. 1984. *Co-wives and Calabashes.* Ann Arbor: University of Michigan Press.

Pridie, E. D., A. E. Lorenzen, A. Cruickshank, J. S. Hovell, and D. R. MacDonald. 1945. *Female Circumcision in the Anglo-Egyptian Sudan.* Khartoum: Sudan Medical Service.

Reaves, Malik Stan. 1997. "Alternative Rite to Female Circumcision Spreading in Kenya." Africa News Service, November 19.

Rushwan, Hamid, Corry Slot, Asma El Dareer, and Nadia Bushra. 1983. *Female Circumcision in the Sudan: Prevalence, Complications, Attitudes and Changes.* Khartoum: Faculty of Medicine, University of Khartoum.

Russell-Robinson, Joyce. 1997. "African Female Circumcision and the Missionary Mentality." *Issue: A Journal of Opinion* (ASA) 26, no. 1:54–57.

Sanday, Peggy Reeves, and Ruth Gallagher Goodenough. 1990. *Beyond the Second Sex: New Directions in the Anthropology of Gender.* Philadelphia: University of Pennsylvania Press.

Sanders, Clinton R. 1989. *Customizing the Body: The Art and Culture of Tattooing.* Philadelphia: Temple University Press.

Sanderson, Lilian Passmore. 1981. *Against the Mutilation of Women: The Struggle Against Unnecessary Suffering.* London: Ithaca Press.

——. 1982. "The Babiker Bedri Scientific Association for Women's Studies Workshops for the Abolition of All Forms of Female Genital Mutilation in the Sudan." *Sudan Notes and Records,* pp. 65–72.

Scheper-Hughes, Nancy. 1991. "Virgin Territory: The Male Discovery of the Clitoris (Commentary to Gordon)," *Medical Anthropology Quarterly* 5, no. 1:25–28.

——. 1992. *Death Without Weeping.* Berkeley: University of California Press.

Shandall, Ahmed Abu El Futuh. 1967. "Circumcision and Infibulation of Females." *Sudan Medical Journal* 5, no. 4:178–212.

Shapiro, Laura. 1998. "A Long Road to Freedom." Review of *Do They Hear You When You Cry?* by Fauziya Kassindja with Layli Miller Bashir. *Newsweek,* March 16, p. 57.

Shaw, Evelyn. 1985. "Female Circumcision." *American Journal of Nursing* 85, no. 6:684–87.

Sheehan, Elizabeth A. 1997. "Victorian Clitoridectomy: Isaac Baker Brown and His Harmless Operative Procedure." In *The Gender/Sexuality Reader,* ed. Roger N. Lancaster and Micaela di Leonardo, pp. 325–34. New York: Routledge.

Shell-Duncan, Bettina, and Ylva Hernlund, eds. 2000. *Female "Circumcision" in Africa: Culture, Controversy, and Change.* Boulder, Colo.: Lynne Rienner.

Sisterhood Is Global Institute. 1999. ⟨*www.sigi.org/Alert/index.htm*⟩, March 17.

Slack, Alison. 1988. "Female Circumcision: A Critical Appraisal," *Human Rights Quarterly* 10 (November): 437–86.

Speth, James G. 1999. *UN Daily Highlights,* March 8.

Sudanese Women NGO Preparatory Committee. 1995. "Platform Document, the Fourth World Conference on Women." Khartoum Forum, August 14–16, Friendship Hall, Khartoum.

Suggs, David N., and Andrew W. Miracle, eds. 1993. *Culture and Human Sexuality.* Pacific Grove, Calif.: Brooks/Cole.

Torsvik, Bente. 1983. *Receiving the Gifts of Allah: The Establishment of a Modern Midwifery Service in the Sudan 1920–1937.* Thesis, University of Bergen, Norway.

Toubia, Nahid. 1985. "The Social and Political Implications of Female Circumcision." In *Women and the Family in the Middle East,* ed. Elizabeth Fernea, pp. 148–59. Austin: University of Texas Press.

———. 1993 (2d ed. 1995). *Female Genital Mutilation: A Call for Global Action*. New York: Women, Ink.

———. 1994. "Female Circumcision as a Public Health Issue." *New England Journal of Medicine* 331, no. 11 (September 15): 712–16.

———. 1996. Interview on "Fresh Air." National Public Radio.

Toubia, Nahid, and Anika Rahman. 2000. *Female Genital Mutilation: A Guide to Laws and Policies Worldwide*. London: Zed Press.

Tubiana, M.-J. 1984. "The Beri." In *Muslim People: A World Ethnographic Survey*, 2d ed., ed. R. Weekes, pp. 499–504. Westport, Conn.: Greenwood Press.

UNICEF/UNIFEM. n.d. *Convention on the Elimination of All Forms of Discrimination Against Women*. (Text and information packet.) New York: UNICEF and UNI-FEM.

United Nations. 1994. "Programme of Action." In *Report of the International Conference on Population and Development* (Cairo, Egypt, September 5–13).

United Nations Commission of the Status of Women. 1999. Press release WOM/1114, March 8.

Vale, V., and Andrea Juno, eds. 1989. *Modern Primitives: An Investigation of Contemporary Adornment and Ritual*. San Francisco: Re/Search Publications.

Van der Kwaak, Anke. 1992. "Female Circumcision and Gender Identity: A Questionable Alliance?" *Social Science and Medicine* 35, no. 6: 777–87.

Verzin, J. A. 1975. "Sequelae of Female Circumcision." *Tropical Doctor* 5, no. 1:163–69.

Walker, Alice. 1992. *Possessing the Secret of Joy*. New York: Harcourt, Brace, Jovanovich.

Walker, Alice, and Pratibha Parmar. 1993. *Warrior Marks: Female Genital Mutilation and the Sexual Blinding of Women*. New York: Harcourt, Brace.

Walley, Christine. 1996. "Searching for 'Voices': Feminism, Anthropology, and the Global Debate Over Female Genital Operations." *Cultural Anthropology* 12, no. 3:405–38.

Walter, Lynn. 1995. "Feminist Anthropology." *Gender and Society* 9, no. 3:272–88.

Washington Post. 1998. "Asylum Bid Cites Female Circumcision." December 5.

Watts, Michael. 1983. *Silent Violence: Food, Famine, and Peasantry in Northern Nigeria*. Berkeley: University of California Press.

Wolkoff, A. Stark. 1976. "Surgery of the Clitoris." In *The Clitoris*, ed. Lowry and Lowry, pp. 104–10.

Women in International Development. Working Papers Series. 1981–. Ed. Rita S. Gallin. Office of Women in International Development, Michigan State University.

Wood, Corinne Shear. 1979. *Human Sickness and Health: A Biocultural View*. Palo Alto, Calif.: Mayfield.

Index

Acknowledgments

I am truly grateful to the many people of Sudan who have generously shared their lives, ideas, cares, joys, and hospitality with me, enabling me to develop a degree of understanding of an extremely complex issue. I am especially grateful to the residents of Abdal Galil, Um Fila, Hallali, Garia Wahid, Rufa'a, and Ayod, to my neighbors in As-Sajjana (Khartoum) and Wad Medani, and to the kind and generous people who invariably appeared wherever I traveled. May their beautiful country find the peace and prosperity it has waited so long to enjoy.

In Sudan, my work was facilitated and my understandings advanced by numerous colleagues. I am especially grateful to Ibrahim Hassan Abdal Galil and Ali M. El-Hassan for facilitating my research; to research assistants Awatif Al-Imam, Saida M. Elamin Ahmed, and Mary Nyagong; and to several valued companions who facilitated participant observation and interviewing, especially Ekhlas Musa. Many colleagues, especially at the University of Khartoum, provided valuable insights and connections: Balghis Badri, Samia El-Hadi El-Nagar, El-Wathig Kamier, Mohammed El-Awad Galal-el-Din, Abdal Ghaffar M. Ahmed, Idris Salim El-Hassan, Salah El-Shazali, Janice Boddy, Asha Mustafa, Nahid Toubia, Amal Hassan Fadlalla, Rogaia Abusharaf, Gerry Hale, and Abdallahi An-Na'im.

I am very grateful to the institutions that provided research support, including the Sudanese Ministry of Social Affairs, the Economic and Social Research Council of the Sudanese National Council for Research, the American Council of Learned Societies, California State University, San Bernardino, and the National Endowment for the Humanities. At California State University, Fresno, Greg Kobzloff assisted me with the bibliography, Bill Slusser with maps, and Randy Vaughn-Dotta with photo processing. Jesse O'Brien assisted me with the index.

I am deeply indebted to Sondra Hale, who provided me with insight, friendship, and encouragement ever since we met in Khartoum in my first year there. I thank her for her unfailing friendship, humor, and collegiality, as well as her helpful suggestions on this manuscript. My dear husband Jay O'Brien shared the wonderful years in Sudan, and I thank him for his innumerable discussions over the years and for his detailed comments. I appreciate the thoughtful comments of an anonymous reviewer of this manuscript, and I am profoundly grateful to Marcia Inhorn for her close reading and enormously helpful suggestions. The encouragement and guidance of my editor, Patricia Smith, played a key role in completing this project.

I owe special thanks to my parents, Ruth and Luther Gruenbaum, whose love of their fellow humans and delight in discovery nurtured my own curiosity and concern. And to my dear family, Jay, Jesse, and Zach O'Brien, thank you. Your love and questions have enriched my life.